CHAMPIONS OF FREEDOM

The Ludwig von Mises Lecture Series

Ludwig von Mises

CHAMPIONS OF FREEDOM

Volume 29

GLOBALIZATION

Will Freedom or World Government Dominate the International Marketplace?

Richard M. Ebeling
Editor

Hillsdale College Press
Hillsdale, Michigan 49242

Hillsdale College Press

Books by the Hillsdale College Press include The Christian Vision series; Champions of Freedom series; and other works.

The views expressed in this volume are not necessarily the views of Hillsdale College.

The Champions of Freedom series
Globalization: Will Freedom or World Government Dominate the International Marketplace?

Printed in the United States of America

Photo credits
Front cover: ©Orion Press/CORBIS
Back cover: Douglas Coon, Director of Creative Media, Hillsdale College

First printing 2002

Library of Congress Control Number 2002105218
ISBN 0-916308-56-1

Contents

Contributors

Doug Bandow is a senior fellow at the Cato Institute and a nationally syndicated columnist with Copley News Service. His articles have appeared in many publications, including *Christianity Today, Harper's, National Interest, National Review,* the *New York Times,* and *The Wall Street Journal.* He has written and edited several books, including *Tripwire: Korea and U.S. Foreign Policy in a Changed World* and *Perpetuating Poverty: The World Bank, The IMF, and The Developing World* (with Ian Vásquez). Formerly a Special Assistant to President Reagan, he received his B.S. in Economics from Florida State University in 1976 and his J.D. from Stanford University in 1979.

Mickey Craig is the Anna Margaret Ross Alexander Professor of Political Science at Hillsdale College. Dr. Craig has taught at Hillsdale since 1986. He also serves as Director of the Washington Hillsdale Intern Program. He received his Ph.D. from the Claremont Graduate School in 1986.

Richard M. Ebeling is the Ludwig von Mises Professor of Economics at Hillsdale College. In addition, he serves as vice president of The Future of Freedom Foundation and writes for its monthly magazine, *Freedom Daily.* He has edited several books, including *The Dangers of Socialized Medicine, The Tyranny of Gun Control, The Case for Free Trade and Open Immigration,* and several volumes in the Hillsdale College Press series *Champions of Freedom.* He has lectured extensively on privatization and monetary reform throughout the United States, Latin America, and the former Soviet Union, where he has consulted with the Lithuanian government, the city of Moscow, and the Russian parliament. Currently he is writing a biography of Ludwig von Mises and editing a series of volumes that will feature Mises' recently unearthed pre-World War II papers. The first, *Selected Writings of Ludwig von Mises: The Political Economy of International Reform and Reconstruction,* was published by Liberty Fund in 2000.

Bryan-Paul Frost is Assistant Professor and the James A. and Kaye L. Crocker Endowed Professor of Political Science at the University of Louisiana at Lafayette. He is editor and co-translator of Alexandre Kojève's *Outline of a Phenomenology of Right,* published by Rowman and Littlefield, as well as co-editor of the forthcoming *History of American Political Thought.* He has published articles on Kojève, Raymond Aron, and Cato the Younger. He received his Ph.D. from the University of Toronto.

James K. Glassman is a resident fellow at the American Enterprise Institute and host of TechCentralStation.com. Mr. Glassman is the co-author of *Dow 36,000,* which has appeared on several business best-seller lists. His previous experience includes writing syndicated columns at the *Washington Post* and hosting CNN's *Capital Gang Sunday* and PBS's *TechnoPolitics.* He is currently a regular commentator on National Public Radio and the *Nightly Business Report* on Public Television. His articles have appeared in the *New York Times, The Wall Street Journal, Reader's Digest,* and many other publications. Among other honors, he was the winner of the 1998 Warren Brookes Award for distinguished journalism from the American Legislative Exchange Council. He is a graduate of Harvard University, where he was editor of the *Harvard Crimson.*

Deepak Lal is James S. Coleman Professor of International Development Studies at the University of California at Los Angeles; Professor Emeritus of Political Economy at University College, London; and co-director of the Trade and Development Unit at the Institute of Economic Affairs in London. He was educated at the Doon School, Dehra Dun; St. Stephen's College, Delhi; and Jesus College, Oxford. He has been a member of the Indian Foreign Service and taught at several schools, including Jesus College, Oxford, and Christ Church, Oxford. Professor Lal is the author of numerous articles and books on economic development and public policy, including *Methods of Project Analysis, The Poverty of Development Economics, Unintended Consequences,* and, most recently, a collection of essays titled *Unfinished Business.*

Mackubin Thomas Owens is Professor of Strategy and Force Planning at the United States Naval War College in Newport, Rhode Island, and a monthly columnist for the *Providence Journal.* His articles on national security issues have appeared in such publications as the *Public Interest,* the *Weekly Standard, Marine Corps Gazette,* the *New York Times,* and *The Wall Street Journal.* He is co-editor of the textbook *Strategy and Force Planning,* and is currently working on a history of U.S. civil–military relations. Before joining the faculty of the War College, he served as Director of Legislative Affairs for the Nuclear Weapons Programs of the Department of Energy during the Reagan administration. Dr. Owens is a Marine Corps veteran of Vietnam, where he served as an infantry platoon commander, was wounded twice, and was awarded the Silver Star. He earned his Ph.D. from the University of Dallas.

Jeremy A. Rabkin teaches international law and American constitutional law at Cornell University. His most recent book is *Why Sovereignty Matters.* His articles on the international criminal court and contemporary international law have appeared in *The Wall Street Journal,* the *Weekly Standard,* and the *Chicago Journal of International Law.* He testified on this subject before the Senate Foreign Relations Committee in 2000 and has lectured on related issues in international law at the China Institute of International Affairs in Beijing, at the University of London, in the Senate Lecture series of the Australian Parliament in Canberra, and at the Gulbenkian Foundation in Lisbon, Portugal. He received his Ph.D. from Harvard University.

Lawrence H. White is Friedrich A. Hayek Professor of Economic History at the University of Missouri–St. Louis. He has been Visiting Professor at the Queen's University of Belfast, visiting fellow at the Australian National University, and visiting scholar at the Federal Reserve Bank of Atlanta. Dr. White is the author of *The Theory of Monetary Institutions* and editor of *The History of Gold and Silver,* among other books. His articles on monetary theory and banking history have appeared in the *American Economic Review,* the *Journal of Economic Literature,* and other publications. He is co-editor of a book series for Routledge titled *Foundations of the Market Economy,* an associate editor of the *Review of Austrian Economics,* and a contributing editor to *Ideas on Liberty.* Dr. White received his Ph.D. from UCLA.

Foreword

Hillsdale College was built under the influence of the American Revolution. In that revolution there was much talk of property rights. These are rights, said Madison, to the material things that we have made and earned. These are also rights to every natural property that belongs to the human being. This means his ability to think and to speak. It means his capacity to worship the Almighty, and his individual responsibility to that highest Being. Property rights are a kind of summation of all of our rights.

In modern times, many great economists have worked to recover the full force of this powerful view, which has been the chief foundation of liberty in the modern world. Among these economists, none is more important than the great Ludwig von Mises.

Hillsdale College has a special connection to Mises. He gave us his personal library, and in making this splendid gift he said these fine words: "Hillsdale, more than any other educational institution, most strongly represents the free market ideas to which I have given my life."

Larry P. Arnn
President
Hillsdale College

Introduction

Globalization has become the new, fashionable catchword for a process that has been developing with increasing intensity for more than two hundred years: the internationalization of the division of labor. Of course, in one sense, international trade is as old as recorded history. From Herodotus to Marco Polo, travelers, adventurers, and merchants made their way to faraway places and returned to their homelands with exotic tales of strange customs, and often laden with stores of sundry commodities to incite the demands of their fellow countrymen. Wherever they went, they all told of ports and cities alive with commerce and trade, populated and visited by merchants and travelers like themselves. Spices and jewels, cloths and tapestries, furs and animal skins, ornaments and household items, these were among the vast number of goods that passed from one part of the world to the other long before modern times. Caravans of commerce brought a certain degree of unity to the human race long before men gave serious thought to the possibilities of a global community of man.

But it was only following the great explorations of the fifteenth and sixteenth centuries, with the opening up of new trade routes from Europe to Africa and Asia and the discovery of a "new world" in the Americas, that the modern era of international trade began its development. It has followed an accelerating trajectory since the eighteenth century as both the technical means and the institutional order has permitted the potentials of global commerce to expand dramatically.

It is worth recalling just how difficult it was to travel and communicate even less than two hundred years ago. In April 1820, Sir Walter Scott traveled from London to Scotland at the rate of ten miles an hour; this speed was considered so extraordinary that it was mentioned in the British *Annual Register.*[1] In the 1840s and 1850s, the famous America clipper ships made the journey across the Atlantic from Liverpool to New York in an average of 15 days, about 240 miles a day, or 10 miles an hour. In the first decade of the nineteenth century it took four days by stagecoach to make the 200-mile trip from Boston to New York. A journey from Boston to Savannah, Georgia, took 18 days of hard riding by stagecoach, or 7 to 25 days by sailing ship, depending upon the winds. These travel times also meant that communication by mail took the same amount of days.[2] Most of us recall that the famous American victory at the battle of New Orleans during the War of 1812 occurred after a peace agreement had already been signed in Europe between the United States and Great Britain. Before the opening of the Suez Canal in 1869, sailing ships traveling from Europe to India and back, going about the Horn of Africa, could expect an average time at sea of between six to eight months; the canal across the Isthmus of Suez in Egypt cut that roundtrip traveling time to only just under thirty days by steamship.[3]

The nineteenth century's ground transportation marvel was the railroad. The first railway line was opened in 1829 between Liverpool and Manchester in Great Britain. It enabled the traveler to make time at the impressive speed of 16 miles per hour.[4] By the end of the nineteenth century, railroads crisscrossed most of Western and Central Europe, and were being extended into Eastern Europe. In 1869—the same year as the opening of the Suez Canal—the first transcontinental railroad system was joined across the United States outside Ogden, Utah. European foreign capital investment was constructing railway networks in South America, Asia, and Australia.

Today, at the beginning of the twenty-first century, a journey of a day and a half by airplane can carry a person to almost any major city on the other side of the world. Now travel across the Atlantic or across the continental United States by air takes hours rather than days or weeks. The development of radio and then television in the twentieth century enabled the transmission of instantaneous voice information and live pictures around the globe. The internet enables personal messages and documents to be sent to any point on the planet within seconds. Time and space have been dramatically shortened, especially during the last one hundred years.

The goods that were carried by caravans and sailing ships from faraway places hundreds of years ago were irrelevant to the daily life of most people. Their food, clothing, and simple daily amenities were produced within the village or narrow regional community within which they lived. Three or four hundred years ago, the vast majority of people anywhere in the world lived out their lives without traveling more than maybe a few dozen miles from their place of birth.

The nineteenth century saw a vast and peaceful movement of people from one end of the globe to another. Between 1840 and 1930 almost 60 million people emigrated from Europe to the other parts of the globe. Eighteen million left Great Britain or Ireland; over 10 million migrated from Italy; from Imperial Russia, 9.2 million; from Austria-Hungary, 5.2 million; from Germany, 4.9 million; from Spain, 4.7 million; from Portugal, 1.8 million; from Sweden, 1.2 million; from Norway 1.1 million, to mention only those countries contributing the largest numbers to this huge movement of humanity. Where did they go? Thirty-four million came to the United States; 6.4 million moved to Argentina; 5.2 million went to Canada; 4.4 million settled in Brazil; 2.9 million made a new home in Australia; and 1.6 million took up residence in the British West Indies, to, again, name only those countries receiving the greatest number of these immigrants.[5]

At the end of the nineteenth century, in 1899, British economist Charles Bastable summarized the result of these momentous changes:

> One of the most striking features of modern times is the growth of international relations of ever-increasing complexity and influence. Facilities of communications have brought about closer and more constant intercourse between the different countries of the world, leading to many unexpected results. This more intimate connection is reflected in all different sides of social activity. International law, that two hundred years ago

> was almost wholly confined to the discussion of war and its effects, now contains a goodly series of chapters treating in detail the conduct of nations during peace.... Literature, Science, and Art have all been similarly affected; their followers are engaged in keenly watching the progress of their favorite pursuits in other countries, and are becoming daily more and more sensitive to any new tendency or movement in the remotest nation. But as might be expected, it is in the sphere of material relations that the increase in international solidarity has been most decisively marked, and can be best followed and appreciated. The barriers that in former ages impeded the free passage of men and goods from country to country have been—it cannot unfortunately be said removed, but very much diminished; and more particularly during the last fifty years the extraordinary development and improvement of transport agencies both by land and sea have gone far towards obliterating the retarding effects of legislative restraints or national prejudices.... In spite of temporary checks and drawbacks, the broad fact stands out beyond dispute, that the transfer of human beings from country to country which is known as "migration," as also the similar movement of goods described as "commerce, is not merely expanding, but, if periods sufficiently lengthy for fair comparison are taken, expanding at an accelerated rate.[6]

The First World War, which began in August of 1914, shattered this trend toward the full globalization of the world's economic activity. In the name of each belligerent's national war effort the trading of goods, the free movement of men, and the international investment of capital came to a halt. Forms of "war socialism" and economic planning were introduced in all of the warring nations—including the United States after its entry into the war in April 1917.

And after World War I, even though many countries attempted to return to the greater freedom that prevailed before 1914, in fact the watchwords of the period between the two World Wars—1918 to 1939—were political and economic nationalism. The economic ideal of many countries became greater national self-sufficiency in the name of industrialization in agrarian countries and agrarianization in industrial countries.[7] Domestic products and labor markets were to be artificially shielded from the competition of manufacturers and workers in foreign lands. Tariffs, import quotas, foreign exchange control, and restrictions on foreign investment, all were manifestations of this new trend. In addition, the relatively high degree of freedom of movement permanently ended with the wartime reinstitution of passports and visas, after almost a century of free migration in North America, Europe, and the European colonial empires.

The process of globalization almost ground to a halt during most of these years as socialism, communism, fascism, Nazism, and the interventionist–welfare state replaced the epoch of economic liberalism. Government planning and control required the regulation of trade, investment, consumption, prices and wages, and the movement of people.[8]

Out of the ashes of the Second World War there was an attempt to reestablish an international order without the economic isolation and political brutality that had marked the trend toward collectivism during the previous twenty-five years. The foundation stones for such a new order were laid down with the establishment of the United Nations, the International Monetary Fund, the World Bank, the International Labor Organization, the World Health Organization, and the General Agreement on Tariffs and Trade (that has now become the World Trade Organization), and numerous others that have come to form the spiders' web of international institutions having power and authority over billions of lives around our planet.[9]

In Europe, over the last ten years, a political process has begun in which the nation–states of that continent are being slowly transformed into what will be lower-level administrative elements in an all-encompassing European State. That is the primary political purpose behind the establishment of a single currency, the Euro. But as the Spanish free market economist Pedro Schwartz has warned, the European Union threatens to become "a mirror image on a larger scale of our interventionist Welfare States, awash with rules and regulations, riddled with subsidized agriculturists, tax cheats, black marketeers, feigned unemployed and imaginary maladies."[10]

And here is the heart of the matter. The existing and proposed international authorities for political control and economic planning are not designed to replace the existing network of government control with a new and liberating regime of individual freedom and economic liberty. Instead, they are designed to manage the personal, social, and economic affairs of billions of people the same way that nation–states have been doing on a territorially smaller scale for several centuries. It is the transfer of sovereignty—the legitimized right to politically rule and command obedience over a geographical area—to a more globally encompassing plane. Some are directed to a wider regional arena of control extending only over some existing nation–states, such as NAFTA or the European Union. Others are truly global in their purpose and functions, such as the International Monetary Fund or the World Bank or the World Trade Organization.

But each of these involves a continuation and often an intensification of the politicization of society. It would be an absurd exaggeration to suggest that these international organizations have had no positive effects. Under the more recent rules of the European Union, for example, citizens of member nation–states have a greater degree of freedom of movement to live and work where they desire, with fewer residency restrictions than previously prevailed in many of these countries. There is a greater degree of flexible capital movement among European Union members, which creates an economic environment conducive to a more rational (i.e., more profit-driven) pattern of investments. And the more petty and extreme regulations and controls that have been in place in some of these European countries have been reduced or repealed to match the regulatory norms of the consensus of the member nations.

But, nonetheless, the premise behind these intergovernmental political organizations is the same planning and social engineering mentality that has guided the governments of the individual nation–states. The methods and types of production are to be strictly regulated, prices and wages must conform to standards of "fairness" and "social justice," and huge welfare state "safety nets" are not only internationalized but imposed and expanded in those member countries that, up to that point, had been less interventionist in their domestic policies. There is no way out for any of the member countries other than leaving the regional or international political order to which they belong.

In this debate over the nature of the new global order there is one alternative that has not been fully presented. It is the case for economic or market liberalism as understood in the nineteenth century. It is the third alternative instead of either political and economic nationalism or international political authority. And it is the only alternative, I would like to suggest, that is consistent with individual freedom, economic liberty, international peace, and global prosperity.

In 1952, free market economist Michael A. Heilperin delivered a lecture on "An Economist's Views on International Organization." He told his audience that, "It is an elementary, but often forgotten, knowledge that policies of national governments have always been the principle obstacle to economic relations between people living in various countries, and that whenever these relations were free from government restrictions, equilibrium and balanced growth would follow by virtue of the spontaneous and anonymous mechanism of the market."[11]

Professor Heilperin was doubtful that the proposals for and implementation of international organizations for economic coordination and prosperity would solve the problems of the world for as long as the mentality and ideology of interventionism and planning continued to dominate the arena of public policy. He concluded that, "In the economic sphere it is government policies which have erected the greatest barriers on the path of international relations between human individuals. It is the market mechanism which creates world unity out of a multitude of business transactions. Let this market mechanism be revived, let economic forces regain the freedom to function, and a decisive step will have been made toward world organization, economic and otherwise."[12]

A few years earlier, in 1947, Michael Heilperin had delivered a lecture in which he explained what such a freer world meant in terms of economic policy. The "kind of world envisaged by the [classical] liberal thinkers of the nineteenth and twentieth centuries," he said, was "a world in which political boundaries would gradually become mere administrative divisions; a world of free trade, free capital movements and free migration; a world in which peace as well as prosperity would be indivisible and sought by common action of all mankind."[13]

This is the vision, the alternative to either political and economic nationalism or international organization for regulation and planning, that needs to be restored for the twenty-first century. The great insight of the classical economists and classical liberals of the eighteenth and nineteenth centuries was their clear demonstration that both freedom and prosperity were possible without government control or direction. Beginning with Adam Smith they offered instead a "system of natural liberty," in which government would be limited to a handful of functions related mostly to securing and protecting people's individual rights to life, liberty, and property.[14] Beyond this, all human relations and interactions would be based on voluntary agreement and peaceful mutual benefit.

Even earlier than Adam Smith's *Wealth of Nations*, Smith's Scottish colleague and friend David Hume had demonstrated that international division of labor and trade benefited all participants. He showed that the mercantilist idea that nation–states were rivals—in which if one country gained, another had to lose—was fundamentally wrong. The very nature of peaceful trade is that each transactor enters into the exchange precisely because he considers that what he will receive is worth more to him than what he has to give up to acquire it. Furthermore, the more prosperous one's trading partners, the better the market for one's goods, since this widens the selection of opportunities for all nations to acquire things that would be more costly or impossible to make at home and, at the same time, have the means to pay for them in trade.[15]

It increasingly came to be seen that wars between nations were both harmful and counterproductive. What was wanted was an international arena of peace, in which rights and property were secure and the individuals of the various nations of the world could go about their private business of improving their own personal circumstances through market exchanges that cumulatively enhanced the prosperity of all in the society.

The Austrian economist Joseph Schumpeter summarized this spirit in the following way in a lecture delivered in 1941. He said that during the second half of the nineteenth century, "the world was rapidly internationalizing itself." The goal and general policy direction was: "Free movement of commodities, restricted if at all only by custom tariffs; freedom, unquestioned in principle, of migration of people and of capital; all this facilitated by unrestricted gold currencies and protected by a growing body of international law that on principle disapproved of force and compulsion of any kind and favored peaceful settlement of international conflicts—that fairly embodies not only what was or was becoming approved practice but also what a majority of people approved." It was a civilization "not favorable to cults of national glory, victory, and so on."[16]

Central to the success of this classical liberal conception of international order was the depoliticization of human relationships. By restricting government involvement in social and economic life to mostly the guarding and guaranteeing of individual rights and property, politics could not and for the most part did not interfere in processes and outcomes of market competition and association. It was not a matter of state whether the citizens or subjects of a particular country purchased more or less of the goods they desired from domestic manufacturers or suppliers in a different land. It was not an affair of national honor whether or not the resources or raw materials in a particular country were owned by the citizens of that land or by individuals who happened to reside in another nation in a different part of the world. It was not an issue of national policy whether individuals chose to leave the land in which they had been born to find more attractive and profitable places to live and work, or whether people born in other countries chose to move into the country under that government's jurisdiction because of its attractiveness as a place to reside and earn a living.

The very nature and requirements of the market economy is that every participant in the social system of division of labor searches out that niche and activity in which he hopes to earn the greatest net gain in his income and return from any investments he undertakes. The labor services an individual offers for hire, the resources and raw materials he employs, and the capital that he invests must be directed to making those goods and services that others in the society value most highly, and from the sale of which each producer hopes to earn the financial wherewithal to reenter the market as a consumer and demand what others have for sale in exchange.

A global network of interdependent exchange emerges from this process, in which the origin and location of employment, resources, and capital are of no importance, other than that they tend to be used where they offer the most economically cost-efficient and profitable application for satisfying the demands of the consumers of the world. The entire planet becomes a world-encompassing community of commerce and trade. The motto of this social order becomes: free trade, peace, and goodwill among nations—the very motto adopted by the British opponents of protectionism and mercantilism in the early nineteenth century.

Such a world of freedom, peace, and prosperity does not need either the end of nations and their administrative sovereignty or their replacement by international organizations asserting super-state powers of control. What is needed is the successful rebirth and triumph of the ideal and practice of freedom as proposed by the classical liberals of earlier times and now. This was explained by the Austrian economist Ludwig von Mises:

> [Classical] Liberalism did not and does not build its hopes upon abolition of the sovereignty of the various national governments, a venture which would result in endless wars. It aims at a general recognition of the idea of economic freedom. If all peoples become liberal and conceive that economic freedom best serves their own interests, national sovereignty will not longer engender conflict and war. What is needed to make peace durable is neither international treaties and covenants nor international tribunals and organizations like the defunct League of Nations or its successor, the United Nations. If the principle of the market economy is universally accepted, such makeshifts are unnecessary; if it is not accepted, they are futile. Durable peace can only be the outgrowth of a change in ideologies.[17]

The ideology of today is that of the interventionist–welfare state. Governments talk of market-oriented reforms, privatization of state enterprises, revamping the welfare state, reducing spending and trying to balance the government's budget, or even managing a budgetary surplus. The rhetoric rings with the sound of economic freedom and a greater individual autonomy and responsibility. Unfortunately, what is meant is greater freedom relative to the now-defunct idea of comprehensive Soviet-style socialist central planning.

And, indeed, by that standard, the world has been moving in the direction of greater liberty.

But the benchmark from which economic freedom and the role of government are judged and evaluated is not one that uses the standard of Adam Smith's system of natural liberty for its point of comparison. Whether it be in the United States or in Western Europe, the domain of the market economy is confined and considered only appropriate within a straightjacket of government regulations, controls, and rules specifying methods of production, ranges in which prices and wages are considered "fair," a "safety-net" of welfare provisions and redistributive schemes to assure "social justice," as well as prohibitions on various types of personal conduct and private choices.[18]

The networks of intergovernmental international organizations that have been established since the Second World War reflect the interventionist ideologies of the member governments. And if these organizations, and new ones that have been proposed, were given even greater regulatory and controlling authority, they would merely extend this ideology in a more uniform and globally encompassing manner. Degrees of freedom still retained, for example, in the United States would be threatened in the process of member governments establishing the rules and standards behind the controls of these international organizations that were given increased political power and authority. Since international treaties take precedence over even the Constitution of the United States, those liberties guaranteed and still respected under the Bill of Rights might be weakened or possibly lost.

In his 1952 lecture, Michael Heilperin argued, "The necessary conditions for a return to economic liberalism on an international scale can be achieved within the various nations only through internal political developments."[19] In other words, international organizations cannot bring the world freedom, peace, and prosperity. Freedom and prosperity begin at home, within each country, with the peoples of those countries discovering and accepting the principles of political, personal, and economic liberty. When the governments of each of those countries begin to practice the principles of freedom at home a network of free peoples encompassing more and more of the world will emerge and develop on its own, without the guiding and planning hand of the state. Each nation practicing the principles of the free market at home and free trade toward its global neighbors will provide the political setting in which individuals will spontaneously generate the private relationships of international association, order, and peace that will bring about the prosperity that people all over the world desire.

At the same time, in not relying upon or being limited by the rules and regulations of international organizations, any countries that wish to go further and faster along the path to economic freedom than some of their global neighbors will not be held back or prevented from doing so.

True internationalism and world peace will come through individual freedom, the free market, and the peaceful and voluntary associations of civil society. This should be our ideal for the twenty-first century.

The essays in this twenty-ninth volume in the Hillsdale College *Champions of Freedom* series are taken from the March 2001 Ludwig von Mises Lecture program and are devoted to the issues surrounding the meaning and significance of free market globalization. They also critically evaluate many of the hurdles standing in the way of establishing an international free market order. It is hoped they will offer some useful guideposts in moving beyond the present political domination of social and economic affairs among nations, so that a truly global society of freedom can be the achievement of the years to come.

Richard M. Ebeling
Ludwig von Mises Professor
of Economics
Hillsdale College

Notes

[1]Harry Pratt Judson, *Europe in the Nineteenth Century* (New York: Charles Scribner's Sons, 1900), p. 315.

[2]Eugene Staley, *World Economy in Transition* (Port Washington, NY: Kennikat Press, [1939] 1971), pp. 3–20.

[3]Judson, *Europe in the Nineteenth Century*, p. 321.

[4]R. R. Palmer, *A History of the Modern World* (New York: Alfred A. Knopf, 1961), p. 426.

[5]Ibid., pp. 564–66.

[6]Charles F. Bastable, *The Commerce of Nations* (London: Methuen, 1899), pp. 1–2.

[7]See Wilhelm Ropke, *International Economic Disintegration* [1942] (Philadelphia, PA: Porcupine Press, 1978), p. 78.

[8]See Richard M. Ebeling, "Liberalism and Collectivism in the 20th Century," in Alexsandras Shtromas, ed., *The End of "Isms"? Reflections on the Fate of Ideological Politics after Communism's Collapse* (London/New York: Blackwell, 1994), pp. 69–84, on the consequences of political and economic collectivism in the twentieth century.

[9]See Richard M. Ebeling, "The Global Economy and Classical Liberalism: Past, Present and Future," in Richard M. Ebeling, ed., *The Future of American Business* (Hillsdale, MI: Hillsdale College Press, 1996), pp. 9–60, for an interpretative analysis of the economic liberalism of the nineteenth century, the political and economic nationalism and collectivism of the twentieth century, and the ideal of international economic freedom for the twenty-first century.

[10]Pedro Schwartz, *Back from the Brink: An Appeal to Fellow Europeans Over the Monetary Union* (London: Institute of Economic Affairs, 1997), p. 26.

[11]Michael A. Heilperin, "An Economist's Views on International Organization," in Lyman Bryson, ed., *Foundations of World Organization* (New York: Harper & Brothers, 1952), p. 53.

[12]Ibid., p. 59.

[13]Michael A. Heilperin, "Prosperity versus Peace: The Political Consequences of a New Economic Fallacy," in Lyman Bryson, ed., *Conflicts of Power in Modern Culture* (New York: Harper & Brothers, 1947), p. 553.

[14]Adam Smith, *The Wealth of Nations* (New York: Modern Library, 1937), Book IV, Chapter IX, p. 651

[15]David Hume, "Of the Jealousy of Trade" in Eugene R. Miller, ed., *Essays: Moral. Political Literary* (Indianapolis, IN: Liberty Classics), pp. 327–31.

[16]Joseph A. Schumpeter, "An Economic Interpretation of Our Time," [1941] in Richard Swedberg, ed., The *Economics and Sociology of Capitalism* (Princeton, NJ: Princeton University Press, 1991), pp. 339–40.

[17]Ludwig von Mises, *Human Action: A Treatise on Economics,* 4th ed. (Irvington-on- Hudson, NY: Foundation for Economic Education, 1996), p. 686.

[18]See Richard M. Ebeling "The Free Market and the Interventionist State," in Richard M. Ebeling, ed., *Between Power and Liberty: Economics and the Law* (Hillsdale, MI: Hillsdale College Press, 1998), pp. 9–46, for a contrast between the principles of the free market economy and the characteristics of the interventionist–welfare state.

[19]Michael Heilperin, "An Economist's Views on International Organization," in Bryson, *Conflicts of Power in Modern Culture,* p. 59.

RICHARD M. EBELING

The Economist as the Historian of Decline: Ludwig von Mises and Austria Between the Two World Wars

Ludwig von Mises and His Place in Austria Between the Two World Wars

In the months immediately after he arrived in the United States in the summer of 1940, Ludwig von Mises set down on paper his reflections on his life and contributions to the social sciences. But his *Notes and Recollections* is less a detailed autobiography and more a restatement of his most strongly held ideas in the context of the times in which he had lived in Europe. It carries in it a tone of despair and dismay about the direction in which European civilization seemed to be moving at the end of the first four decades of the twentieth century. In clear anguish and frustration, he summarized how he viewed his efforts as an economist in Europe in general and Austria in particular during those years between the two world wars:

> Occasionally I entertained the hope that my writings would bear practical fruit and show the way for policy. Constantly I have been looking for evidence of a change in ideology. But I have never allowed myself to be deceived. I have to come realize that my theories explain the degeneration of a great civilization; they do not prevent it. I set out to be a reformer, but only became the historian of decline.[1]

In the years between 1918 and 1938 Mises' activities were divided into two interrelated categories: his scholarly writings on various themes in economic theory and political economy, and his work as an economic policy analyst and advocate for the Vienna Chamber of Commerce, Crafts, and Industry.[2] Even before the First World War, he had already established himself as a leading monetary theorist with the publication of *The Theory of Money and Credit* in 1912. Besides its many other theoretical contributions, Mises formulated what became known as the Austrian theory of the business cycle. Inflation and depression were not inherent to a capitalist economy, but were the result of government control and mismanagement of the monetary system through manipulation of market rates of interest.[3]

In the months following the end of the war in November 1918, Mises wrote *Nation, State and Economy.* He attempted to present a classical liberal analysis of and explanation for the problems of nationality and nationalism, the failures of German and Austrian liberalism that culminated in the First World War, and the economic consequences from the implementation of wartime collectivism and socialism in Imperial Germany and the Austro–Hungarian Empire. He ended the book with an appeal for reason and rationality in designing postwar policies in Germany that would enable an enduring peace and a renewal of prosperity through a return to a regime of economic liberalism and a political philosophy of individualism under the rule of law.[4]

But an article he published in 1920, and which two years later he expanded into a book-length treatise on *Socialism,* caused the whirlwind of debate that surrounded him for the rest of his life. In this work, Mises demonstrated that the central planners of a socialist state would have no way of knowing how to use the resources of the society at their disposal for least-cost and efficient production. Without market-generated prices, the planners would lack the necessary tools for "economic calculation." The reality of the promised socialist utopia would be poverty, economic imbalance, and social decay. Furthermore, Mises argued that any type of collectivism that was applied comprehensively would result in a terrible tyranny, since the state would monopolize control over everything needed for human existence. While written as a response to those who were advocates of socialist central planning in general, it is also worth keeping in mind that his 1920 article, in particular, was written—and first delivered as a lecture in 1919 at the Austrian Economic Society—against the backdrop of the proposals being made for "nationalization" and "socialization" of the means of production in Austria and Germany during the year following the end of the war, when Social Democrats were in positions of power in both countries.[5]

In 1927, Mises published *Liberalism,* in which he presented the classical liberal vision of the free and prosperous society, one in which individual freedom would be respected, the market economy would be free, open, and unregulated, and government would be limited to the primary functions of protecting life, liberty, and property.[6] He followed this work with *Critique of Interventionism* in 1929, a collection of essays in which he tried to explain that the interventionist–welfare state was not a "third way" between capitalism and socialism, but a set of contradictory policies that, if fully applied, would eventually lead to socialism through incremental increases in government regulation and control over the economy—and that Germany in the 1920s was heading down a dangerous political road that would lead to the triumph of national socialism.[7]

Not surprisingly, both Marxists and Nazis viewed Ludwig von Mises as a serious intellectual enemy. In fact, in 1925, the Soviet journal *Bolshevik* published an article calling him a "theorist of fascism."[8] What was Mises' "crime" deserving of such a charge? In a 1925 article, "Anti-Marxism," Mises explained the process by which Marxian thought came to have such a strong hold on German intellectuals and the division of these intellectuals into different anticapitalist camps. Looking over the ideological and political landscape of Germany in the middle of the 1920s, Mises argued that the rising force in opposition to Marxian socialism was "national socialism." The national socialists argued that "proletarian interests" had to be submerged in the wider interests of the "fatherland." The strong state would control and repress the profit motive of the private sector and pursue an aggressive foreign policy. Mises also said in this article that Marxist Russia and a "national socialist" Germany would be natural allies in a war in Eastern Europe—thereby anticipating the infamous Nazi–Soviet Pact of August 1939, which served as the prelude to the beginning of the Second World War.[9]

In an accompanying article, "Social Liberalism," which Mises published the following year in 1926, he warned that a growing number of people in Germany were "setting their hopes on the coming of the 'strong man'—the tyrant who will think for them and care for them."[10] What Mises clearly saw and explained in the mid-1920s were the political, cultural, and ideological forces at work in Germany that were creating the conditions for the victory of Adolf Hitler and the Nazi movement in 1933.

Mises' efforts in various areas of public policy in Austria grew out of his position at the Vienna Chamber of Commerce where he was hired in October 1909, first as an assistant for the drafting of documents and then in 1910 as a deputy secretary. Mises was promoted to "first secretary" of the Vienna Chamber *(Leitenden Kammerssekertars)* when he returned to his duties after his service as an officer in the Austrian Army during the First World War. He was in charge of the Chamber's finance department, which was responsible for banking and insurance questions, currency problems, foreign exchange regulations, and public finance and taxation. He also consulted on issues relating to civil, administrative, and constitutional law. Indeed, because of his wide interests and knowledge, practically every facet of the Chamber's activities concerning public policy and regulation fell within his expertise.[11]

Mises also was assigned special tasks. From November 1918 to September 1919, he was responsible for financial matters relating to foreign affairs at the Chamber. In 1919–1921, he was in charge of the section of the Austrian Reparations Commission for the League of Nations concerned with the settling of outstanding prewar debt.[12] His activities in these assignments were highly regarded and praised for their accomplishments. For example, after he stepped down as one of the directors of the Office of Accounts for the settlement of these prewar debts, *The Laws for Peace,* a publication reporting on matters relating to the execution of the terms of the Treaty of St. Germain that ended the war between Austria and the Allied Powers, summarized his contribution in the following way:

> Due to his responsibilities as a deputy director in the offices of the Vienna Chamber of Commerce, Crafts and Industry, he has had to resign from his activities in the Office of Accounts.

> As an economic theorist, Professor Mises has made a name for himself in the German-speaking scientific world far beyond the boundaries of Austria. His wide knowledge and his accurate, clear way of thinking are combined with an extraordinary, practical understanding and a detailed knowledge of the economic life in Vienna and Austria. Given Austria's present economic and financial difficulties, that the arranging of the debentures for the settlement of prewar debts has been facilitated under such comparatively favorable conditions we owe to his farseeing and able handiwork. With foresight into the requirements necessary for success, he sketched out the rules for the committee overseeing the settlement of the debentures. And it was his proposals for the issuance of the debentures that were adopted by the consortium of nations. It was just as important and beneficial for the work of the Office of Accounts that Mises applied, in a strictly objective way, his knowledge of the economic situation in the selection of the Office's personal. Already as a staff member of the Chamber of Commerce, he had won the confidence of wide circles in the business world, and he has kept that confidence in his work with the Office of Accounts.[13]

At the Chamber, Mises explained, "I created a position for myself." While always having a superior nominally above him, he basically came to operate on his own with the assistance of a few colleagues. Though he felt that his advice was not often taken, he viewed himself as "the economist of the country," whose efforts were "concentrated on the crucial economic political questions" and that "[i]n the Austria of the postwar period I was the economic conscience."[14]

Friends often suggested to him that he could have had more of a positive impact on Austrian economic policy if he had been willing to give a little and modify his principled stance on various issues. But Mises' only regret, as he looked back on his years at the Chamber, was that he often felt that he compromised too much, though he stated that he had always clearly understood that in politics compromise was inevitable. The challenge was to "give" on the less important issues so as to have a better chance to succeed on the essential ones. This is how he viewed the positions he often took within the Chamber so as to get the organization to publicly back policies that he considered crucial at various times during these years.[15]

By the early 1930s, Mises understood that a Nazi victory in Germany would threaten Austria. As a classical liberal and a Jew, he could be sure that after a Nazi takeover of Austria the Gestapo would come looking for him. So when in March 1934 he was offered a way out by William E. Rappard, co-founder and director of the Graduate Institute of International Studies in Geneva, Switzerland, who offered him a position as Professor of International Economic Relations, Mises readily accepted and moved to Geneva in October 1934.[16] After he accepted the appointment in Geneva he went on extended leave from the Chamber, though he continued to return to Vienna periodically to consult on various policy matters until February 1938.[17]

But by the time he left Vienna in October 1934, Mises believed that he had done little more than fight a series of rear-guard actions to delay the decay and destruction of his beloved Austria. "For sixteen years I fought a battle in the Chamber in which I won nothing more than a mere delay of the catastrophe.... Even if I had been completely successful, Austria could not have been saved," Mises forlornly admitted. "The enemy who was about to destroy it came from abroad [Hitler's Nazi Germany]. Austria could not for long withstand the onslaught of the National–Socialists who soon were to overrun all of Europe." But he had no regrets over the efforts he had made. "I could not act otherwise. I fought because I could do no other."[18]

Austria Between the Two World Wars, 1918–1938

One day in 1927, Ludwig von Mises stood at the high window of his office at the Vienna Chamber of Commerce. Looking out over the *Ringstrasse* (the main grand boulevard in the center of Vienna), he said to his young friend and former student Fritz Machlup, "Maybe grass will grow there, because our civilization will end."[19] To understand why Mises would have drawn such a dark picture of Vienna's and Austria's future, and his attempts to influence Austrian economic policy during this period between the two world wars, requires an appreciation of the political and economic catastrophe that followed from the First World War in this part of the European continent.[20]

Prewar Austria–Hungary under the Habsburg monarchy had been a vast polyglot empire in Central and Eastern Europe encompassing a territory of approximately 415,000 square miles with a population of over 50 million. The two largest linguistic groups in the Empire were the German-speaking and Hungarian populations, each numbering about 10 million. The remaining 30 million were Czechs, Slovaks, Poles, Romanians, Ruthenians, Croats, Serbs, Slovenes, Italians, and a variety of smaller groups of the Balkan region.

During the last decades of the nineteenth and the opening decade and a half of the twentieth centuries, the Empire increasingly came under the strain of nationalist sentiments by these various groups, each desiring greater autonomy and some forcefully demanding independence. The First World War brought the 700-year-old Habsburg dynasty to a close.[21] The war had put severe political and economic strains on the country. Power was centralized in the hands of the military command, civil liberties were greatly curtailed, and the economy was controlled and regulated.[22] But the more that power was concentrated and the more that the fortunes of war turned against the Empire, the more the national groups—most insistently the Hungarians and then the Czechs, Croats, and Poles—demanded self-determination to form their own nation states.[23]

The Empire formally began to disintegrate in October 1918, when first the Czechs declared their independence, followed by the Hungarians and the Croats and Slovenes. On November 11, 1918, the last of the Habsburg emperors, Karl, stepped down from the throne, and on November 12, a provisional national assembly in Vienna proclaimed a republic in German–Austria, as this remnant of the Empire was now named. But in the second article of the document of independence, it was stated that "German–Austria is an integral part of the German Republic." Thus the new Austria was born—reduced to 32,370 square miles with a population of 6.5 million inhabitants, one-third of whom resided in Vienna—with a significant portion of the population not wishing their country to be independent but unified (an *Anschluss)* with the new republican

Germany. From the moment the new Austria was born, it was plagued by three problems: the disintegration of the Austro–Hungarian monetary system; socialist-welfare programs, budget deficits, and inflation; and threatened political disintegration within the boundaries of the new smaller Austrian state.

For almost five months after the Empire had politically broken apart, the Austro–Hungarian National Bank continued to operate as the note-issuing central bank within German–Austria, Czechoslovakia, and Hungary. The Czechs, however, increasingly protested that the Bank was expanding the money supply to cover the expenses and food subsidies of the German–Austrian government in Vienna. In January 1919, the new Yugoslavian government declared that all notes of the Austro–Hungarian Bank on their territory would be stamped with a national mark, and only such stamped money would then be legal tender. The Czech government announced the same in late February 1919. The Czech border was sealed to prevent smuggling notes into the country and the notes on Czechoslovakian territory were stamped between March 3 to 10. Soon after, both Yugoslavia and Czechoslovakia began to issue their own national currencies and exchange the stamped Austrian notes for their new monetary units.

In Hungary the situation was more chaotic. In March 1919 a Bolshevik government took power in Budapest, and began printing huge quantities of small denomination notes with Austro–Hungarian Bank plates in their possession, as well as larger notes of their own design, causing a severe inflation. The Bolshevik government was overthrown in August 1919 by invading Romanian armies. The Austrian Bank notes were not embossed with a national stamp until March 1920, and a separate national currency was introduced in Hungary in May 1921.

The Austrian government, in response, to the monetary decisions by the Yugoslavians and the Czechs, began their own official stamping of Austro–Hungarian Bank notes within its territory between March 12 and 24, 1919.[24] But the limiting of notes considered legal tender in the new Austria did not end the problem of monetary inflation. In a matter of weeks after the declaration of the Austrian Republic, the coalition government made up of the Social Democrats, the Christian Socialists, and the Pan-German Nationalists began the introduction of a vast array of social welfare programs. They included a mandatory eight-hour workday, a guaranteed minimum one- to two-week holiday for industrial employees, a continuation and reinforcement of the wartime system of rent controls in Vienna, centrally funded unemployment and welfare payments, and price controls on food supplies that were supplemented with government rationing and subsidies.[25] The cost for these latter programs was huge and it kept growing. In 1921, half of the Austrian government's budget deficit was caused by the food subsidies.[26]

To cover these expenditures the Austrian government resorted to the printing press.[27] Between March and December 1919, the paper money of the Austrian Republic increased from 831.6 million crowns to 12.1 billion crowns. By December 1920, it had increased to 30.6 billion crowns; by December 1921 to 174.1 billion crowns; by December 1922 to 4 trillion crowns; and to 7.1 trillion crowns by the end of 1923. Prices rose dramatically through this period. A cost of living index, excluding housing, (with July 1914 = 1) stood at 28.37 in January 1919; by January 1920 it had risen to 49.22; by January 1921 it had gone up to 99.56; in January 1922 it stood at 830; by January 1923 it had shot up to 11,836; and in April 1924 it was at 14,850.

The foreign exchange value of the Austrian Crown also dramatically fell during this period. In January 1919, one dollar could buy 16.1 crowns in the Vienna foreign exchange market; by May of 1923, a dollar traded for 70,800 crowns.[28]

Adding to the monetary and financial chaos was the virtual political disintegration of what remained of Austria. Immediately after the declaration of the Austrian Republic, political power devolved to the provinces and the local communities, which showed little loyalty to the new national government and great animosity toward the capital city of Vienna. In 1919 some provinces even entered into independent negotiations with Switzerland and Bavaria about possible political incorporation into these neighboring countries. But a primary motivation for this provincial "nationalism" or "particularism" was the food and raw materials crisis.

The imperial government had forcefully requisitioned food from the agricultural areas of German–Austria during the war. The new republican government in Vienna continued the practice of forced requisition at artificially low prices, using a newly formed

Volkswehr (People's Defense Force) to seize the food supplies sold in Vienna at controlled prices for ration tickets.[29] The provincial governments used their local power to prevent the export of their agricultural products to Vienna at these below market prices. The governments in the provinces blocked the provincial borders and imposed passport controls to enter or exit their respective jurisdictions, with baggage and body searches at the provincial checkpoints to determine whether food or other "contraband" were being smuggled among the regions of Austria. But in spite of this, Vienna received food from the countryside through a vast black market network that operated throughout the country. Anything could be had—for (illegal) market prices.[30]

Men, women, and children would scrape together enough money to make weekly railway trips to the countryside to beg and buy food from the farmers in the outlying areas. They would also make excursions to the Vienna Woods to bring back firewood to heat their apartments, hauling on their backs heavy cords of wood they had chopped down. One observer described seeing "men and women of all ages, children as young as five struggling under crushing loads of wood, fighting their way into the trains, falling exhausted upon the roads and incidentally ruining by ignorant felling the timber resources of the country. Moreover this daily migration into the country means withdrawal from productive labor of thousands of the best workers in Vienna."[31]

The food crisis was reinforced by an economic blockade, one that was continued for a brief time after the armistice by the Allied powers, but mostly imposed by the Czechs, Hungarians, and Yugoslavians. Coal supplies throughout 1919 and early 1920 were often very scarce. The Czechs and Hungarians refused to supply coal and other resources unless they received payment in manufactured goods in trade or the hard currencies of the Western powers. But the inability to acquire coal and other essential raw materials resulted in Austrian, and especially Viennese, industry grinding to a halt, with no way to produce the goods necessary to pay for the resources required for production.

Throughout 1919 to 1922, Vienna was on the verge of mass starvation, with food and milk rations almost nonexistent except for the very young. The streets of central Vienna often saw children of all ages begging for food at the entrances to restaurants and hotels. Only relief supplies provided by both the Allied powers and private charities saved thousands of lives in the city. How desperate the economic condition was in Vienna at this time was described by Austrian economist Friedrich von Wieser in a paper he wrote in the autumn of 1919 for a conference on famine in Europe:

> Milk can only be supplied to babies and invalids. In peacetime the daily consumption in Vienna amounted to between 800,000 and 900,000 liters. Now, barely 70,000 liters are available, because Hungary and Czechoslovakia have completely stopped their milk supply to Vienna, and milk production in the Austrian provinces are much reduced. In Vienna today no milk can be given to children over two years of age. Children up to one year receive one liter a day, and those between one and two years receive three-quarters of a liter. We need not dwell on the horrible effects on child mortality.... The nourishment of the population is extremely inadequate, the state of public health very low, and death claims many victims. The number of crimes committed in this extremity, and the number of suicides is extraordinarily high.... The coal shortage and the transport difficulty connected therewith are so severe that we fear we may not be able to forward in time, to the consumer, even the foodstuffs which can be procured. The railroads have no stocks of coal, and when the lines will be blocked by the winter snow, traffic will have to cease everywhere.... Shortage of coal and the transport crisis hamper our industrial production. Even the farmer has to wait for the coal that he needs to thrash his harvest. In the towns, especially Vienna, the supply of gas and electric light is reduced to a minimum, and we fear from day to day that it may have to be stopped altogether. For the two million inhabitants of Vienna, there is at present [autumn of 1919] only enough coal to cover the most urgent kitchen requirements. Till now no supplies are available for the heating of rooms.... Deprived of millions of her own race, who have been assigned as subjects to alien national States; cut off from her industrial undertakings, which she had established and guided throughout the former empire; without food for more than half her inhabitants, almost without coal, without raw materials from abroad—with her railways and workshops worn out, bowed down

> under the burdens of the War and under those of the Peace Treaty—we [Austrians] must indeed doubt whether she [Austria] will be capable of surviving when once the time has come when she may use her powers in peaceful and free competition.[32]

In October 1920 a new constitution was promulgated as the law of the land. Written primarily by the Austrian legal philosopher Hans Kelsen, it defined the lines of authority between the central government and the provinces. The provinces were given wide powers at the local and regional level but the constitution established the supremacy of the federal authority over essential political and economic matters that ended the provincial nationalism and "particularism.[33] One new element resulting from the constitution was that the city of Vienna was now administratively recognized as having a separate "provincial" status. So neither the surrounding province of Lower Austria nor the federal government located in Vienna had jurisdiction over the affairs of the city. From 1920 until 1934, the city became known as "Red Vienna."

Throughout the interwar period, Austrian politics were dominated by the battle between the Social Democrats and the Christian Socialists. The Social Democrats, while rejecting the Bolshevik tactic of dictatorship to achieve their ends, were dedicated to the ideal of marching to a bright socialist future. But outside Vienna (where they consistently won a large electoral majority) they were thwarted in this mission by the Christian Socialists who held the majority in the Alpine provinces of Austria, and therefore in the National Assembly that governed the country as a whole. The Christian Socialists based their support in the agricultural regions of the country where there was a suspicion and dislike for socialist radicalism. The Christian Socialists, however, were willing to use, in turn, domestic regulations, trade restrictions, and income transfer programs to benefit segments of the rural population at the expense of the larger municipalities, and especially Vienna.

The battle between these two parties had first been fought out in 1921 and 1922 when government expenditures and the mounting increases in the money supply to pay for them were threatening runaway inflation and financial and economic collapse. International loans totaling over $170 million and charitable expenditures of about $50 million provided temporary support. In May 1922, Monsignor Ignaz Seipel of the Christian Socialist Party became Chancellor of Austria. After several appeals to the Allied powers, Seipel made a dramatic appearance at the League of Nations in Geneva in August 1922 and arranged for the League to extend a $131.7 million loan to the Austrian government to repay outstanding debts left over from the war and to temporarily cover current expenditures.[34]

In return the League supervised a demanding austerity plan that required sizable cuts in government spending, including the end of expensive food subsidies for the urban population and the firing of 80,000 civil servants. In addition, the League assisted in the construction of a new Austrian National Bank, for which Mises played a central role in the writing of the charter and bylaws. In November 1922 the new Bank was established and the inflation of bank notes was soon ended. By November 1923, the Austrian Federal budget had been brought into balance, a half year earlier than called for under the terms of the loan from the League of Nations. And in March 1925, a new Austrian schilling was introduced to replace the old inflated Austrian crown, and it became redeemable in gold in June 1925.

But in Vienna the Social Democrats were determined to press on with creating a model socialist community. Huge sums of money were spent in the 1920s on building dozens of schools, kindergartens, libraries, and hospitals in the "working class" districts of the city. They also constructed vast new housing complexes, sometimes built literally like fortresses ready to be defended against any counter-revolutionary attacks; one of the most famous of these complexes was *Karl Marx Hof,* three-fifths of a mile long and containing almost 1,400 apartments. In other parts of the city rent control kept the cost of apartment housing artificially low at the expense of the landlords. Municipal social and medical insurance programs provided cradle-to-grave protection—including free burials—for the constituents of the Social Democratic Party in Vienna.[35]

To pay for these programs and projects, the Social Democrats imposed a "soak the rich" tax system. Among them were 18 categories of "luxury" taxes, including entertainment levies that placed a 10 percent tax on opera, theater, and concert tickets and a 40 percent tax on movie theater tickets, which was meant to induce the "working class" to listen to classical music rather than watch Hollywood films. The tax for attending horse races or boxing matches was 50 percent, under the presumption that these were the spectator sports of the wealthy and the comfortable middle class. There was a 33 percent tax levied on any person giving a luncheon or dinner party, or if music was played at a funeral, again under the assumption that only the rich had such parties or could afford to hire musicians. There were heavy taxes on "luxury" apartments and automobiles, as well as on horses used for riding or for drawing a carriage. There was a tax on the employment of more than one servant in a household, with the rate set at 50 schillings a year for the second servant, if female, 300 schillings for the third, and an extra 250 schillings per year for each additional servant after that. There were steep taxes for food and drink served to patrons in bars, cabarets, variety clubs, concert cafes, and restaurants, *Huerigen und Buschenschenken* (popular taverns and inns in the suburbs of Vienna), and liqueur and breakfast houses; the tax rates on these establishments were set anywhere between 2 and 15 percent at the discretion of the tax officials, depending on how they classified the income categories of the clientele in each.[36] One newspaper referred to the city's fiscal system as "the success of the tax vampires," especially since to cover these municipal expenditures the tax base and rates soon enveloped a large portion of Vienna's middle class as well as "the rich."[37]

Parallel to the electoral combat between Social Democrats and the Christian Socialists were paramilitary battles around the country. In 1919 and 1920, under the threat of foreign invaders, especially the Yugoslavian armed forces along Austria's ill-defined southern border and the plundering expeditions of private gangs and the government's *Volkswehr*, who attempted to seize food supplies from the rural population, the farming communities created a *Heimwehr* (Home Defense Force). It soon became the paramilitary army of the Christian Socialists. In turn, the Social Democrats created the *Schutzbund* (Protection League), as their private armed force. Armed with war surplus and other weaponry, they both had training camps, parades, and military drills, and held maneuvers in the countryside, during which they would sometimes engage in actual combat. By 1931, the *Heimwehr* had an armed force of 60,000 men, while the *Schutzband* had an armed and trained membership of 90,000. In comparison, under the peace treaty that ended the First World War, the Austrian Army was limited to a force of 30,000 men.[38]

One of the most serious of these clashes occurred in January 1927 in a town near the Hungarian border southeast of Vienna. Several people were killed in the fighting, including a small child. In July 1927, three members of the local *Heimwehr* where the combat occurred were put on trial in Vienna but soon were acquitted. Mobs from the "working class" districts of the city, who were led by known communists, rampaged through parts of the center of Vienna; they burned the Federal Palace of Justice, requiring the police to use deadly force to put down the violence. In response, the Social Democratic mayor of the city declared the police "incompetent" and set up a new parallel police force, the *Wiener Gemiendewache* (Vienna Municipal Guard), manned mostly by recruits from the Social Democrat's *Schutzbund,* all at the taxpayers' extra expense.

Throughout the 1920s, Austria lived a precarious economic existence. Heavy taxes and domestic regulations hampered private investment in the country with both the private sector and the municipal authorities dependent upon foreign lenders and domestic credit expansion for financing many of their activities. Indeed, the burden of rising taxes and social insurance costs, increasing wage demands by labor unions and tariff regulations actually resulted in *capital consumption* in the Austrian economy through the 1920s.[39] In a report for the Austrian government that Ludwig von Mises had co-authored in 1931, it was shown that between 1925 and 1929 taxes had risen by 32 percent, social insurance by 50 percent, industrial wages by 24 percent, agricultural wages by 13 percent, and transportation costs by 15 percent. Meanwhile, an index of the prices of manufactured goods bearing these costs had increased only 4.74 percent between 1925 and early 1930.[40]

This was the political and economic situation in the country as Austria entered the Great Depression in 1929. Austria's crises in the early 1930s were both political and economic. Between 1929 and 1932, Austria had four changes in the government, with Engelbert Dollfuss becoming Chancellor in May 1932. The economic crisis became especially severe after May 1931. One of Austria's old imperial-era banks, the *CreditAnstalt,* had taken over the *Boden-KreditAnstalt* in October 1929. The latter bank had branches throughout Central Europe and suffered heavy financial losses through most of 1929 into 1930. To sustain the *Boden-KreditAnstalt* and its own financial position, *CreditAnstalt* borrowed heavily in the short-term market. In May 1931, panic set in that *CreditAnstalt* would not be able to meet its financial obligations, which precipitated a run on the bank. At the same time, there was a rush to exchange Austrian schillings for foreign currencies and gold.

The Austrian government responded by passing a series of emergency measures between May and December 1931. Concerned about continuing losses of hard currency reserves, the Austrian government instituted foreign exchange control. But distortions, imbalances, and corruption resulting from the law lead to three revisions during the first year, each one loosening the controls a little bit more.

In February 1932, for example, the Austrian National Bank permitted the use of a system of "private clearings": exporters earning foreign currency from sales abroad could sell at least a portion of their foreign exchange holdings directly to Austrian importers of foreign raw materials, and at a rate of exchange above the official rate. Also that same month, the Austrian National Bank, in cooperation with the Vienna Chamber of Commerce, established a "certificate system." The Chamber was permitted to issue "certificates" allowing exporters of manufactured goods to retain the foreign currency proceeds they had earned from sales abroad so that they would have the necessary funds to purchase the imported raw materials essential to the continuation of production in their enterprises. The controls were phased out in 1933 and 1934 after the Austrian government received loans from a group of foreign sources.[41]

In June of 1931, Austria appealed for financial assistance to provide funds needed to stem the massive loss of gold and foreign exchange following the collapse of the *CreditAnstalt* bank in May. On June 16, the Bank of England provided a 150-million schilling credit to the Austrian National Bank. This was immediately followed by a 100-million schilling credit from the Bank for International Settlements in Basel, Switzerland. In August 1931, the Austrian government appealed to the League of Nations in Geneva for a 250-million schilling loan. Representatives of the Financial Section of the League traveled to Vienna to evaluate the situation. On October 15, 1931, the Bank of England and the Bank for International Settlements postponed repayment of their loans. On May 9, 1932, Austria sent another appeal to the League of Nations for a loan.

After Austria declared a partial moratorium on payment of its international debts, the League signed the Geneva Protocol on July 15, 1932, stating a willingness on the part of Great Britain, France, and Italy to extend a loan to the Austrian National Bank. But the actual loan, in the amount of 296 million schillings (237.4 million in devalued schillings), was not transferred to the National Bank until August 1933. It enabled the Bank to repay the 100 million schillings owed to the Bank of England and the 90 million schillings owed to the Bank for International Settlements, as well as 50 million schillings still owed to the League from 1923. Refinancing the loan a short time later at a lower rate of interest significantly reduced Austria's total foreign debt.

But the events that were to seal Austria's fate were being played out in the political arena. The League loan, like the one in 1922, required that a League representative supervise the allocation and use of the funds and insisted upon austerity measures to reduce government expenditures, in addition to a renewal of the pledge against an *Anschluss* with Germany.[42] The Social Democrats and Pan-German Nationalists in the Austrian Parliament unsuccessfully attempted to block passage of the loan bill, which left a bitter and tense relationship between these two parties and Dollfuss' Christian Socialists.

In March 1933, a procedural argument arose during a parliamentary vote and the leading members of each major party stepped down from the rostrum, bringing the proceedings to a halt. The next day, Chancellor Dollfuss used this as an excuse to suspend the parliament and announce that he was going to rule by decree. In May 1933, Dollfuss decreed a new constitution for Austria that established a fascist-type corporativist political structure in place of the constitution written by Hans Kelsen in 1920.[43]

Tensions continued to mount for the next year until the situation exploded into civil war in February 1934. Based on information that units of the *Schutzbund,* the paramilitary arm of the Social Democratic Party, were going to initiate a coup attempt, the Christian Socialist's *Heimwehr* attempted to disarm them in several cities around the country, including Linz. When fighting broke out, the Austrian Army was called into action to put down the combat.

In Vienna, the Social Democrats called for armed insurrection in "self-defense" against the "reactionary" forces of the Austrian Army and the *Heimwehr.* For four days deadly and destructive fighting went on in the outer districts of Vienna, with hundreds either killed or wounded and the government forces using artillery pieces to bombard Social Democratic strongholds. When the fighting ended, the Social Democratic forces were completely defeated, most of the its leadership fled the country, and the party was declared illegal.

Then in July 1934, a group of Austrian Nazis, inspired by Hitler's rise to power in Germany the preceding year, attempted a coup. They seized the Chancellery building, captured and killed Dollfuss, and proclaimed a National Socialist government. They were swiftly defeated by forces loyal to the Austrian government, as was another Nazi-led uprising in the region of Styria at the same time. When Mussolini declared Italy's intention to preserve Austria's independence by sending military forces to the Brenner Pass at the Italian–Austrian border, Hitler repudiated his Austrian followers (for the time being).

Kurt von Schuschnigg became Chancellor following Dollfuss' death, continuing to rule in the same authoritarian manner as his predecessor. On March 12, 1938, the German Army crossed the Austrian border. When Adolf Hitler arrived in Vienna on March 15, he announced that his native Austria had been incorporated into Nazi Germany. Over the next several weeks the Gestapo arrested tens of thousands of Viennese. An estimated seventy thousand were soon imprisoned or sent to concentration camps, including Schuschnigg. Among the immediate victims were the Jews of Vienna, who were harassed, beaten, tortured, murdered, or humiliated by being made to scrub the streets of Vienna on their hands and knees with toothbrushes while surrounded by tormenting crowds of onlookers.[44] Thus ended Austria's tragic twenty-year history between the two world wars.

Monetary Disintegration, Inflation, and Institutional Reform 1918–1923

When the First World War ended, Ludwig von Mises was serving as an economic consultant with the Austrian General Staff in Vienna. He had seen action on the Russian front as an artillery officer, three times decorated for bravery under fire. Following the signing of the Treaty of Brest–Litovsk, which ended the war between Imperial Germany and Austria–Hungary with Lenin's new Bolshevik government in Russia in March 1918, Mises was appointed the officer in charge of currency control in Austrian-occupied Ukraine, with his headquarters in Odessa. He was transferred to Vienna in the summer of 1918. Back in the capital, he picked up his writings on policy matters, when not occupied with his military responsibilities.

For the General Staff, he prepared a paper in which he offered some "Remarks Concerning the Establishment of a Ukrainian Note-Issuing Bank." In February 1918, an independent Ukraine had been declared in Kiev, and Mises outlined the institutional rules that should be followed by a Ukrainian central bank. All bank notes issued and outstanding should be at all times covered with gold or foreign exchange redeemable in gold equal to one-third of the bank's liabilities. Bank assets in the form of secure short-term loans should back the remaining two-thirds of the notes in circulation. Mises admitted that there were particular institutional and historical circumstances that would have to be taken into consideration in setting the conditions under which certain types of borrowers might have access to the lending facilities of the Ukrainian central bank. What was crucial for Ukraine to have a sound monetary system were relatively high reserves for redemption of bank notes on demand and limits on the term-structure of the loans made by the central bank.[45]

But the more important problem, looking forward to the end of the war and a return to peacetime economic conditions, was the reestablishment of the Austrian monetary system. On July 23, 1914, the Austro–Hungarian National Bank had 2,130 million crown notes in circulation with a 74.6 percent cover in gold. Shortly after the war began in August 1914, the government suspended gold redemption for crown notes, and turned to the central bank to finance a large proportion of the wartime expenses. By October 26, 1918, crown notes in circulation had increased to 33,529 million with only a 1 percent gold cover. The actual state of the bank's financial condition was not widely known due to wartime censorship.[46]

In two articles in the autumn of 1918 that were subject to the censor's red pen,[47] Mises restated the quantity theory of money, explained the inherent non-neutrality of money on the structure of prices, argued against those who claimed that the general rise in prices during the war years was singularly due to the decrease in the quantities of goods and services available on the market during wartime, and reasoned that such a general and sustained rise in prices can only have come about from a sizable expansion of the money supply.

The task ahead would be to end the inflation and restore the soundness and stability of the Austrian currency when the fighting stopped. Mises made clear that monetary theory, as a social scientific endeavor, offered no answer to the question as to which policy was best to follow in the postwar period. One option would be to end the printing of bank notes and allow the value of the Austrian crown to stabilize in terms of its current depreciated market value in exchange for gold and foreign currencies. A new fixed rate of exchange could be established, Mises suggested, say, one year from the day the war ended. If, on the other hand, there were a strong preference to return to the status before the war began in 1914, including a restoration of the prewar foreign exchange value of the Austrian crown, it would be necessary for the government to run a budget surplus and pay off its debt to the Austro–Hungarian Bank, which would then take the bank notes out of circulation. The monetary contraction would have to continue until the value of the crown had once again risen to its prewar parity.

Mises emphasized that such a monetary deflation would have various disruptive social consequences in the transition to the higher foreign exchange rate for the crown. Whether to contract the money supply or stabilize the value of the crown at its depreciated value was a political question that economic theory could not answer, other than to explain the consequences that were likely to follow from either course of action.[48]

These essays looked forward to a return to peace, but they contain nothing suggesting the actual cataclysm of events that were to follow. Indeed they almost have a surrealistic quality to them in suggesting a postwar period in which there would be a calm, stable, and relatively smooth transition to a restructured monetary system as a complement to the return to a tranquil peacetime economy. Instead, the problems that Mises attempted to grapple with when the war was over in November 1918 concerned the actual situation of monetary disintegration, high inflation, political disorder, and general economic chaos.

With the end of the war, Mises returned to his position with the Vienna Chamber of Commerce. And he was shortly to take on responsibility for the Austrian Section of the League of Nations Reparations Commission. His written contributions during the next year and a half seem almost Herculean, considering that he was working far more than a nine-to-five day. His two most well-known works from this period are *Nation, State and Economy* and his essay on "Economic Calculation in the Socialist Commonwealth." People who knew Mises at this time suggested that there was the possibility that he might have been called to serve as Austrian Finance Minister.[49] But he was not. Instead, through most of 1919, the Austrian Minister of Finance was Joseph A. Schumpeter.

But, nonetheless, he formulated several possible monetary policies during the first half of 1919, meant to deal with the onrush of events during those uncertain months. In three fairly lengthy papers he dealt with three distinct but interrelated questions. How shall a previously unified monetary system be separated into different national currencies? How might the private banking sector create a transition to a new currency after government mismanagement of the monetary system will have brought about a sudden inflationary collapse of the currency? And, how might two separate national currency systems be unified or reunified into a single monetary regime?

As we have seen, the first monetary crisis in early 1919 was the disintegration of the unified monetary system of the now collapsed Austro–Hungarian Empire. The newly independent successor states had started embossing official stamps on Austro–Hungarian Bank Notes on their territories, declaring that only these would be considered legal tender within their respective nation–states.

In April 1919, shortly before the Austrian delegation left for France to be given the formal terms for peace from the Allied Powers, Mises prepared a paper titled "The Austrian Currency Problem Prior to the Peace Conference,"[50] in his role as the senior economist responsible for financial matters relating to foreign affairs at the Chamber of Commerce. He outlined alternative possibilities that might be followed in establishing a new monetary order in the wake of the collapse of the Austro–Hungarian Empire and its unified currency system. He discussed the possibilities of maintaining a common single currency area with a single central bank, or a monetary union with independent central banks, or completely independent national currencies issued and managed by separate central banks.

Mises assumed that none of the successor states would opt for the first alternative. So, whether the successor states were to finally adopt a monetary union of national central banks or national central banks each making independent monetary policies, the matter concerned how all the people presently holding notes issued by the Austro–Hungarian National Bank would convert them into units of the respective new national currencies. He suggested that those residing in the respective successor states should have the freedom of converting their old notes into either the national currency of the new country in which they resided or into the currency of any other of the successor states as they found most convenient and useful. The same free choice of currency conversion should apply to those holding quantities of the old notes in countries outside the territory of the former Empire, as well.

The additional problem to which the currency conversion would be tied, Mises said, was the distribution of the Austro–Hungarian prewar and wartime debt among the successor states. He offered a detailed formula of how the distribution of this debt and the conversion of the old notes into new currencies might be reasonably balanced without an undue financial burden on any one of the new countries.[51]

But in the spring of 1919, a far greater problem confronted the new Austria: the danger of runaway or hyperinflation. With state spending seemingly out of control because of the welfare-redistributive programs introduced by the Social Democratic and Christian Socialist coalition government, and especially the cost of subsidized food for the urban populations, the monetary system seemed headed for collapse. In the first half of 1919, the Austrian money supply increased from 831.6 million crowns in March to 8.3 billion crowns in July. The note issue reached 12 billion crowns by December 1919.

In a paper marked "confidential" that he prepared for the bankers and businessmen connected with the Chamber in May 1919, Mises presented a proposal "On the Actions to be Taken in the Face of Progressive Currency Depreciation."[52] He was cautious to say that it was neither certain nor inevitable that a currency collapse had to occur. But if it did, Austria, and particularly Vienna with its large urban population, could be faced with social disintegration, food riots, and mass destruction and theft of property as the value of the medium of exchange fell to zero.

Such violence had already been seen on the streets of Vienna. In an account given by the Austrian Social Democrat Otto Bauer, on April 18, 1919, Austrian communists had instigated a riot by "a few hundred hungry, ignorant, and despairing unemployed and disabled men" to attack the parliament buildings. "At the same time the incident threw ghastly light upon the terrible privation which existed in Vienna. The demonstrators threw themselves upon the fallen horses of the police, tore out pieces of flesh from the still warm bodies of the dead animals, and carried them home as delicacies which had not been enjoyed for a long time."[53]

If the currency were to suffer a rapid collapse, the government would have lost all legitimacy and trust in relation to monetary matters. It would fall on the shoulders of the private sector—banks and businesses—to devise the mechanism to bridge the gap between any such dramatic and rapid collapse of the old currency and the spontaneous shift to the use of alternative monies by the citizens of the society.

Why did the private sector have to prepare for such a contingency? Because, Mises said, "We can hardly expect the government to be of any help." For five years they had done nothing but follow "a disastrous inflationary course." Therefore, he stated, "It is up to us citizens to try to do on our own what the government is failing to do for us. All we can hope from the government is that it will not stymie the endeavors of its private citizens. In their own interest and in the interest of the community, the banks as well as large industrial and commercial enterprises must take the necessary preparatory steps to avert the catastrophic consequences that will follow from the collapse of the currency."[54]

Mises presented a plan to these elements in the private sector to use export revenues and sales of assets to accumulate cash reserves of small denomination units of Swiss money to use as the temporary emergency medium of exchange. He estimated that the amount needed for the purpose was approximately 30 million Swiss francs. There were approximately 1.5 million employees who were neither self-employed nor working in the agriculture or timber sectors of the economy. Assuming that the average monthly income was 1,500 crowns, the total monthly income to be covered would be 2,250 million crowns. At the going exchange rate that came to 22.5 million Swiss francs. Assuming a need for an additional 150 million for government monthly subsistence, unemployment and pension incomes, that added another 1.5 million Swiss francs. To meet any unplanned contingencies, Mises suggested adding an extra 25 percent, to be on the safe side, for a total of 30 million Swiss francs.

The money would be used to pay salaries and pensions and to loan to the government and other employers in the market so that the population would have access to a medium of exchange they could have confidence in. This would be necessary only until normal export sales and capital transfers supplied the required quantities of gold or foreign currencies to use as the permanent substitute monies in a postinflationary Austrian economy.

These were "expedients for the moment of the collapse," Mises explained. Because, "As soon as government interference in the monetary system is eliminated by the collapse of the currency, free market forces will automatically come into play that will supply the economy with the exact amount of money it needs. Sales to other countries will build up at that moment, and will attract the requisite money into the country." Goods might have to be sold at very low prices on the world market, "but that is the inescapable consequence of the disastrous currency policy that will have been pursued earlier."[55]

He also explained the process by which private banks could form an informal consortium to jointly cover the costs and clearings of providing alternative small-note private currencies. "The collapse of the currency will almost certainly have so thoroughly undermined general confidence in the state's monetary system," Mises suggested, "that it will take some length of time before the public will again be willing to use any form of money issued by the state."[56]

While Mises alluded to the possibility of a private monetary order without a central bank in the wake of a currency collapse, realistically central banking was and would remain the prevailing monetary regime. The question then arose as to whether the new Austria should have its own independent central bank and national currency or instead should be integrated into a common currency area with the new Germany. Indeed, Mises stated that, "It is beyond doubt that some day we will carry through a political union with Germany. It is perfectly clear that at such a time the fusion of the Austrian and the German currency systems will take place." But, he also said, "We must remember that the time of such a currency merger is especially critical," for various political and international reasons.[57]

We pointed out earlier that when Austria was declared to be a republic in November 1918, the second article of the document stated that "German–Austria is an integral part of the German Republic." Both inside Austria and among the Allied Powers, there was a strong opinion that an independent Austria as it had been constituted with the break-up of the Austro–Hungarian Empire was not viable as a separate political entity. The Pan-German Nationalist Party in Austria believed that race, language, and culture required the unification of all German people in one German Reich. Many Social Democrats—the most vocal being Otto Bauer, who served as Foreign Minister in the first coalition government—desired unification because it would strengthen the socialist cause in Austria if the country was joined with the new Germany Republic, which possessed a large Social Democratic movement. The Christian Socialists were more reluctant to endorse Austro–German unification, but found it a useful ploy in bargaining for aid, loans, and political support from the Western Allied Powers.

When he looked back at this period immediately after the First World War in his *Notes and Recollections,* written in 1940, Mises said that on the issue of Austrian unification with Germany, "The situation [of Austria's apparently paralyzed political and economic situation at this time] sometimes made me vacillate in my position on the annexation program. I was not blind regarding the danger to Austrian culture in a union with the German Reich. But there were moments in which I asked myself whether the annexation was not a lesser evil than the continuation of a policy that inescapably had to lead to catastrophe."[58] Yet in certain passages in essays written in 1919 it is clear that at the time Mises was persuaded that unification with Germany was a "political and moral necessity."[59]

In 1919, he said that Germany was in the throes of its own inflationary disaster. This made it wiser at this moment to devise a way for Austria to find its own way out of the monetary collapse that might be in front of it. "We are not abandoning the idea of a

Greater Germany when we envision a currency merger as a means to a joint ascension rather than a means to a joint decline." If Austria solved its monetary problem it would be offering to Germany "an example for the proper conduct in critical times like these."[60]

In spite of the fact that in the Treaty of St. Germain, which was presented by the Allied Powers to the Austrian delegation in France in June 1919, it was stated directly that Austria was to be barred from unification with the new German Republic, the sentiment for *Anschluss* persisted. At the end of June 1919, Mises finished a lengthy paper on the very theme of "The Reentry of German–Austria into the German Reich and the Currency Question."[61]

Here one sees Mises as not only a monetary theorist but as the monetary historian. He first lays out a detailed account of how the Austrian monetary system had evolved, from it earlier monetary linkage with the German principalities to its monetary expulsion from the German Confederation in the 1860s after Austria's war with Prussia in 1866, and to its establishment of a gold standard in the 1890s through the inflationary funding of Austria–Hungary's war expenditures between 1914 to 1918.

Political unification of Austria with Germany necessarily would mean monetary unification as well. If the two countries were respectively on the gold standard, the unification would be relatively simple; but the dilemma, Mises pointed out, was that both countries were on paper currencies. No successful unification would be possible until Austria and Germany had abandoned inflationary methods of financing their government expenditures. But this, in turn, would require a coordination of fiscal policies, and in Mises' view this meant a subordination of Austrian financial policy to that of Germany's. "This agreement can hardly be conceived as determining anything but a settlement under which Germany assumes over German–Austria all those powers of expenditure and revenue that she has in the other federal [German] states," including the conversion of Austrian debt into the national debt of Germany.[62] Independent budgetary policies—including deficit spending—during the period leading up to conversion of the currencies could only create pressures for inflationary policies or continuing accumulations of debt that would only forestall the unification process.

Another central reason for the ending of inflationary policies in both countries leading up to unification, Mises argued, was that monetary expansions were non-neutral and took time to work their full effect through the structure of prices.[63] For the market to settle upon a rate of exchange for purposes of the currency conversion between the Austrian crown and the German mark, which would more or less reflect their equilibrium purchasing power parities, there needed to be a period over which the inflationary influences would have worked their final effects on the respective price systems in Austria and Germany.

For the transition to a common currency, Mises suggested the German mark could first be introduced as a "core" or reserve currency in Austria, with a specified ratio of exchange at which the Austrian bank would be obliged to redeem Austrian notes for German marks, and vice versa.[64] Increases and decreases in the number of units of Austrian currency in circulation would be dependent upon deposits or withdrawals of marks from the Austrian banking system. The Austrian National Bank would no longer be an independent authority that determined the quantity of money in the country (similar to the idea behind a currency board). Final unification would then come through the German central bank redeeming all Austrian bank notes for marks at a specified ratio of conversion, after which there would be only one monetary system and one currency in use in both countries.

But no great advantage would accrue from monetary unification for either Austria or Germany unless it was permanently joined by a renunciation of inflationary monetary policies. "The positive effects of having overcome the pernicious effects of monetary 'particularism,'" Mises concluded, "will not be enjoyed by the entire German people unless in matters of currency policy they will have taken a stance in favor of renouncing any inflationary measures."[65]

But a far more immediate problem in 1919 was the disintegration of trade and commerce between the provinces and regions making up the new Austria, a disintegration that threatened the very existence of the country as a political entity. Mises offered his analysis and solutions for Austria's economic future in his paper titled "Vienna's Political Relationship with the Provinces in the Light of

Economics," delivered as a lecture at the Association of Austrian Economists in December 1919.[66] The causes behind the problem, he argued, were preferential abuse of the fiscal structure through the system of differential tax incidence borne by the rural areas in comparison to the urban population, and Vienna in particular. The price controls on food supplies and the government's subsidies for Vienna residents at the financial expense of the farmers reinforced the tension.

Throughout the war, rural property owners had borne a differentially smaller fraction of the costs of the war. While the prices of agricultural goods rose from 40 to 100 times what they had been before the war, the tax on land had not even doubled. Even the income taxes paid by landowners did not keep up with the rental price on land. The agrarian sector in general had been left financially no worse off than they had been before the war.

The tax burden for the war had fallen predominantly on the shoulders of commercial and industrial sectors situated in the cities, especially in Vienna. Not only did taxes go up dramatically, but the government took no account of the effects of inflation on the real cost of assets and their maintenance. They taxed away as "war profits" the greater nominal sums that the entrepreneurs and businessmen needed merely to maintain their capital intact, given the higher crown expense of replacement and repair, and replenishment of inventory and stock. Capital was consumed.[67] "Thus, the result from this fiscal policy followed during the war," Mises said, "is that primarily the agrarian provinces received tax relief, while on the other hand the greater part of all liquid capital was seized by the state, transformed into consumer goods, and used for non-productive purposes during the war."[68]

What the farmers objected to and revolted against was the requisitioning policy introduced during the war, under which, rather than pay higher taxes from the sale of their agricultural goods, the government demanded in-kind payments at implicitly far-below market prices calculated on the basis of gross revenues earned from the land. "The farmers of the Alpine provinces sent their sons willingly into the hopeless war from which many were never to return," Mises explained. "But their loyalty to the Emperor quickly made an about-face the moment the military commercial inspectors for the district began the forced collection of the imposed quota. In the struggle between the brute force of the military and the cunning of the peasantry, the latter won. The collection results worsened from day to day."[69] From the perspective of the landowners and the peasants, they were being made to sacrifice the means of their livelihood at the point of a gun or a bayonet to feed the middle class and the well-off workers of the factories in the cities—especially Vienna—about whom they had always been suspicious.

On the other hand, in the cities—and especially in Vienna—both the working and middle classes were so captured by the myth of class conflict and the supposed exploiting aspect to wartime profits and speculation that they supported the far-below-market imposed maximum prices that both destroyed the supplies of food coming into the city and only enflamed the anger and resentment of the farmers in the rural provinces from whence the city's food needed to come. These same segments of the urban population, enthusiastically supporting the taxing of wartime and inflationary profits, did not realize that,

> In light of the depreciation of our national currency, taxing away war profits signifies that owners of liquid capital, i.e., capital that is recorded in the books of businesses or represented in the form of securities, will be divested through taxation of their financial means for investment.... The city's working population is so much under the spell of the ideas of class struggle and irreconcilable differences of interest between the entrepreneur and the worker, that they do not realize that due to this fiscal policy the basis of their very existence is being reduced through the erosion of liquid capital. The difficulties with which our industry has to struggle nowadays are primarily due to the fact that because of the lack of liquid capital they cannot successfully compete against foreign industry. The level of real wages in our country will have to be kept below that of the foreign worker until, as the result of many years of hard work and economizing, we will again be financially sound and, thus, more competitive.[70]

The central government was reduced to either attempting to use force to requisition food supplies from the outlying provinces

—which only served to drive the provincial governments further away from wanting to be politically a part of the new Austria—or begging for rations of food from the countryside. Either method was a path to political disintegration and economic destruction.

Matching this, considering that Vienna was on the verge of mass starvation, was the loss of the bourgeois spirit of enterprise and work that is both the hallmark and the necessity of city life:

> City residents have to live on what they make through commerce and trade. This is already reflected in the very concept and nature of the city.... If we, the Viennese, want to eat, then we must do business and produce and sell commercial products, so that we can use the profits to procure what we are not able to produce ourselves, namely raw materials and foodstuffs.... Our public's opinion and our ideas about economic policy regarding raw material supplies are completely untenable. We demand from our farmer that he supply us with foodstuffs at a price that is below the price quoted on the world market, and we demand from foreign countries that they make us a present of their foodstuffs and raw materials.... Our ideas about supplying our cities do not correspond to the reality of a city whose working population is made up of entrepreneurs and workers, but reflects the notion of an idle city proletariat that wants to live off the fruits of the farmer's diligence.[71]

A city must be open to commerce and trade. Because the Austrian provinces attempted to economically lock themselves away through provincial trade restrictions and passport controls did not mean that it was in the interest of Vienna to do so in retaliation. "But it is definitely a mistake when the city of Vienna retaliates by restricting entry into Vienna," Mises insisted. "A city whose livelihood depends on commerce and selling industrial products has to rely on visits by people from elsewhere; it must desire and foster such visits and not restrict it under any circumstances.... It is village politics of the worst kind that we are pursuing and not by any means the policy of a great city."[72]

All of Vienna's and Austria's economic difficulties would be gone with a return to a free market. "All these conflicts of interest that exist today between Vienna and the provinces would disappear under free trade," Mises explained. "There would be no conflict over the seizure of grain, the supply of foodstuffs, entry visas, nationalization questions, compensations, and similar matters. As soon as we get rid of the idea that a city can obtain its foodstuffs by means other than commerce and industry, as soon as we understand once again that we have to produce and sell, then foreign countries will perceive us in a completely different light."[73]

Why Vienna had been reduced to this state of affairs, Mises argued, was due to the loss of the spirit of enterprise. "What we lack are not foodstuffs and raw materials, but the spirit that has to pervade a non-agrarian population if it wants to survive, and that is the modern, capitalist spirit of profit-making commerce.... An industrial state can survive without coal, but not without the spirit of a modern economy." The Viennese were living by selling the accumulated wealth of the past. And if their civilization collapsed, Mises concluded, "we will not have perished due to a lack of coal and food, but because we lacked the spirit that builds cities and makes them flourish: the bourgeois spirit."[74]

Free trade and division of labor on the basis of market prices was the only path to salvation if the new Austria were to survive.

What brought Austria back from the precipice was the appointment of Monsignor Ignaz Seipel as Chancellor of Austria in May 1922. In *Notes and Recollections,* Mises describes his interactions with "this noble priest whose world view and conception of life remained alien to me," but whom Mises considered "a great personality." Seipel's "ignorance in economic affairs was that which only a cleric could have," Mises said. "He saw inflation as an evil, but otherwise was rather unacquainted with financial policy." And even when Mises explained to the Monsignor that following the end of inflation would come an unavoidable "stabilization crisis" that no doubt would be blamed on Seipel's Christian Socialists, with the inevitable short-run negative effects for his party, the Chancellor replied that a necessary policy had to be undertaken even if it injured his party's standing. "There were not many politicians in Austria who thought that way," Mises declared.[75]

Seipel did bear severe criticism, both from outside and inside his party, for following this economic policy. The Social Democrats ridiculed his "conversion" to "Manchester liberalism," with an underlying anti-Semitic tone by suggesting a Jewish element at work behind him. His own Christian Socialists accused him of moving from a socialist course to "a consciously and deliberately capitalistic" one. In reply, Seipel said, "A people does not just perish, however, desperate its economic situation." "Spend less and save more" was the remedy for Austria's economic ills.[76]

As we explained earlier, through the assistance of the League of Nations in 1922 to 1923, Austrian inflation was stopped before total collapse (as did happen in Germany during this time).[77] The Austrian federal budget was balanced ahead of schedule (in fact, in 1924 and 1925 the budget went into a modest surplus), and a new Austrian central bank was instituted on a gold basis with redeemability. Over 85,000 government jobs were eliminated by 1925, and modest progress was made in revising the tax schedules.[78]

Monetary Policy, Interventionism, and Fiscal Policy 1924–1930

But Mises' fight against interventionism, socialism, and fiscal mismanagement did not end, especially after the League's supervision of Austrian finances under the terms of the loan agreement expired in 1926. In this period of the mid- to late 1920s, he recalled that his work at the Chamber "was even more routine than during the earlier periods. It was a daily fight against ignorance, inability, indolence, malice, and corruption."[79]

In the area of monetary policy Mises was heartened by "The Return to Gold," following the catastrophic inflations in Austria, Germany, and a number of other countries.[80] The move back to gold had been to a gold-exchange standard, under which the primary reserves of most European nations had become the redeemable hard currencies of a small number of nations—of which the United States was the leading one. Austria was one of those countries that had added nothing to its gold reserves, only adding to its supply of hard currencies as a backing for increases in the issue of schilling notes.[81] But Mises still considered this as "the first step on the way to rehabilitating the ruined monetary situation."[82]

But what he did feel called upon to critically evaluate were the proposals being made by John Maynard Keynes in Great Britain and Irving Fisher in the United States for replacing the traditional gold standard with "managed currencies." The battle to end inflation, he argued, now was replaced with a debate over the most appropriate monetary system. Mises argued the merits of a gold standard, most especially the fact that a gold-based currency removed direct control of the printing press from the grasping hand of government. He also critically evaluated the counterproposals of Irving Fisher and John Maynard Keynes for government-managed currencies, the value of which would be manipulated to stabilize the price level or assure a desired level of employment and output.[83]

He reasoned out the limits and shortcomings in all index number methods that make it near impossible to construct a measure of the purchasing power of money that is not open to disagreement about the goods to be included, the weights to be assigned to the items in the selected basket, the difficulty of estimating changes in the qualities of the goods whose prices are tracked through time, and the fact that new goods are constantly entering the market as old goods are being eliminated. In Mises' estimation, this meant that any monetary policy geared toward changes in "the price level" as calculated on the basis of index numbers would always be open to political manipulation on behalf of various interest groups that would benefit if the index was constructed and weighted one way rather than another.

How, then, could the world move back to actual gold-backed currencies, instead of either managed paper currencies or a gold-exchange standard? The League of Nations should be employed to use political pressure:

> Of course, in this sphere, as well as in others, it is no longer acceptable that each individual country carries on its own economic policy without any consideration for neighboring countries. In the realm of monetary systems it will be necessary to make international agreements. The goal of these international agreements must be to reintroduce the gold standard in every single country of the world, which can be achieved without difficulty if the League of Nations imposes a punitive duty on the exports of

> those countries that refuse to stabilize their monetary system. If the nations of the world once again agree to accept the gold standard we will once more have a monetary system that is not dependent on the influence of one or several individual governments. This monetary system would also guarantee the stability of foreign exchange rates and thereby the stability of international capital and bank transactions.[84]

It was equally in the realm of fiscal policy that Mises believed that both Austria and most other European countries desperately needed to introduce reform and retrenchment in their spending and narrow the arena of government activities. Once there was a time, Mises explained in a lecture delivered in Hungary on "Restoring Europe's State Finances," that conventional wisdom assumed that taxes were an evil and to be minimized.[85] Low, indirect taxes on various items of consumption did not have to impose an egregious burden on the citizenry. While "In the eyes of the older liberals, taxation of income and the interest on capital had the negative effect of slowing down the process of capital formation and hence retarded economic progress.[86]

But now the presumption was that no government spending, no matter for what or how extravagant, had a limit on it. Particularly pernicious in Mises' view was the shift from indirect to direct taxes. Under the assumption that direct taxes could be used to impose a burden only on the wealthy and the owners of property, the tax structure was shifted to weigh more heavily against those presumed to be the rich. "Feelings of envy such as this generated the belief that the impoverishment of entrepreneurs and the owners of capital was beneficial to the economy," he said. "The fact that the economy as a whole, not just the owners of capital, became poorer was completely disregarded."[87]

Equally as detrimental was the growth in government borrowing to cover the expenses and deficits of nationalized industries and municipal services. Most had been financial disasters. "The old fable about Midas has been turned on its head: whatever gold governments touch turned to dust," Mises quipped. And in his view there was only one answer. "There is only one remedy for this problem. Governments and local agencies must sell off all these enterprises and turn them over to private entrepreneurs who will know how to run them at a profit." Unfortunately, Mises admitted, such a proposal ran against the entire tide of public opinion. What were needed was understanding and the will to do what was necessary. "What is needed is frugality" in government spending, he concluded. "The ability to economize, not the invention of new taxes, is the hallmark of a good finance minister."[88]

But nowhere was there a greater lack of such finance ministers and political figures than in his native Austria. In looking at "The Balance Sheet of Economic Policies Hostile to Property" in 1927, Mises stated that the deficit in the Austrian government's budget was almost totally attributable to the large losses in the state-run enterprises and the national railway system.[89] Indeed, the deficit from these two sectors of the economy was greater than the expenditures in the Austrian defense budget. Even the national forestry administration had a deficit, in spite of the profitability of timber sales and exports.

Taxes and government expenditures had to be cut back to restore balance and profitability to the Austrian economy, especially since Austria was a small country heavily dependent upon maintaining its competitiveness in a global market to which it had to adjust and conform. "Reductions in the costs of production only can be effected through a lowering of domestic wages or taxes," Mises said. "If we cannot succeed in reducing taxes and the social burdens that the private producer has to bear, then wages will inevitably have to go down or unemployment will have to go up. The reduction of the tax burden on our enterprises is therefore in the interest of all sectors of the population, not only in the interest of businessmen but also and especially in the interest of the labor force." High taxes and government spending "undermines the necessary conditions for the nation's economic productivity, it is a policy of decline and destruction that must be opposed with all possible strength."[90]

But the heart of the fiscal problem was the philosophy of spending and taxing that was behind the Austrian government's budget. In an address before the Vienna Industrial Club in 1930,[91] Mises pointed out that between 1925 and 1929 spending at all levels of government in Austria had increased 31.4 percent, or almost 8 percent a year. Direct federal taxes alone had increased by 35 percent during this period. Both the Austrian federal government and the city of Vienna were budgeting for even larger increases in the years to come.

The premise behind this growth in government expenditure, Mises said, was the idea that the constraints on private individual and enterprise spending did not apply to government. Whereas in the private sector the financial means available limited the expenditures that could be undertaken, in the public sector it was presumed that taxes were to be increased to cover any desired level of expenditure with little or no thought to the opportunities foregone as a result.

> The worst of these misconceptions is the...idea that the main difference between the state's and the private sector's budget is that *in the private sector's budget expenditures have to be based on revenues, while in the public sector's budget it is the reverse, i.e., the revenue raised must be based on the level of expenditures desired.* The illogic of this sentence is evident as soon as it is thought through. There is always a rigid limit for expenditures, namely the scarcity of means. If the means were unlimited, then it would be difficult to understand why expenses should ever have to be curbed. If in the case of the public budget it is assumed that its revenues are based on its expenditures and not the other way around, i.e., that its expenses have to be based on its revenues, the result is the tremendous squandering that characterizes our fiscal policy. The supporters of this principle are so shortsighted that they do not see that it is necessary, when comparing the level of public expenditures with the budgetary expenditures of the private sector, to not ignore the fact that enterprises cannot undertake investments when the required funds are used up instead for public purposes. They only see the benefits resulting from the public expenditures and not the harm the taxing inflicts on the other parts of the national economy.[92]

The second dangerous premise that guided Austrian fiscal policy was that direct taxation on property was always preferred to indirect taxes on consumption. The effect from following this fiscal course in Austria had been extremely damaging, Mises insisted:

> Property taxes impede the creation of capital. And when the taxation of enterprises goes too far, it results in the consumption of capital. To a large extent, this has been the case here in Austria for the last 18 years. Capital consumption is detrimental

> not only for the owners of property but for the workers as well. The more unfavorable becomes the quantitative ratio of capital to labor, the lower is the marginal productivity of the work force and, consequently, the lower are the wages that can be paid. That the Austrian economy is only able to compete and survive on the basis of the relatively low wages that are paid today is primarily due to the fact that very significant amounts of the capital belonging to Austrian entrepreneurs has been eaten up during the past 18 years.[93]

These two premises had led to seemingly "unlimited demands ... by all and sundry for access to public monies." But when the case to rein in government spending was made, Mises pointed out, the response was to say that many of these expenditures are "inevitable," since they are built into various legislative acts and entitlements. But Mises replied: "What exactly does 'inevitable' mean in this context? That the expenditures are based on various laws that have been passed in the past is not an objection if the argument for eliminating these laws is based on their damaging effects on the economy. The metaphorical use of the term 'inevitable' is nothing but a haven in which to hide in the face of the inability to comprehend the seriousness of our situation. People do not want to accept the fact that the public budget has to be radically reduced."[94]

The bull had to be taken by the horns. Merely dismissing public employees—as had been done under the terms of the loan agreement with the League of Nations in 1922—did not eliminate the core of the problem. Only a reduction in government responsibilities and institutional reform could solve the problem in the long run. Mises detailed various Austrian government agencies that either were unnecessary or duplicative in their activities in the Austrian bureaucracy at the local, provincial, and federal levels that could be eliminated or streamlined to reduce taxing and regulatory burdens on business and the taxpayer. He proposed that they first be introduced in the smaller, rural Austrian provinces to see how effective they were, and when they had demonstrated their effectiveness they could then be extended to the rest of the country.

At the same time, subsidies to state enterprises and to various private sectors, such as in agriculture, had to be abolished. If the criterion of "economic hardship" continued to be the rationale for government subsidies "then probably most of the branches of production will be able to request such entitlements." The threat and existence of capital consumption due to taxes to pay for these and other expenditures were already a problem. Mises concluded that, "Corporate taxes, as well as the income tax, have to be cut, because if they are kept at their present high level, they impede industrial production and allow unemployment to grow at the speed of an avalanche. In whatever way the political situation may develop, fiscal policy in coming years," he insisted, "must be directed at cutting taxes on property and shifting the state's budgetary source to taxation of the general public. . . . In the coming years, the Public Budget Administration will have a far more difficult task. Namely to get along on less in order to adjust public expenditure to the financial capacity of an impoverished economy."[95]

The Great Depression and Austrian Economic Policy 1931–1936

But living beyond its means is exactly what the Austrian government continued to do with the onslaught of the Great Depression. In 1929, the Austrian federal budget had a small surplus that was almost equal to 10 percent of tax revenues. But from 1930 on, the Austrian government's budget was in the red, with expenditures exceeding tax revenues between 1930 and 1934 in the range of 13 to 16 percent for all but one year. During this time, the deficit for all but one year was between 11.5 and 14 percent of total federal expenditures.[96]

To try to stem the tide toward greater intervention, government spending, and economic planning, Mises, along with a group of like-minded economists in Vienna attempted to influence public opinion. In the early 1930s, Mises regularly met with Gottfried Haberler, Oskar Morgenstern, and Fritz Machlup in the home of Julius Meinl, an importer of coffee and various foodstuffs, to plan out what themes were most important for them to focus on in the articles they would submit to the daily Vienna newspapers. Between September 1931 and May 1934, Machlup alone published 148 articles in the Austrian newspapers, many in a regular column he titled "Two Minute Economics."[97]

Mises applied himself in this direction as well, though to a far more limited extent, in articles and lectures. In February 1931, he delivered an address to a group of German industrialists, "The Causes of the Economic Crisis," which shortly thereafter was published as a monograph.[98] He wrote a variety of newspaper articles: "The Economic Crisis and Capitalism," "The Gold Standard and Its Opponents," and "Planned Economy and Socialism." He contributed to collections of essays in which he wrote on the themes of "The Myth of the Failure of Capitalism," "The Current Status of Business Cycle Research,"[99] and "Problems of Monetary Stabilization and Foreign Exchange Rates." And he contributed to journals such articles as "Interventionism as the Cause of the Economic Crisis" and "The Return to Freedom of Exchange."[100]

Central to Mises' argument in all of these articles was to refute the charge that the Great Depression was caused by capitalism and that more interventionism or even socialist planning was now needed to replace the market economy. The Depression, Mises explained over and over again, had been caused by the monetary mismanagement of governments in the years leading up to 1929. Interest rates had been artificially pushed below the market rate at which savings and investment would have tended toward equality. Instead, credit expansion had fed misdirections of resources and capital malinvestments that set the stage for an inevitable correction and readjustment of the economy once the money and credit expansion had slowed down or come to an end.

The duration and depth of the Depression was not due to any inherent defects in the market economy. No, the severity of the Depression was also the product of government interventionism that supported trade unions that resisted money wage cuts in the face of a decreasing demand for labor in the misdirected sectors of the economy; that supplied support for union resistance to wage adjustment through the "dole" that subsidized those who had priced themselves out of the labor market; and that provided subsidies and protection for industries and enterprises that used political pressure to secure their market situation from competition, capital write-offs, and lower prices that would make clear their loss-making or even bankrupt status.

The "Interventionist State" had bred corruption, "pull," and antimarket conduct throughout the economy. It had created a generation of political rather than market entrepreneurs who knew had to use the corridors of politics more than the avenues of consumer-oriented commerce. Mises explained this process concisely:

> In the Interventionist State it is no longer of crucial importance for the success of an enterprise that the business should be managed in a way that it satisfies the demands of consumers in the best and least costly manner. It is far more important that one has "good relationships" with the political authorities so that the interventions work to the advantage and not the disadvantage of the enterprise. A few marks more tariff protection for the products of the enterprise and a few marks less tariff for the raw materials used in the manufacturing process can be of far more benefit to the enterprise than the greatest care in managing the business. No matter how well an enterprise may be managed, it will fail if it does not know how to protect its interests in the drawing up of the customs rates, in the negotiations before the arbitration boards, and with the cartel authorities. To have "connections" becomes more important than to produce well and cheaply.
>
> So the leadership positions within enterprises are no longer achieved by men who understand how to organize companies and to direct production in the way the market situation demands, but by men who are well thought of "above" and "below," men who understand how to get along well with the press and all the political parties, especially with the radicals, so that they and their company give no offense. It is that class of general directors that negotiate far more often with state functionaries and party leaders than with those from whom they buy or to whom they sell.
>
> Since it is a question of obtaining political favors for these enterprises, their directors must repay the politicians with favors. In recent years, there have been relatively few large enterprises that have not had to spend very considerable sums for various undertakings in spite of it being clear from the start that they would yield no profit. But in spite of the expected loss it had to be done for political reasons. Let us not even mention contributions for purposes unrelated to business—for campaign funds, public welfare organizations, and the like.[101]

To overcome the problem of unemployment, governments searched for indirect methods that would permit them to avoid having to confront trade union power directly. Instead, they used currency devaluation and monetary depreciation as ways to decrease the high cost of labor by raising prices through inflation in the hope that unions would accept cuts in their members' real wages by not insisting (at least not immediately) on higher money wages in the face of lost purchasing power:

> First of all, there is the problem of wages and unemployment. In many countries wages did not fall as low as the depressed state of trade required. The salaries and wages of public servants in some countries are too high relative to public revenue. It seems impossible to restore budgetary equilibrium except by a reduction of the pay roll. In trade and industry, wages in some countries are too high in comparison with the prices at which the products can be sold. The rigidity of wages has so far been successful, as real wages did not fall in the years of the slump. But on the other hand, with falling prices and unchanged nominal wages, the volume of unemployment increased as entrepreneurs were unable to employ the same number of hands as before.
>
> It is obvious that the proposals to do away with the rigidity of wages are very unpopular. But it is not fair to charge those who see no other means of escape with the accusation of hardheartedness. Those who prefer devaluation of the currency also aim, ultimately, at a reduction in real wages. All the proposals in favor of devaluation are based upon the tacit assumption that nominal wages will remain unchanged, and that with rising prices for commodities real wages will drop. Of course, they do not expressly mention this point. But when speaking of reductions in costs they mean nothing other than a reduction both in gold wages and in commodity wages while nominal wages remain unchanged at least for some time following the devaluation of the currency. The reduction in the costs of production that is meant to stimulate exports is to a large extent a reduction in the cost of labor.[102]

This policy offered no long-run solution to the problem of unemployment. First, there was no certainty that trade unions would allow the real wages of their members to decline due to inflation over time. Second, inflationary policies to reemploy only a part of the work force was setting the stage for another downturn and period of necessary correction after another wave of malinvestments and misdirections of resources had been generated. Furthermore, this spelled even lower real wages for workers in the future. By taxing away capital to support the unemployed and wasting scarce capital by misdirecting it through credit expansion, real wages would be pushed down as a result of the marginal product of labor being reduced because of this consumption and squandering of capital.

Finally, Mises once again defended the gold standard and the long-run benefits from stable and certain foreign exchange rates. The gold standard was being opposed and overthrown precisely because it stood in the way of government manipulation of money, credit, and the purchasing power of the monetary unit. He responded to those who warned of "imbalances" in trade, or a "scarcity" of gold, or who wanted to give government the ability to arbitrarily manipulate interest rates and the value of money. "Good banking policy makes well-ordered currency relationships possible," Mises said. "Bad banking policy jeopardizes the currency. That interest rates in Central Europe are extraordinarily high is the long-term consequence of the capital-consuming policies that have been pursued with veritable fanaticism for two decades. This evil cannot, however, be remedied by banking policy trickery. All that the policy of artificially lowering the rate of interest can achieve is destruction of the currency."[103]

But besides his writings to inform and influence public opinion in Austria during the early 1930s, Mises was also working to influence economic policy through his work at the Vienna Chamber of Commerce. As we saw earlier, the Great Depression began to have its full impact in Austria when one of Central Europe's most important banks, *CreditAnstalt,* was threatened with collapse due to huge financial losses.[104]

In a series of addresses before meetings of the members of the Vienna Chamber of Commerce in 1932, Mises persuaded them to take certain public policy stances on a number of crucial issues, including the government system of foreign exchange control, the gold parity, the need to rein in government spending and taxation, and on the international loan to assist Austria in reestablishing its domestic and international finances.[105]

In a letter written to F. A. Hayek (who at this time had moved to England and taken up a position as a professor at the London School of Economics) on December 7, 1931, Mises reported how when he got back from a trip the previous the month, "I was greeted on all sides upon my return to Vienna with the universal outcry: 'We most urgently need a central authority for exchange control.' Even today everybody is blaming the whole trouble on the delay in creating the central authority, it should already have been established in May. You can see that I keep harping on this matter. I fret about it day and night and have to deal with it a lot in the Chamber. Unfortunately, I am also a member of the advisory board for foreign exchange, a totally powerless, hence superfluous institution."[106]

The Chamber first formally dealt with the problem of foreign exchange control in February 1932 in a session at which Mises explained the reasons for its imposition and the harmful, contrary-to-purpose results that already were emerging. The decision of the Austrian National Bank to cover the losses being suffered by *Credit-Anstalt* through credit expansion required the Bank to stop redeeming schillings for foreign currencies on demand. Fearful that the schilling's value on the foreign exchanges would fall, the Bank imposed exchange control at the legally prescribed rate of exchange that had been established in 1923 at a ratio of 0.21172086 grams of gold per schilling.

What this did immediately, considering that on the foreign exchange markets in other countries the value of the schilling declined by about 20 percent, was to create an artificial stimulus for imports and an artificial barrier to exports. At the controlled rate of exchange, Austrian importers received more units of foreign money per schilling exchanged than they would at the free market rate. At the same time, since exporters had to trade in their foreign exchange earnings at an officially fixed rate they received fewer schillings for each unit of foreign exchange they traded in.

Furthermore, in an attempt to keep domestic prices from rising, the foreign exchange agency had rationed more of the foreign currencies in short supply to those importing consumer items, and less of the available foreign currencies to those needing to import raw materials and semifinished goods for the Austrian manufacturing sectors. The latter policy undermined Austria's industrial production, weakened the country's exporting capability, and threatened increased unemployment in the manufacturing and exporting sectors of the economy. The only thing preventing an even worse deterioration in Austrian manufacturing and the exporting trade was the fact that "the system of foreign exchange control is riddled with loopholes." Indeed, Mises went as far to suggest that it was only the system of "private clearings" and "certificates" (which we explained earlier) that permitted Austria's export industry and a number of other sectors of the economy to survive at all.[107]

The Austrian National Bank, through the exchange control process, had attempted to prevent schillings held abroad from returning to Austria and adversely affect the domestic purchasing power of the monetary unit, as well as its foreign exchange value by more schillings being traded on the exchange markets in Vienna. But the latter effect had not been prevented by this policy. Schilling-denominated debt was merely transferred by consignment to be sold on foreign markets where its value was competitively determined, and at about a 20 percent discount from the officially mandated foreign exchange rate.

What then was to be done? Mises outlined "An Agenda for Alleviating the Economic Crisis" at a session of the Vienna Chamber of Commerce in March 1932. First, the official gold parity of the schilling had to be reestablished. There were too many Austrian enterprises—financial institutions, agricultural companies, and federal, state, and municipal governments—that owed debts in gold and foreign currency, and who would be shouldered with impossible costs if the schilling were to be devalued. It would also undermine international confidence in the Austrian economy, coming only a few years after the country's currency had once more been stabilized and legally placed on a fixed gold parity.

The Austrian National Bank would have to contract the supply of money and credit until the value of the schilling had been raised to a level that once more equaled the official gold parity. But this had to be done relatively quickly, Mises argued, before the domestic structure of price had fully adjusted to the depreciated value of the schilling. Otherwise, the monetary deflation might impose too excessive a burden on the economy to bring the domestic level of prices back down. The non-neutral effects from a monetary deflation could be just as adverse as from a monetary inflation:

> The reestablishment of the legal gold parity must not be delayed until the time when the prices of all goods in general as expressed in schillings have risen into line with the decreased foreign valuation of the schilling. Otherwise the reestablishment of the gold parity would require a sharp reduction in prices, along with a period of severe adjustment.
>
> A reduction in the number of bank notes in circulation is essential for reestablishing the legal gold parity of the schilling. The note-issuing central bank must, therefore, follow a restrictive credit policy as an unavoidable necessity, even though it may create unfortunate difficulties for the economy and impose certain sacrifices on the society.[108]

The contrary policy of even greater money and credit expansion that some were calling for would only create more difficulties for the Austrian economy down the road, an economy already suffering from living beyond its means and capital consumption.

Mises then formulated the official Chamber of Commerce policy prescriptions that would enable Austria to overcome the economic crisis. Exchange controls were to be ended as soon as possible with the reestablishment of full freedom of trade. For the transition leading up to that, the Chamber advocated that all further coercive methods had to stop. All regulations that restricted foreigners from controlling and trading their schilling-denominated accounts in Vienna banks should be abolished. The prohibitions on the free exporting and importing of schilling notes should be lifted. And all existing institutions that facilitate export trade and importing of raw materials and semifinished products used in Austrian manufacturing—the private clearings and the certificate system—should not be interfered with. "Every attempt at isolating the country from world commerce must have the most harmful effects," Mises concluded. "Things imposed on us from aboard, and which cannot be prevented through any policy of our own, must be tolerated as unavoidable. What we must not do is to promote our own isolation from the world market."[109]

Shortly after the Austrian government arranged for a new loan through the League of Nations in the middle of July 1932, the Vienna Chamber of Commerce again met in full session. Mises took the floor to discuss the case for accepting the loan. He pointed out to the Chamber representatives that most of the loan would be used to pay back the credits that had earlier been extended to the Austrian National Bank by the Bank of England and the Bank for International Settlements in Switzerland. At the most, this would leave 150 million schillings for domestic use to overcome budgetary problems. This was a relatively small amount, he said, when consideration was given to the fact that the Federal Transportation Department had total current debts outstanding of 137 million schillings, and the overall federal deficit for the year was estimated to be 450 million schillings, with 72 million of this required to cover unemployment relief for the year. Thus, from the Treasury's perspective, the League's loan offered merely a momentary relief.

So how should the loan be viewed, then, in terms of domestic Austrian economic policy? It could serve one purpose and one purpose alone: "breathing space" for immediate implementation of long neglected but absolutely necessary domestic economic reforms.

> It is absolutely essential that all those measures of frugality that the economy has required for a long time—but which have always been delayed or sabotaged—be put into effect as quickly as possible. For this loan is nothing more than breathing room for the carrying out of those absolutely necessary reforms and retrenchments. Not for one moment should the government or the political parties assume that the loan should be looked upon as anything removing the necessity for these reforms....
>
> It must be stated that just as the loan has to be considered as only offering short-term breathing room for the government to introduce reforms and retrenchment measures, so too it must not be seen as a way to continue our trade, and social and budgetary policies of the past. Nor can it be assumed that the same monetary policy that has been followed for months can be continued because we have received the means to do so....
>
> So if the National Bank were simply to continue the present system, Austrian trade would continue to contract, with all the same consequences for foreign exchange and monetary policy that have been seen in recent months. It would be a grave error to believe that the foreign exchange needed to obtain the raw materials, semi-finished products and foodstuffs that we import

from abroad can simply be withdrawn from a fund that was once filled up by confiscatory measures and now is supposed to be replenished by the loan. The economy is an on-going institution, and it can only keep on receiving the needed foreign exchange by constantly replenishing the required funds through exports, foreign trade, business activity and the like. The idea that we have a certain given amount of capital upon which we can permanently operate would lead to a currency catastrophe.[110]

Failure to accept the loan and follow its stringent requirements for domestic reform and institutional change, Mises warned, would have serious international repercussions. It would undermine all confidence in the international market that Austria could again be a trustworthy trading and credit partner, with whom financial commitments could be undertaken. It was on this basis alone, Mises insisted, that the Austrian Chambers of Commerce endorsed the government's agreement to the terms of the loan. While the conditions of the loan were being imposed from aboard, the crucial reforms would "have to be carried out in Austria by Austria." Thus, the conditions specified by the League of Nations were to be supported, Mises argued, only because they would require the Austrian government to institute the budgetary austerities that it apparently lacked the domestic will to implement without external pressure.

Near the end of 1932, at the general meeting of the Austrian Chambers of Commerce in October, Mises returned once more to the problems with the system of foreign exchange control in his remarks to the assembly. He stated that of all the damaging economic policies instituted by the Austrian government in the face of the economic crisis the most pernicious measure had been foreign exchange control. Mises again explained how the controls had artificially fostered imports and restricted exports, with an extremely negative effect on the manufacturing sectors of the economy. It served as a severely damaging "tax" on the importation of all those inputs upon which the export trade was totally dependent. "This burden is intolerable for Austrian exports and must be eliminated without delay," he insisted.[111]

What made the system especially harmful was the lack of expertise by those determining the rationing of foreign currency:

> The agents of the National Bank responsible for forming authoritative judgements about various trade policy problems appear to be totally incompetent, whether due to their educational background or their lack of prior experience. Yet these people, who most certainly cannot be considered qualified experts, have the discretionary power to finally decide whether particular export firms will be "favored" with permission to enter into a private clearing agreement or not. A refusal for this so-called favoring" is the same thing as a prohibition on export businesses; therefore, in the final analysis, it means an increase in unemployment.[112]

The decision as to which types of transactions were permitted to be undertaken through the system of "private clearings" was completely arbitrary. Every month, for example, one million schillings were provided through the private clearings to pay the pensions of those Austrians living abroad. But payment of royalties from abroad for intellectual work by authors was excluded from the private clearings. There seemed to be no rhyme or reason to the logic of the decisions.

Furthermore, the rationing of foreign exchange served as another policy tool for economic privilege and favoritism. Foreign currency earned by an export industry had to be remitted to the foreign exchange control agency, which then allocated that foreign currency to the agricultural sector for the importing of fodder and fertilizer. "Foreign exchange control, therefore, also represents a link in the chain of economically unjustifiable privileges for agricultural producers," Mises said, "at the expense of all the other strata of the population."[113]

After critically evaluating a number of other policies connected with foreign exchange control, including the "clearing agreements" under which the Austrian government had entered into reciprocal barter trading arrangements with other countries at artificial rates of exchange that misallocated goods and resources, Mises presented the policy proposals of the Chamber of Commerce. First, no obstacles should be put in the way of the operation of the private clearings at the designated institutions. The Austrian National Bank should only prohibit transactions in the private clearings if it could be shown that such dealings were a cover for illegal activities. All currency transactions were to take place through the institutions assigned for private clearings, including all buying and selling of foreign exchange by the National Bank, with the latter transactions being made at the market prices established by the clearing process. And all barter "clearing agreements" entered into by the Austrian government with foreign governments should be terminated.

In additional concluding remarks Mises added that "only the shortest amount of time is suitable for the carrying out of appropriate measures. There is no reason to postpone them even for one day, measures like the ones that have been proposed." But he observed that, "Unfortunately, when it is a question of introducing appropriate measures, the history of Austrian currency policy in recent years has provided new proof of the correctness of Grillparzer's characterization of Austrian politics: 'To strive halfheartedly half the way toward a half deed with half measures.'[114] Only where something completely wrong is to be undertaken are we accustomed to seize it quickly and completely."[115]

The following year, Mises delivered an address on "The Return to Freedom of Exchange" at the Vienna Congress of the International Chamber of Commerce meeting in May 1933, in which he once more explained the harmful effects of foreign exchange controls. But he also analyzed what were the preconditions for a permanent and successful elimination of the controls. The fundamental problem in most countries that had introduced foreign exchange control, including Austria, was the structure of bank debt. Many banks had invested long term with short-term credits that had been extended to them by financial institutions abroad. Foreign exchange control give these debtor banks an excuse to inform their foreign creditors that they could not pay because their government did not allot the funds for them to do so. But this stopgap policy device needed to be replaced with a long-term solution. This required structural changes in the debtor nations. And this could be most effectively done, Mises argued, through the participation and coordination of various international organizations:

> The restructuring of the insolvent banks must therefore precede the abolition of foreign exchange control. The banks whose balances are in severe deficit must be liquidated, and the losses that have occurred must be recognized as complete

> losses. It is useless to postpone the liquidation of these enterprises. The losses will only be greater by delaying a final settling of accounts. Fortunately, the balances of the majority of the banks in question are not bankrupt but only insolvent. These banks would be in a sound condition if the maturity dates of their own debt obligations coincided with the dates when they received claims owed to them. It is necessary to make every effort to reach an arrangement through agreements between these banks and their foreign creditors, in collaboration with the governments of the various countries involved as well as with international organizations (the League of Nations, the Bank of International Settlements, the International Chamber of Commerce). This is all the more feasible considering that it is not in the interest of creditors that the banks in which they have placed their capital should fail and suffer further losses, only adding to the harm to themselves in the process. These arrangements should be initiated and carried out as soon as possible. Once they are, there will no longer be any obstacles, from this source, to delay the abolition of foreign exchange control.
>
> It would be superfluous, in this regard, to provide special legislation requiring that banks maintain their own liquidity in the future. The banks will do this in their own interest, particularly if it is clear that any bank that poorly manages it own affairs can have no hope of being kept afloat by government intervention at the expense of the rest of society.[116]

In addition, Mises said, the problems of long-term debt obligations needed to be worked out as well, especially since many of these debts were owed by state and municipal governments that had sunk borrowed funds into various nationalized industries and municipal projects. These often had no long-term solution, given governments' inability to raise enough taxes to meet their obligations. Mises offered no concrete solution to this problem, other than the implicit suggestion that many of these debts would have to be completely written off. Mises concluded his remarks by emphasizing the essential importance of international trade for all nations, but especially for relatively poorer ones dependent upon foreign capital investment for their economic development, and that these benefits from international trade could never be fully taken advantage of as long as foreign exchange control stood in the way.

At the end of 1934, shortly after Mises had departed for Geneva to take up his teaching appointment at the Graduate Institute of Economic Studies, he wrote a short piece, "The Direction of Austrian Financial Policy: A Retrospective and Prospective View."[117] Democratic government had ended in Austria, a brief civil war had been fought and had crushed the Social Democrats, and now Mises hoped that a new calm in the country could serve as the backdrop for returning to the path of economic reform and recovery. He reviewed the course of Austrian economic policy during the preceding fifteen years since the end of the First World War. And he emphasized that what the country still needed was less government spending and taxing, more flexibility in the country's price and wage structure, a stable currency, and acceptance that as a small nation in a large global economy Austria had to adjustment to the international conditions of supply and demand. Alas, in less than four years Austria's fate would be sealed for the duration of the Second World War.

Conclusion: Warning Signs and Guideposts for a Future Generation

From his new vantage point in Geneva at the Graduate Institute, Mises was freed from the everyday affairs of Austrian economic policy that had been the focus of his attention at the Vienna Chamber of Commerce. On March 10, 1934, William Rappard, the co-founder and director of the Graduate Institute, had written to Mises in Vienna offering the chair in International Economic Relations for the academic year 1934–1935.

Rappard explained to Mises that "the professors of this Institute have only a very few formal university duties: one hour of seminar and two hours of lecture per week. We try to allow them the greatest leisure possible to continue their research work here. It is of course understood that in addition to these three hours of *ex cathedra* teaching, they will make themselves available to students who wish to consult them about their own work. If I take the liberty of asking you about the possibility of your accepting a chair here for a year, it is because we would be particularly happy to have the collaboration of one of the contemporary economists whose intellectual value we prize most highly and whose main professional interests fit best within the framework of this Institute."[118]

After an exchange of letters, Mises formally accepted on March 30, 1934, informing Rappard that he would teach his course in English, and allow the language used in the seminar (English or French) to be decided by the students. For his course, Mises chose the subject, "The International Aspects of Monetary Policy." And for his seminar, "International Finance," which he said was "sufficiently broad to allow me to treat in the seminar all problems relative to the present situation of the economic relationships among nations."[119]

In *Notes and Recollections,* Mises said, "For me it was a liberation to be removed from the political tasks I could not have escaped in Vienna, and from the daily routine in the Chamber. Finally, I could devote myself completely and almost exclusively to scientific problems."[120] As he said in the foreword to the first edition of *Human Action,* "In the serene atmosphere of this seat of learning. . . . I set about executing an old plan of mine, to write a comprehensive treatise on economics."[121]

In Geneva he had no false hopes for the future of Austria. The Social Democrats had made the work of the Nazis that much easier, Mises said, because they—and especially Otto Bauer—had long made the unification of Austria and Germany one of their leading goals before their destruction in the short-lived civil war in February 1934. If not for Mussolini's intervention during the brief Nazi coup-attempt in July 1934, Austria might have been swallowed up by Germany right then. The politicians in charge of guiding Austria's foreign relations were not up to the task, Mises argued. The authoritarian government of Kurt von Schuschnigg was unable to ward off the increasing pressures from across the border in Nazi Germany that culminated in the *Anschluss* of March 1938.[122]

When Mises neared the end of his narrative in *Notes and Recollections,* he did so with romantic and heroic words: "Only one nation on the European continent attempted seriously to oppose Hitler, namely the Austrian nation."[123] However the fact was that when Hitler arrived in Vienna, an ocean of jubilant Austrian faces filled the streets to see the man who had "liberated" them from their independence and had reunited them with the German *Volk.* At the Vienna Chamber of Commerce the employees went to work the day after Hitler had arrived and greeted each other with "Heil Hitler," with several turning out to be Nazis.[124]

Mises' despair (that we quoted at the beginning of this paper)—that he had "set out to be a reformer, but only became the historian of decline"—is tragically understandable in the context of the course of Austrian events in the twenty years between the two world wars. But precisely because of this, his policy writings offer us a clearer understanding of why it was that in the countries of Europe between 1918 and 1938, inflation, interventionism, socialism, and economic nationalism lead to stagnation, social disruption, a Great Depression, and finally to a new world war.

In spite of his pessimism, Mises was not a fatalist. He said more than once in his writings that trends can change, that they had changed in the past and could change again in the future.[125] With this in mind, after coming to the United States he devoted part of his time to working out the political and economic policies and reforms that could bring about a rebirth of freedom and prosperity in Europe after the Second World War.[126]

Likewise, from the perspective of these first days of the twenty-first century, Mises' writings from this period offer important instructions for the present and the future. Within his writings criticizing the direction of Austrian economic and social policy are also many ideas and prescriptions for free market-oriented alternatives in the areas of monetary and fiscal policy, government regulation and planning, and the social institutional order, which would move a society along the path that leads to freedom and prosperity. In fact, I would suggest that is precisely how Mises would want the modern reader to view his efforts and his writings in that period between the two world wars. He said this very clearly in the preface he prepared for the 1932 second edition of his treatise on *Socialism:*

> I know only too well how hopeless it seems to convince impassioned supporters of the Socialist Idea by logical demonstration that their views are preposterous and absurd. I know too well

> that they do not want to hear, to see, and above all to think, and they are open to no argument. But new generations grow up with clear eyes and open minds. And they will approach things from a disinterested, unprejudiced standpoint, they will weigh and examine, will think and act with forethought. It is for them that this book is written.[127]

His articles and essays, originally penned more than sixty and seventy years ago in the context of the economic and political policy controversies of those times, were, therefore, also written for us. They are warning signs and guideposts left behind by one of the greatest economists of the twentieth century to assist us in thinking about and designing better policies for our own times.

F. A. Hayek made the following remark when looking back at the events in Austria during the 1920s and 1930s: "That they had one of the great thinkers of our time in their midst, the Viennese have never understood."[128] Mises' body of writings—on theory and policy—from this period enables us to understand what they, to their great misfortune, did not.

Notes

[1]Ludwig von Mises, *Notes and Recollections* [1940] (South Holland, IL: Libertarian Press, 1978), p. 115.

[2]For an exposition of Mises' ideas on the theory of human action, the market economy, socialism, and intervention, see Richard M. Ebeling, "A Rational Economist in an Irrational Age: Ludwig von Mises," in Richard M. Ebeling, ed., *The Age of Economists: From Adam Smith to Milton Friedman* (Hillsdale, MI: Hillsdale College Press, 1999), pp. 69–120.

[3]Ludwig von Mises, *The Theory of Money and Credit* (Indianapolis, IN: Liberty Classics, [1912; 1924; 1952] 1981). For an exposition of the Austrian theory of money and the business cycle in the context of the Great Depression and in contrast to the Keynesian approach, see Richard M. Ebeling, "The Austrian Economists and the Keynesian Revolution: The Great Depression and the Economics of the Short-Run," in Richard M. Ebeling, ed., *Human Action: A 50-Year Tribute* (Hillsdale, MI: Hillsdale College Press, 2000), pp. 15–110; for a comparison of Mises' theory of money and the business cycle with that of the Swedish economists during this period, see Richard M. Ebeling, "Money, Economic Fluctuations, Expectations and Period Analysis: The Austrian and Swedish Economists in the Interwar Period," in Willem Keizer,

Bert Tieben, and Rudy van Zip, eds., *Austrian Economics in Debate* (London/ New York: Routledge, 1997), pp. 42–74.

[4]Ludwig von Mises, *Nation, State and Economy: Contributions to the Politics and History of Our Time* [1919] (New York: New York University Press, 1983).

[5]Ludwig von Mises, "Economic Calculation in the Socialist Commonwealth," [1920] in F. A. Hayek, ed., *Collectivist Economic Planning: Critical Studies in the Possibilities of Socialism* (London: George Routledge, 1935), pp. 87–130; reprinted in Israel M. Kirzner, ed., *Classics in Austrian Economics. A Sampling in the History of a Tradition,* Vol. 3: "The Age of Mises and Hayek" (London: William Pickering, 1994), pp. 3–30; and Mises, *Socialism: An Economic and Sociological Analysis* (Indianapolis, IN: Liberty Classics [1922; 1936; 1951] 1981). For an exposition of Mises' critique of socialist planning in the context of the critics of socialism who preceded him, see Richard M. Ebeling, "Economic Calculation Under Socialism: Ludwig von Mises and His Predecessors," in Jeffrey M. Herbener, ed., *The Meaning of Ludwig von Mises* (Norwell, MA: Kluwer Academic Press, 1993), pp. 56–101.

[6]Ludwig von Mises, *Liberalism: The Classical Tradition* [1927] (Irvington-on-Hudson, NY: Foundation for Economic Education, 1996).

[7]Ludwig von Mises, *Critique of Interventionism: Inquiries into the Economic Policy and the Economic Ideology of the Present* [1929] (Irvington-on-Hudson, NY: Foundation for Economic Education, 1996). For an exposition of some aspects of the Austrian ideas on interventionism, see Richard M. Ebeling, "The Free Market and the Interventionist State," in Richard M. Ebeling, ed., *Between Power and Liberty: Economics and the Law* (Hillsdale, MI: Hillsdale College Press, 1998), pp. 9–46.

[8]F. Kapeluch, "'Anti-Marxism': Professor Mises as a Theorist of Fascism," *Bolshevik,* No. 15 (August 15, 1925): 82–87. This article has been translated from Russian and is included as an appendix to Richard M. Ebeling, ed., *Selected Writings of Ludwig von Mises,* Vol. 2: "Between the Two World Wars: Monetary Disorder, Interventionism, Socialism and the Great Depression" (Indianapolis, IN: Liberty Fund, 2002).

[9]Ludwig von Mises, "Anti-Marxism" [1925] reprinted in *Critique of Interventionism,* pp. 71–95.

[10]Ludwig von Mises, "Social Liberalism" [1926] reprinted in *Critique of Interventionism,* pp. 43–70; the quote appears on p. 67.

[11]See Alexander Hortlehner, "Ludwig von Mises und die Österreichische Handelskammerorganisation" [Ludwig von Mises and the Austrian Chamber of Commerce] *Wirtschaftspolitische Blätter,* No. 4 (1981): 141–42.

[12]On the general working of the Austrian Section of the Reparations Commission, see, 0. de. L., "The Reparations Commission in Austria," *Contemporary Review* (July 1921): 45–50.

[13]*Friedensrecht, Ein Nachrichtenblatt über die Durchfuhrung des Friedenvertrages Enthaltend die Verlautbarungen des Österreichischen Abrechnungsamtes* [*The Laws for*

Peace, A Newsletter for the Execution of the Peace Treaty, Containing Announcements of the Austrian Office for the Settlement of Accounts] (February 1925): 9–10.

[14]Mises, *Notes and Recollections,* pp. 74–75.

[15]Ibid.

[16]See Richard M. Ebeling, "William E. Rappard: An International Man in an Age of Nationalism," *Ideas on Liberty* (January 2000): 33–41.

[17]Mises, *Notes and Recollections,* pp.76 & 91.

[18]Ibid., pp. 91–92.

[19]Fritz Machlup in *Tribute to Mises, 1881–1973* (Chislehurst, England: Quadrangle, 1974), p. 12; from a paper delivered at The Mont Pèlerin Society session at Brussels on September 13, 1974.

[20]The following summary of the course of Austrian political and economic history between 1918 and 1938 is taken, mostly, from the following works, J. van Walre de Bordes, *The Austrian Crown: Its Depreciation and Stabilization* (London: P. S. King, 1924); Otto Bauer, *The Austria Revolution* [1925] (New York: Bert Franklin, 1970); W. T. Layton and Charles Rist, *The Economic Situation in Austria: Report Presented to the Council of the League of Nations* (Geneva: League of Nations, 1925); *The Financial Reconstruction of Austria: General Survey and Principal Documents* (Geneva: League of Nations, 1926); Carlile A. Macartney, *The Social Revolution in Austria* (Cambridge: Cambridge University Press, 1926); Leo Pasvolsky, *Economic Nationalism of the Danubian States* (New York: Macmillan, 1928); John V. Van Sickle, *Direction Taxation in Austria* (Cambridge: Harvard University Press, 1931); Malcolm Bullock, *Austria, 1918–1919: A Study in Failure* (London: Macmillan, 1939); David F. Strong, *Austria (October 1918–March 1919): Transition from Empire to Republic* [1939] (New York: Octagon Books, 1974); Antonin Basch, *The Danubian Basin and the German Economic Sphere* (New York: Columbia University Press, 1943); Mary MacDonald, *The Republic of Austria, 1918–1934: A Study in the Failure of Democratic Government* (Oxford: Oxford University Press, 1946); Frederick Hertz, *The Economic Problem of the Danubian States: A Study in Economic Nationalism* (London: Victor Gollancz, 1947); K. W. Rothschild, *Austria's Economic Development Between the Two Wars* (London: Frederick Muller 1947); Charles A. Gulick, *Austria: From Habsburg to Hitler,* 2 Vols. (Berkeley: University of California Press, 1948); Klemens von Klemperer, *Ignaz Seipel: Christian Statesman in a Time of Crisis* (Princeton, NJ: Princeton University Press, 1972); Eduard Marz, *Austrian Banking and Financial Policy: Credit-Anstalt at a Turning Point, 1913–1923* (New York: St. Martin's Press, 1984); David Clay Large, *Between Two Fires. Europe's Path in the 1930s* (New York: W. W. Norton, 1990); Helmut Gruber, *Red Vienna: Experiment in Working Class Culture, 1919–1934* (Oxford: Oxford University Press, 1991); and Gordon Brook-Shepherd, *The Austrians: A Thousand-Year Odyssey* (New York: Carroll & Graf Publishers, 1996.

[21]See, Edmond Taylor, *The Fall of the Dynasties: The Collapse of the Old Order, 1905-1922* (New York: Doubleday, 1963), pp. 69–96 & 337–56.

[22]See Joseph Redlich, *Austrian War Government* (New Haven, CT: Yale University Press, 1929).

[23]On the nationalist currents in Austria–Hungary, see Oscar Jaszi, *The Dissolution of the Habsburg Monarchy* (Chicago: University of Chicago Press, 1929).

[24]On the introductions of separate currencies within the successor states of the former Austro–Hungarian Empire, see John Parke Young, *European Currency and Finance,* Vol. II (Washington, D.C.: Government Printing Office, 1925), on Austria, pp. 9–25; Czechoslovakia, pp. 55–77; and Hungary, pp. 103–24.

[25]Eduard Marz, *Austrian Banking and Financial Policy: Creditanstalt at a Turning Point, 1913–1923,* pp. 290–317. On the effects of rent controls in Vienna in the 1920s, see F. A. Hayek, "The Repercussions of Rent Restrictions" [1930] reprinted in *Rent Control, A Popular Paradox* (Vancouver: Fraser Institute, 1975), pp. 67–83.

[26]Between 1919 and 1922 the budget deficits in nominal terms grew from 2.7 billion crowns in 1919 to 137.7 billion crowns in 1922. The deficits averaged between 40 and 67 percent, as a fraction of total federal government expenditure in Austria during this period of time. See Kurt W. Rothchild, *Austria's Economic Development between the Two Wars,* p. 24.

[27]In 1925, at a meeting of the *Verein für Sozialpolitik* [Society for Social Policy], Mises told the following story: "Three years ago a colleague from the German Reich, who is here in this hall today, visited Vienna and participated in a discussion with some Viennese economists. Everyone was in complete agreement concerning the destructiveness of inflationist policy. Later, as we went home through the still of the night, we heard in the *Herrengasse* [a main street in the center of Vienna] the heavy drone of the Austro–Hungarian Bank's printing presses that were running incessantly, day and night, to produce new bank notes. Throughout the land, a large number of industrial enterprises were idle; others were working part-time; only the printing presses stamping out notes were operating at full speed. Let us hope that industry in Germany and Austria will once more regain its prewar volume and that the war- and inflation-related industries, devoted specifically to the printing of notes, will give way to more useful activities." See Bettina Bien Greaves and Robert W. McGee, eds., *Mises: An Annotated Bibliography* (Irvington-on-Hudson, NY: Foundation for Economic Education, 1993), p. 35.

[28]J. van Walre de Bordes, *The Austrian Crown: Its Depreciation and Stabilization.* pp. 48–50, 83, 115–39.

[29]See Joseph Redlich, "Austria and Central Europe," *Yale Review* (January 1923): 243–44: "The tendency of the old Austrian war government to suppress economic freedom and to monopolize for the state the disposition of all the economic activities of the people can easily be explained... [by] a

general state of dictatorship that arose in all the belligerent countries.... Yet state socialism of this kind has been preserved in republican Austria [and is] the consequence of a general and strong, but vague, idea entertained by the leading party, the Social Democrats, that economic omnipotence should be maintained by a public administration, which must henceforward execute only the will of the masses of the people, as a first large step towards the great Social-Democratic goal, namely, the 'socialization' of the means of production and distribution of goods."

[30] Carlile A. Macartney, *The Social Revolution in Austria,* pp. 94–95; David F. Strong, *Austria (October 1918–March 1919): Transition from Empire to Republic,* pp. 193–99; Charles A. Gulick, *Austria: From Habsburg to Hitler,* Vol. I, pp. 90–92; Malcolm Bullock, *Austria, 1918–1938: A Study in Failure,* p. 21; and Joseph Redlich, "The Problem of the Austrian Republic," *Quarterly Review* (July 1920): 209–10.

[31] Samuel Hoare, "Vienna and the State of Central Europe," *The Nineteenth Century and After* (March 1920): 409–23; for pictures of the conditions in Vienna at this time—the begging on the streets, the hauling of firewood into the city by family members, of people returning from journeys to the countryside to barter for food, etc., see Solita Solano, "Vienna—A Capital Without a State," *The National Geographic Magazine* (January 1923): 77–102.

[32] Friedrich von Wieser, "The Fight Against the Famine in Austria," in Lord Parmoor, et al., *The Famine in Europe: The Facts and Suggested Remedies* (London: Swarthmore Press, 1920), pp. 49–56; and also the contributions about the situation in Austria by Friedrich Hertz, "What the Famine Means in Austria," pp. 17–26; and Dr. Ellenbogen, "The Plight of German Austria," pp. 39–48. For other contemporary accounts of the starvation and general hardship conditions in Vienna in 1919 and 1920, see Philip Gibbs, "The Tragedy of Vienna," *Living Age* (January 3, 1920): 5–9; "A Dying Metropolis," *Living Age* (January 24, 1920): 198–200; Ludwig Hirschfeld, "Pictures from a Shivering Vienna," *Living Age* (February 21, 1920): 461–63; "Vienna Paying the Tragic Price of War, and Defeat," *Literary Digest* (March 20, 1920): 83–91; Renato la Valle, "Two Aspects of Vienna," *Living Age* (August 7, 1920): 382–86; and D. H. Loch, "Austria Revisited," *Contemporary Review* (November 1920): 628–37; also, Lothrop Stoddard, "Berlin and Vienna: Likenesses and Contrasts," *Scribners Magazine* (December 1923): 651–55; one of the most detailed accounts of daily life in Vienna during this time is found in Anna Eisenmenger, *Blockade: The Diary of an Austrian Middle-Class Woman, 1914–1924* (New York: R. Long and R. R. Smith, 1932).

[33] For a detailed analysis of the Austrian constitution and changes in it during the 1920s, see Mary MacDonald, *The Republic of Austria, 1918–1934; A Study in the Failure of Democratic Government,* op. cit.; also W. Leon Godshall, "The Constitution of New Austria," *Current History* (May 1923): 281–85; and Malbone W. Graham, "The Constitutional Crisis in Austria" *American Political*

Science Review (February 1930): 144–57; on the legal philosophy behind Kelsen's writing of the Austrian constitution, see Erich Voegelin, "Kelsen's Pure Theory of Law," *Political Science Quarterly* (June 1927): 268–76.

[34]Klemens von Klemperer, *Ignaz Seipel: Christian Statesman in a Time of Crisis,* pp. 186–219.

[35]See Helmut Gruber, *Red Vienna: Experiment in Working-Class Culture, 1919–1934,* op. cit.; also Anson Rabinbach, *The Crisis of Austrian Socialism: From Red Vienna to Civil War, 1927–1934* (Chicago: University of Chicago Press, 1983).

[36]The tax on luxury goods imposed by the city of Vienna was abandoned in April 1923 when the federal government of Austria put into affect a general "turnover tax" of one percent that was raised to 2 percent in 1924. Through most of the remainder of the 1920s, it provided approximately one-third of the total that was raised in joint taxes that were divided among the provinces, cities, and towns.

[37]Gulick, *Austria: From Habsburg to Hitler,* Vol. 1, pp. 354–406; Malcolm Bullock, *Austria, 1918–1 938: A Study in Failure,* pp. 112–15.

[38]Walter C. Langsam, *The World Since 1914* (New York: Macmillan, 1933), pp. 422–24. Mises described these private armed forces in his memoirs, *Notes and Recollections,* pp. 88 & 90: "It was even more significant that the Social-Democratic Party had at its disposal a Party Army that was equipped with rifles and machine guns—even with light artillery and ample ammunition—an army with manpower at least three times greater that the government troops, such as the Federal Forces, state and local police. . . . The Social-Democratic Army, officially called the 'Organizers,' *[Ordner]* conducted open marches and field exercises which the government was unable to oppose. Unchallenged, the Party claimed the 'right to the street'. . . . The terror caused by the Social Democrats forced other Austrians to build their defenses. Attempts were made as early as winter 1918–1919. After various failures, the 'Home Guard' *[Heimwehr]* had some organizational success. . . . I watched with horror this development that indeed was unavoidable. It was obvious that Austria was moving toward civil war. I could not prevent it. Even my best friends held to the opinion that the force (actual and potential) of the Social-Democratic Party could be opposed only by violence. The formation of the Home Guard introduced a new type of individual into politics. Adventurers without education and desperados with narrow horizons became the leaders, because they were good at drill and had a loud voice to give commands. Their bible was the manual of arms; their slogan, 'authority.' These adventurers—petty *Il Duces* and *Führers*—identified democracy with Social-Democracy and therefore looked upon democracy 'as the worst of all evils.' Later they clung to the catchword, 'corporate state.' Their social ideal was a military state in which they lone would command."

[39]See Mises, *Socialism,* p. 414: "Capital consumption can be detected statistically and can be conceived intellectually, but it is not obvious to everyone.

To see the weakness of a policy that raises the consumption of the masses at the cost of existing capital wealth, and thus sacrifices the future to the present, and to recognize the nature of this policy, requires deeper insight than that vouchsafed to statesmen and politicians or to the masses who have put them in power. As long as the walls of the factory building stand, and the trains continue to run, it is supposed that all is well with the world. The increased difficulties of maintaining the higher standard of living are ascribed to various causes, but never to the fact that a policy of capital consumption is being followed." On the theory of capital consumption, see, F. A. Hayek, "Capital Consumption," [1932] in *Money, Capital, and Fluctuations: Early Essays* (Chicago: University of Chicago Press, 1984), pp. 136–58.

[40]Ludwig von Mises, Engelbert Dollfuss, and Edmund Palla, *Bericht über die Ursachen der Wirtschaftsschwierigkeiten Österreichs* [*A Report on the Causes of the Economic Difficulties in Austria*] (Vienna: 1931); for a summary of some of the report's conclusions and related data on capital consumption and the shortage of capital in Austria during this time, see Frederick Hertz, *The Economic Problem of the Danubian States,* pp. 145–68; see also Nicholas Kaldor, "The Economic Situation of Austria," *Harvard Business Review* (October 1932): 23–34; and Fritz Machlup, "The Consumption of Capital in Austria," *Review of Economic Statistics* (January 15, 1935): 13–19, especially p. 13, n2: "Professor Ludwig v. Mises was the first, as far as I know, to point to the phenomenon of consumption of capital. As a member of a committee appointed by the Austrian government... he also emphasized comprehensive factual information." The process of capital consumption due to economic miscalculation under inflation was explained by Mises immediately after the war in his work, *Nation, State and Economy: Contributions to the Politics and History of Our Time* [1919] pp. 161–63; also, *The Theory of Money and Credit,* pp. 234–37.

[41] For accounts of Austria's experience with foreign exchange controls between 1931 and 1934, see Howard Ellis, *Exchange Control in Central Europe* (Cambridge: Harvard University Press, 1941), pp. 27–73; and Oskar Morgenstern, "Removal of Exchange Control: The Example of Austria," *International Conciliation,* No. 333 (October 1937): 678–89.

[42]In March 1931, the German and Austrian governments signed a protocol for the establishment of an Austro–German customs union. Under opposition from the governments of Great Britain, France, Italy, and Czechoslovakia, the customs union was prevented from operating after the World Court at the Hague found it to be inconsistent with the international agreements that Austria had signed in 1922; see Mary Margaret Ball, *Postwar German–Austrian Relations: The Anschluss Movement, 1918–1936* (London: Oxford University Press, 1937), pp. 100–85.

[43]Arnold J. Zurcher, "Austria's Corporative Constitution," *American Political Science Review* (August 1934): 664–70.

[44]See Joachim C. Fest, *Hitler* (New York: Harcourt Brace Jovanovich, 1973), pp. 549–50; and Ian Kershaw, *Hitler, 1936–1945: Nemesis* (New York: W. W. Norton, 2000), pp. 84–85; Saul Friedlander, *Nazi Germany and the Jews*, Vol. I: "The Years of Persecution, 1933–1939" (New York: HarperCollins, 1997) pp. 242–44; also Getta Sereny, *The German Trauma: Experiences and Reflections, 1938–2000* (London: Penguin Press, 2000), pp. 6–8; Getta Sereny, who was a teenager in Vienna at the time of the German occupation, is the stepdaughter of Ludwig von Mises. For a more detailed account of the events in Austria following the Nazi annexation of the country, see Dieter Wagner and Gerhard Tomkowitz, *Anschluss: The Week Hitler Seized Power* (New York: St. Martin's Press, 1971); and Walter B. Maass, *Country Without a Nation: Austria under Nazi Rule, 1938–1945* (New York: Frederick Unger Publishing Co., 1979).

[45]Ludwig von Mises, "Remarks Concerning the Establishment of a Ukrainian Note-Issuing Bank," [1918] in Richard M. Ebeling, ed., *Selected Writings of Ludwig von Mises*, Vol. 2: "Between the Two World Wars: Monetary Disorder, Interventionism, Socialism and the Great Depression" (Indianapolis, IN: Liberty Fund, 2002).

[46]Strong, *Austria (October 1918–March 1919): Transition from Empire to Republic*, pp. 202–3; for a detailed summary of the inflationary policies of the Austro–Hungarian National Bank during the First World War, see, George A. Schreiner, "Austria–Hungary's Financial Debacle," *Current History* (July 1925): 594–600.

[47]See Mises, *Notes and Recollections*, p. 66: "Toward the end of the war, I published a short essay on the quantity theory in the journal of the Association of Banks and Bankers, a publication not addressed to the public. The censor did not approve my treatment of the inflation problem. My tame academic essay was rejected. I had to revise it before it could be published."

[48]Mises, "The Quantity Theory" and "On the Currency Question," [1918] in Ebeling, ed., *Selected Writings of Ludwig von Mises*, Vol. 2.

[49]F. A. Hayek, "Ludwig von Mises (1881–1973)" in Peter G. Klein, ed., *The Collected Works of F.A. Hayek*, Vol. 4: "The Fortunes of Liberalism," (Chicago: University of Chicago Press, 1992), pp. 132–33: "There was a time then when we thought he would soon be called to take charge of the finances of the country. He was so clearly the only man capable of stopping inflation and much damage might have been prevented if he had been put in charge. It was not to be."

[50]Mises, "The Currency Problem Prior to the Peace Conference," [1919] in Ebeling, ed., *Selected Writings of Ludwig von Mises*, Vol. 2.

[51]The peace treaties divided the Austro–Hungarian prewar debts into two categories, secured and unsecured. Secured debts, e.g., railroads against which the property had been secured for the loan, were charged to the county in whose territory the property was now located. If the property was located

across more than one of the successor states, each country was responsible for the portion of the debt corresponding to the amount of the secured property under its jurisdiction. Unsecured debt was distributed among the successor states on the basis of the fraction of the tax revenue its territory had supplied to the Austro–Hungarian monarchy. For a more detailed summary of the debt allocation process following the signing of the peace treaties, see Leo Paslovsky, *Economic Nationalism of the Danubian States* (New York: Macmillan, 1928), pp. 42–47.

[52]Mises, "On the Actions to be Taken in the Face of Progressive Currency Devaluation" [1919] in Ebeling, ed., *Selected Writings of Ludwig von Mises,* Vol. 2.

[53]Otto Bauer, *The Austrian Revolution,* pp. 105–6.

[54]Mises, "On the Actions to be Taken in the Face of Progressive Currency Devaluation."

[55]Ibid.

[56]Ibid.

[57]Mises, "The Reentry of German–Austria into the German Reich and the Currency Question," [1919] in Ebeling, ed., *Selected Writings of Ludwig von Mises,* Vol. 2.

[58]Mises, *Notes and Recollections,* p. 87.

[59]Mises, "Vienna's Political Relationship with the Provinces in Light of Economics" [1920] in Ebeling, ed., *Selected Writings of Ludwig von Mises,* Vol. 2.

[60]Mises, "The Reentry of German–Austria into the German Reich and the Currency Question" [1919].

[61]Ibid.

[62]Ibid.

[63]Ibid.

[64]Ibid.

[65]Ibid.

[66]Mises, "Vienna's Political Relationship with the Provinces in Light of Economics" [1920] op. cit.

[67]See also Mises, "Viennese Industry and the Tax on Luxury Goods" [1921] in Ebeling, ed., *Selected Writings of Ludwig von Mises,* Vol. 2, for his analysis of how a tax-the-rich policy undermined an essential Viennese export trade.

[68]Mises, "Vienna's Political Relationship with the Provinces in Light of Economics" [1920], op. cit.

[69]Ibid.

[70]Ibid.

[71]Ibid.

[72]Ibid.

[73]Ibid.

[74]Ibid.

[75]Mises, *Notes and Recollections,* pp. 79–80.

[76]Klemperer, *Ignaz Seipel: Christian Statesman in a Time of Crisis,* p. 180.

[77]For Mises analysis of the Great German Inflation, see "Stabilization of the Monetary Unit—From the Viewpoint of Theory" [1923] in Percy L. Greaves, Jr., ed., *Von Mises, On the Manipulation of Money and Credit* (Dobbs Ferry, NY: Free Market Books, 1978), pp. 1–49; also Mises, "The Great German Inflation," [1932] in Richard M. Ebeling, ed., *Money, Method and the Market Process.'Essays by Ludwig von Mises* (Norwell, MA: Kluwer Academic Press, 1990), pp. 96–103.

[78]Arthur Salter, "The Reconstruction of Austria," *Foreign Affairs* (June 15, 1924): 630–43; W. T. Layton and Charles Rist, *The Economic Situation in Austria* (Geneva: League of Nations, 1925); Emil Lengyel, "Austria's Emergence from Bankruptcy," *Current History* (January 1926): 539–42; and *The Financial Reconstruction of Austria: General Survey and Principal Documents* (Geneva: League of Nations, November 1926).

[79]Mises, *Notes and Recollections,* p. 83.

[80]Mises, "The Return to Gold" [1924] in Ebeling, ed., *Selected Writings of Ludwig von Mises,* Vol. 2.

[81]See J. van Walre de Bordes, *The Austrian Crown: Its Depreciation and Stabilization,* pp. 219–20: "Austria has therefore at present a *gold exchange standard,* and in the purist form—*with practically no gold*. . . . There is no gold in circulation, and the gold reserve of the Austrian National Bank is insignificant. At the end of 1923 the gold reserve amounted to 6.5 million gold crowns, and there was a foreign exchange reserve of 298.6 million. On several occasions during 1923 the Bank sold gold, probably because it preferred to have a reserve of interest-bearing foreign bills than of unproductive gold." [Emphasis in the original.]

[82]Mises, "The Return to Gold," op. cit.

[83]Ibid.

[84]See also Mises, *The Theory of Money and Credit,* p. 434, where he repeats the idea that "[i]t would be easy to force countries into such an agreement by means of penal customs duties."

[85]Mises, "Restoring Europe's State Finances," [1924] in Ebeling, ed., *Selected Writings of Ludwig von Mises,* Vol. 2.

[86]Ibid.

[87]Ibid.

[88]Ibid.

[89]Mises, "The Balance Sheet of Economic Policies Hostile to Property," [1927] in Ebeling, ed., *Selected Writings of Ludwig von Mises,* Vol. 2.

[90]Ibid.

[91]Mises, "Adjusting Public Expenditures to the Economy's Financial Capacity," [1930] in Ebeling, ed., *Selected Writings of Ludwig von Mises,* Vol. 2.

[92]Ibid.

[93]Ibid.

[94]Ibid.

[95]Ibid.

[96]The data is derived from the figures provided in the League of Nations' *Statistical Yearbooks* for this period.

[97]Fritz Machlup, "My Early Work on International Monetary Problems," *Banca Nazionale del Lavoro Quarterly Review* (June 1980): 135.

[98]Mises, "The Causes of the Economic Crisis: An Address" in Percy L. Greaves, Jr., ed., *Von Mises, On the Manipulation of Money and Credit,* pp. 173–203.

[99]Mises, "The Current Status of Business Cycle Research and Its Prospects for the Immediate Future," [1933] in Percy L. Greaves, Jr., ed., *Von Mises, On the Manipulation of Money and Credit,* pp. 207–13.

[100]Mises, "The Economic Crisis and Capitalism" [1931], "The Gold Standard and Its Opponents," [1931], "The Myth of the Failure of Capitalism," [1932], "Interventionism as the Cause of the Economic Crisis: A Debate Between Otto Conrad and Ludwig Mises," [1932], "Planned Economy and Socialism" [1933], "The Return to Free Exchange" [1933], and "Two Memoranda on the Problems of Monetary Stabilization and Foreign Exchange Rates" [1936] in Ebeling, ed., *Selected Writings of Ludwig von Mises,* Vol. 2.

[101]Mises, "The Myth of the Failure of Capitalism," ibid. Mises also pointed out that corruption was the only mechanism that permitted the economy to continue functioning, while at the same time that very corruption undermined the moral foundations upon which the market economy was ultimately based; see Mises, "Interventionism" [1926] in *Critique of Interventionism,* p. 13.

[102]Mises, "Two Memoranda on the Problems of Monetary Stabilization and Foreign Exchange Rates" [1936], op. cit. At the very time in February 1936 that Mises made these criticisms of devaluation as a roundabout method to bring about a decline in real wages through a rise in prices while nominal (or money) wages are presumed to remain the same, there appeared that same month John Maynard Keynes' *The General Theory of Employment, Interest and Money* [1936] (Cambridge: Cambridge University Press, 1973). Keynes justified using just such a method for reducing real wages on the rationale that (p. 264): "In fact, a movement by employers to revise money-wage bargains downward will be much more strongly resisted than a gradual and automatic lowering of real wages as a result of rising prices." But already in 1931, Mises pointed out in his monograph, "The Causes of the Economic Crisis: An Address," in Percy L. Greaves, ed., *Von Mises, On the Manipulation of Money and Credit,* pp. 199–200: "Only one argument is new, although on that account no less false. This is to the effect that the higher than unhampered market wage rates can be brought into proper relationship more easily by an inflation. This argument shows how seriously concerned our political economists are to avoid displeasing the labor unions. Although they cannot help but recognize that wage rates are too high and must be reduced, they dare not openly call for a halt to such overpayments. In-

stead, they propose to outsmart the unions in some way. They propose that the actual money wage rate remain unchanged in the coming inflation. In effect, this would amount to reducing the real wage. This assumes, of course, that the unions will refrain from making further wage demands in the ensuing boom and that they will, instead, remain passive while their real wage rates deteriorate. Even if this entirely unjustified optimistic expectation is accepted as true, nothing is gained thereby. A boom caused by banking policy measures must still lead eventually to a crisis and a depression. So, by this method, the problem of lowering wage rates is not resolved but simply postponed." And, again, in 1945, Mises pointed out in his essay "Planning for Freedom" in *Planning for Freedom and Sixteen Other Essays and Addresses* (South Holland, IL: Libertarian Press, 1980), p. 14: "If in the course of an inflation the rise in commodity prices exceeds the rise in nominal wage rates, unemployment will drop. But what makes unemployment shrink is precisely the fact that real wage rates are falling. Lord Keynes recommended credit expansion because he believed that the wage earners will acquiesce in this outcome; he believed that 'a gradual and automatic lowering of real wage rates as a result of rising prices' would not be so strongly resisted by labor as an attempt to lower money wage rates. It is very unlikely that this will happen. Public opinion is fully aware of the changes in purchasing power and watches with burning interest the movements of the index of commodity prices and of cost of living. The substance of all discussions concerning wage rates is real wage rates, not nominal wage rates. There is no prospect of outsmarting the unions by such tricks."

[103]Mises, "The Gold Standard and Its Opponents" [1931], op. cit.

[104]Mises anticipated the coming of a banking crisis in Austria years earlier. Fritz Machlup recounted, in his *Tribute to Mises* (p. 12), that, "As his assistant in the University seminar which met every Wednesday afternoon, I usually accompanied him home. On these walks we would pass through a passage of the *Creditalstalt* in Vienna. From 1924, every Wednesday afternoon as we walked through the passage for pedestrians he said: 'That will be a big smash.' Mind you, this was from 1924 onwards; yet in 1931, when the crash finally came, I still held some shares of the *Creditalstalt*, which of course had become completely worthless."

[105]Mises, "Foreign Exchange Control and Some of Its Consequences," "An Agenda for Alleviating the Economic Crisis: The Gold Parity, Foreign Exchange Control and Budgetary Restraint," "An International Loan as the 'Breathing Room' for Austrian Economic Reform," "On Limiting the Adverse Effects of a Proposed Increase in the Value-Added Tax," and "Foreign Exchange Policy" [all 1932] in Ebeling, ed., *Selected Writings of Ludwig von Mises*, Vol. 2.

[106]Letter from Ludwig von Mises to F. A. Hayek, dated December 7, 1931, in Ebeling, ed., *Selected Writings of Ludwig von Mises*, Vol. 1 (Indianapolis, IN:

Liberty Fund, forthcoming, 2003). Years later, Mises told about his appointment to this foreign exchange control advisory board, and its peculiar impact on various people needing foreign exchange for travel abroad: "I want to tell you an experience of how foreign exchange [control] interferes with everything in business, in private affairs, in religion, etc. In 1931, the Austrian government introduced overnight foreign exchange control. An advisory board was named and they immediately published the names of the men appointed to the board. My name was among them. I read it in the newspapers. I knew that the next day there would be several hundred letters from businessmen because they realized that I was the only man who was friendly to them. Then I went home and in the evening the maid told me that the Archbishop had telephoned me. Now the Archbishop doesn't telephone at all. But the maid said that he would telephone the next morning. And sure enough, the legal advisor of the Archbishop, the Canon of the University whom I knew, phoned. He told me it was important for some students from the educational institutions in Rome. He said we have to have a sum of money. I promised him that I would try to get it for him. But you see the first reaction of the foreign exchange [control] was not from business, not from people who want to flee with the capital from a foreign country, it was from a regular affair of education in a neighboring country (in Rome). You have to realize that students from Austria went to Rome to study and no authority interfered with it before. But as soon as foreign exchange enters, at once the thing is no longer free. I want to add only that I didn't remain very long on this advisory board." This quote is taken from Mises' "Lectures on Political Economy" delivered at The Inn, Buck Hill Falls, Pennsylvania, June 13–24, 1955, from the stenographic notes of Bettina Bien Greaves. Other undesirable effects from foreign exchange controls were also emphasized by Mises, see "Noninflationary Proposal for Postwar Monetary Reconstruction" [1944] in Richard M. Ebeling, ed., *Selected Writings of Ludwig von Mises,* Vol. 3: *The Political Economy of International Reform and Reconstruction* (Indianapolis, IN: Liberty Fund, 2000), p. 95: "At any rate, foreign exchange control is tantamount to the full nationalization of foreign trade.... Where every branch of business depends, to some extent at least, on the buying of imported goods or on the exporting of a smaller or greater part of its output, the government is in the position to control all economic activity. He who does not comply with any whim of the authorities can be ruined either by the refusal to allot him foreign exchange or to grant him what the government considers as an export premium, that is, the difference between the market price and the official rate of foreign exchange. Besides, the government has the power to interfere in all the details of every enterprises' internal affairs; to prohibit the importation of all undesirable books, periodicals, and newspapers; and to prevent everybody from traveling abroad; from educating his children in foreign schools; and from consulting foreign doctors. Foreign exchange control was the main vehicle of European dictatorships."

[107]Mises, "Foreign Exchange Control and Some of Its Consequences" [February 1932].

[108]Mises, "An Agenda for Alleviating the Economic Crisis" [March 1932].

[109]Ibid.

[110]Mises, "An International Loan as the 'Breathing Room' for Austrian Economic Reform" [July 1932].

[111]Mises, "Foreign Exchange Policy" [October 1932].

[112]Ibid.

[113]Ibid.

[114]Franz Grillparzer (1791–1872) was an Austrian dramatist considered to have written some of the greatest works ever performed on the Austrian stage.

[115]Mises, "Foreign Exchange Policy."

[116]Mises, "The Return to Freedom of Exchange" [May 1933], op. cit.

[117]Mises, "The Direction of Austrian Financial Policy: A Retrospective and Prospective View," [1935] in Ebeling, ed., *Selected Writings of Ludwig von Mises,* Vol. 2.

[118]Letter from William E. Rappard to Ludwig von Mises, dated March 10, 1934, in Ebeling, ed., *Selected Writings of Ludwig von Mises,* Vol. 1 (forthcoming, 2003).

[119]Letter from Ludwig von Mises to William E. Rappard, dated March 30, 1934, in Ebeling, ed., *Selected Writings of Ludwig von Mises,* Vol. 1 (forthcoming, 2003).

[120]Mises, *Notes and Recollections,* p. 137

[121]Ludwig von Mises, *Human Action, A Treatise on Economics* (New Haven, CT: Yale University Press, 1949), p. iii. This first edition of *Human Action* was handsomely reprinted in 1998 by the Ludwig von Mises Institute of Auburn, Alabama, with an introduction by Jeffrey M. Herbener, Hans-Hermann Hoppe, and Joseph T. Salerno, which tells the history of how the volume came to be published in the United States. In Geneva, between 1934 and 1940, Mises had written the German-language forerunner to *Human Action,* titled, *Nationalökonomie: Theorie des Handelns und Wirtschaftens* [1940] (Munich: Philosophia Verlag, 1980).

[122]Mises, *Notes and Recollections,* p. 139–41.

[123]Ibid., p. 142.

[124]Comments of Mises' assistant at the Chamber of Commerce, Therese Wolf-Thieberger, November 26, 1971, in the notes of Bettina Bien Greaves.

[125]Ludwig von Mises, "Trends Can Change" [1951] and "The Political Chances for Genuine Liberalism" [1951] in *Planning for Freedom,* pp. 173–84.

[126]That is precisely the theme and purpose of the essays that he wrote in the early 1940s, see Richard M. Ebeling, ed., *Selected Writings of Ludwig von Mises,* Vol. 3: "The Political Economy of International Reform and Reconstruction" (Indianapolis, IN: Liberty Fund, 2000); see also Richard M. Ebeling,

"Planning for Freedom: Ludwig von Mises as Political Economist and Policy Analyst" in Richard M. Ebeling, ed., *Competition or Compulsion? The Market Economy versus the New Social Engineering* (Hillsdale, MI: Hillsdale College Press, 2001), pp. 1–85.

[127]Mises, *Socialism,* p. 13.

[128]Hayek, "Ludwig von Mises (1881–1973)," p. 159.

Deepak Lal

Globalization and Culture

Elementary economics tells us that the growing integration of the world economy through increasingly free movement of goods and capital—though not of people[1]—labeled "globalization," which essentially creates a common economic space, is a potentially beneficial process. As an economic process in itself, it is value-neutral. It cannot be an ideology. There are, however, many concerns expressed about its impact that may have an ideological basis. The major concerns relate to its distributional consequences, its political and cultural nature as a form of American imperialism—both concerns relating to values—and its possible fragility because of the instability caused by the "creative destruction" of global capitalism—a question of fact. Thus, there are demands from a wide part of the political spectrum for the process to be regulated and tamed through the creation or expansion of various international institutions to deal with the problem of "global public goods."[2]

Here I will deal with the questions of globalization and culture, the question of values, by examining first the need for a globalized world economy for someone to maintain a global Pax, and second, the fears of many cultural nationalists in developing countries that globalization will destroy cherished ways of living.

Globalization and Empire

The first point to be made about the process of integrating previously loosely linked or even autarkic countries and regions through freeing flows of goods and services and capital—globalization—is that it is not a new phenomenon. Globalization has been a cyclical phenomenon for millennia, being associated with the rise and fall of empires. By integrating previously separated areas into a common economic space under their Pax, these empires promoted those gains from trade and specialization emphasized by Adam Smith, leading to what I have labeled Smithian intensive growth.[3] Thus the Graeco–Roman empires linked the areas around the Mediterranean; the Abbasid empire of the Arabs linked the worlds of the Mediterranean and the Indian Ocean; the various Indian empires created a common economic space in the subcontinent; while the expanding Chinese empire linked the economic spaces of the Yellow River with those of the Yangtze. In more recent times the British knit the whole world through their Empire.

But most of these empires have been ephemeral. Given the existing technology and the inevitable predatoriness of the State, most of these empires overextended themselves.[4] Their decline was followed by a disintegration of the enlarged economic spaces they had created. In our own times, the death of the nineteenth-century liberal economic order (LIEO) built by Pax Britannica on the fields of Flanders led to a near century of economic disintegration and disorder that has only been repaired with the undisputed emergence of the United States as the world hegemon in the last decade.[5] Once again this new Imperium—the American—is associated with the resurrection of another LIEO, so that the world economy is roughly back to where it was at the end of the nineteenth century.[6]

Apart from the creation of a common economic space (which is what globalization amounts to) there was another reason why past empires promoted prosperity. For economic prosperity, a State is needed to provide the classical public goods that protect the life, liberty, and property of its citizens. Liberty needs to be protected against external predation. Life and property against both external and domestic predators. Hence the essential public goods are to provide for external defense and internal law and order.

The centers of the ancient civilizations in Eurasia, where sedentary agriculture could be practiced and yielded a surplus to feed the towns (*civitas*, the emblem of civilization), were bordered in the North and South by areas of nomadic pastoralism: the steppes of the North and the semidesert of the Arabian peninsula to the South.

In these regions the inhabitants had kept up many of the warlike traditions of our hunter-gatherer ancestors and were prone to prey upon the inhabitants of the sedentary "plains," and at times attempted to convert them into their chattel, like cattle.[7] This meant that the provision of one of the classical public goods—protection of its citizens from invaders—required the extension of territory to some natural barriers that could keep the barbarians at bay. The Roman, Chinese, and various Indian empires were partly created to provide this Pax, which was essential to keep their labor-intensive and sedentary forms of making a living intact. The Pax of various Imperia has thus been essential in providing one of the basic public goods required for prosperity.

These empires can further be distinguished as being either *multi-ethnic* or *homogenizing*. The former included the Abbasids, the various Indian empires, the Ottoman Empire, the Austro–Hungarian Empire, and the British Empire, where little attempt was made to change "the habits of the heart" of the constituent groups—or if it was, as in the early British Raj, an ensuing backlash led to a reversal of this policy.

The homogenizing empires, by contrast, sought to create a "national" identity out of the multifarious groups in their territory. The best example is China, where the ethnic mix was unified as Hans through the bureaucratic device of writing their names in Chinese characters in a Chinese form and suppressing any subsequent discontent through the subtle repression of a bureaucratic authoritarian state.[8] In our own time the American "melting pot," which creates Americans out of a multitude of ethnicities by adhering to a shared civic culture and a common language, has created a similar homogenized imperial state.

Similarly, the supposedly ancient "nations" of Britain and France were created through a state-led homogenizing process. India, by contrast is another Imperial State whose political unity is a legacy of the British Raj, but whose multi-ethnic character is underwritten by an ancient hierarchical structure that accommodates these different groups as different castes.

With the end of the Cold War and the fears it engendered, which kept this broad structure of nation–states with their distinct forms of "national identity" intact, we are seemingly moving into a postmodern world where there are varying currents that undermine these familiar structures.

In the multi-ethnic imperial nation–states, on the one hand, we have assertions of cultural self-determination, leading in many cases to bloody conflicts: from the successor states of the former Yugoslavia, the Kurds in Turkey, the Kashmiris and Sikhs in India, the Tamils in Sri Lanka, the various regional separatists in Indonesia, and numerous ethnic conflicts in Africa of which that between the Hutus and the Tutsis was the most bloody. This desire to assert a distinct cultural identity is not limited to the multi-ethnic imperial nation–states. It is also happening in the "homogenized" nation–states. The partial deconstruction of the United Kingdom—with the establishment of Scottish, Welsh, and Irish parliaments—the continuing demands for Quebec to secede from Canada, the continuing tensions between the Wallons and the Flemish in Belgium, and the rise of separatist movements (still without mass appeal) in the United States are all part of this trend.

But side-by-side with these centrifugal decentralizing tendencies are centripetal ones, as represented by the attempt to resurrect a new Holy Roman Empire through the ongoing process of European integration, as well as the growing demands, which are being partially and fitfully satisfied, from a host of international nongovernmental organizations (NGOs) for the creation of a new international moral order. The latter is part of a general revolt of the "border" against the "center"[9] and the questioning of the international system of the nation–states established by the Peace of Westphalia. This system got a fillip when at the end of the First World War, President Wilson pronounced the dawn of a worldwide Age of Nations and the ending of that of empires. Most of the Third World has naturally embraced this globalization of the Westphalian system, while it is in the West that it is increasingly coming into question.

This Age of Nations has also let the ethnic genie out of the bottle, and the most common form of deadly conflict today is a civil war in the name of cultural self-determination.[10] Apart from the obvious detrimental effect on the prosperity of the countries concerned there are also spill-over effects from these civil wars on other countries, for instance, through the mounting number of refugees.[11]

Some interesting recent research by Paul Collier of Oxford and his associates[12] on the causes of civil wars finds that the relationship of ethnolinguistic fragmentation in a state and the risk of civil war is shaped like an inverted U. The most homogenous as well as the most fragmented state are the least at risk of civil war. Thus there is likely to be a bipolarity in the institutions best able to deal with ethnic diversity. One—complete fragmentation—is to be found in empires. The other—homogeneity—is surprisingly a course advocated by Keynes during the Second World War when speculating about the ideal political postwar order in Europe. Skidelsky reports on one of Keynes' fancies:

> A view of the post-war world which I find sympathetic and attractive and fruitful of good consequences is that we should encourage *small* political and cultural units, combined into larger, and more or less closely knit, economic units. It would be a fine thing to have thirty or forty capital cities in Europe, each the center of a self-governing country entirely free from national minorities (who would be dealt with by migrations where necessary) and the seat of government and parliament and university center, each with their own pride and glory and their own characteristics and excellent gifts. But it would be ruinous to have thirty or forty entirely independent economic and currency unions.[13]

But as Skidelsky notes "this pleasing picture of a re-medievalised Europe did not survive in later drafts." This homogenized solution, which as Keynes recognized could involve "ethnic cleansing," has clearly been eschewed by the West, as witness its actions in Bosnia and Kosovo. This reflects the hopes of much progressive thought over the last two centuries stemming from the Enlightenment that, transnational and "modern" forms of association such as "class" would transcend primordial forms of association such as "ethnicity" and "culture," of which nationalism is an offshoot. But, contemporary history continues to show the power of these primordial forces. The much derided sociobiology provides some cogent reasons for their survival.

Evolutionary anthropologists and psychologists maintain that human nature was set during the period of evolution ending with the Stone Age; there has not been enough time since for further evolution.[14] One salient feature of this Stone Age environment was that rapid "species"-relevant judgments had to be made on the basis of quick impressions. Our brains, according to the evolutionary psychologists, have been hardwired to deal with the problems faced in the primordial environment, the savannahs of Africa. Here it was a matter of life and death to judge from whatever signs were available that a dangerous member of a predatory species was at hand. The decision moreover had to be instantaneous, without any time spent on continued sampling to confirm one's conjecture that the striped yellow shape in the distance was indeed a tiger. This has meant, say the evolutionary psychologists, that we are naturally primed to make instantaneous "species" judgments.[15]

Given the divergence between different human groups in physiognomy and culture, once our ancestors spread throughout the world and then rarely came in contact with their genetic cousins—as with the ending of the Ice Age when the ice bridges linking the continents melted—it is hardly surprising that when we do come across another ethnic group we are primed to look upon it as a different species. Intermarriage and long familiarity might change these natural instincts, but as the bloody outcome in the successor states of Yugoslavia demonstrate this might be a very long run. This provides one important reason, rooted in our biology, why the Enlightenment hopes of the reduction, if not the end, of ethnic differences and conflicts have not been fulfilled.

So, at least in principle, the Keynes solution seems to be in keeping with human nature. Since in a globalized economy size does not matter for prosperity, as demonstrated by the shining examples of the city–states of Hong Kong and Singapore, his solution would also be feasible, as long as there is someone to maintain a global Pax.

But in this confused and confusing picture, the effectiveness of the current global hegemon, the United States, to provide this effective Pax, is increasingly in question, largely due to its domestic politics. And the continuing domestic resonance of the "idealism" in its foreign policy emphasized by Woodrow Wilson has the potential of creating a backlash against the LIEO it has helped to recreate.

Given its domestic homogenizing imperial tendencies, the United States (along with various other Western countries, which Huntington has aptly described as a directorate seeking to run the world)[16] is attempting to legislate its "habits of the heart" around the world—"human rights," democracy, egalitarianism, labor and environmental standards, and so on. Its claim that it is thereby promoting universal values is unjustified.

On Culture

To understand this we need to look more closely at the concept of culture. I have found a definition adopted by ecologists particularly useful.[17] Ecologists emphasize that, unlike other animals, the human is unique because its intelligence gives it the ability to change its environment by learning. It does not have to mutate into a new species to adapt to a changed environment. It learns new ways of surviving in the new environment and then fixes them by social custom. These social customs form the culture of the relevant group, which then are transmitted to new members of the group (mainly children)who do not then have to invent these "new" ways *de novo* for themselves.

This definition of culture fits well with the economists' notion of equilibrium. Frank Hahn describes an equilibrium state as one where self-seeking agents learn nothing new so that their behavior is routinized. It represents an adaptation by agents to the economic environment in which the economy "generates messages which do not cause agents to change the theories which they hold or the policies which they pursue." This routinized behavior is clearly close to the ecologists' notion of social custom that fixes a particular human niche. On this view, the equilibrium will be disturbed if the environment changes, and so, in the subsequent process of adjustment, the human agents will have to abandon their past theories, which would now be systematically falsified. To survive, they must learn to adapt to their new environment through a process of trial and error. There will then be a new social equilibrium, which relates to a state of society and economy in which "agents have adapted themselves to their economic environment and where their expectations in the widest sense are in the proper meaning not falsified."[18]

In *Unintended Consequences*,[19] I argued that it is useful to distinguish between what I label the material and cosmological beliefs of different cultures and civilizations. The former relate to ways of making a living, the latter, in Plato's words, to "how one should live."

There is considerable cross-cultural evidence to show that material beliefs are fairly malleable, altering rapidly with changes in the material environment. There is greater hysteresis in cosmological beliefs—in how people view their lives: its purpose, meaning, and relationship to others. The cross-cultural evidence shows that rather than the environment it is the *language group* that influences these world views.

This distinction between material and cosmological beliefs is important for economic performance because it translates into two distinct types of "transactions costs," which are important in explaining not only "market" but also "government or bureaucratic failure."[20] Broadly speaking, transactions costs can be distinguished usefully as those costs associated with the efficiency of *exchange*, and those that are associated with *policing* opportunistic behavior by economic agents. The former relate to the costs of finding potential trading partners and determining their supply-demand offers, the latter to enforcing the execution of promises and agreements.

The great Eurasian agrarian civilizations had more similarities in their material and cosmological beliefs than they had differences. They can be described broadly as "communalist." They maintained a social and economic stratification among three classes of men: those wielding the sword, the pen, or the plough. The basic human instincts of the supremely egotistical human animal would prove dysfunctional in the new environment of settled agriculture. (These human animals, however, evinced "reciprocal altruism" in the "tit for tat" response of the prisoners' dilemma game played by hunter-gatherers in the Stone Age, as well as their basic economic instinct to "truck and barter," which is also of Stone Age vintage.) Reciprocal altruism would be insufficient to curb opportunism in the larger number of one-shot prisoners' dilemma games involving strangers in the new environment. To reduce the resulting increase in "policing" transactions costs, which would have dissipated the mutual gains from co-operation, agrarian civilizations internalized restraints on such "antisocial" action through internalized moral codes that were part of their "religions," which were really more "ways of life" since they did not necessarily depend upon a belief in God. The socialization process began in infancy using the moral emotion of shame to internalize moral codes embodied in cultural traditions. These cosmological beliefs can be described as "communalist."

The basic instinct to trade would also be disruptive for settled agriculture because traders are motivated by instrumental rationality that maximizes economic advantage and thus threatens communal bonds. These agrarian civilizations took a dim view of merchants and markets, tolerating them at best as a necessary evil. The material beliefs of the agrarian civilizations were not conducive to promoting modern economic growth.

I have argued that the rise of the West was due to its breaking away from this agrarian past as a result of the twin revolutions of Pope Gregory the Great in the sixth century and Pope Gregory VII in the eleventh century.[21] The former created a "family revolution" that broke with the cosmological beliefs of its fellow agrarian civilizations in the domestic domain by essentially promoting the independence of the young and "individualism." To curb the threat this might have posed to its material business of settled agriculture, which requires settled households, the Church created a fierce guilt culture built on Original Sin, which in effect kept a lid on the "antisocial" behavior the promotion of "individuals" might have unleashed. It was only later—when the scientific, Darwinian, and sexual revolutions undermined the belief in God on which this adherence to "traditional" morality was based—that the "morals" of the "Christian" West and the Rest really began to deviate.

The second Papal Revolution of Pope Gregory VII brought the Church into the world with his proclamation that the City of God was now to be placed above Caesar, and its will was to be enforced through the powerful sanction of excommunication. This led the Church-state to create all the legal and commercial infrastructure for a market economy, which provided the essential institutional infrastructure for the Western dynamic that led to the European miracle—Promethean growth.

Global Peace

Although the twin papal revolutions leading to the change in the cosmological beliefs of the West were historically conjoined, they no longer have to be, as we shall see.

There is an important difference between the cosmological beliefs of what became the Christian West and the other ancient agrarian civilizations of Eurasia. Christianity shares a number of distinctive features with its Semitic cousin Islam, but not entirely with its parent Judaism, and which are not to be found in any of the other great Eurasian religions. The most important is its universality. Neither the Jews nor the Hindu nor the Sinic civilizations had religions that claimed to be universal. You could not choose to be a Hindu, Chinese, or Jew: You were born as one. This also meant that, unlike Christianity and Islam, these religions did not proselytize. Third, only the monotheistic Semitic religions have also been egalitarian. Nearly all other Eurasian religions believed in some form of hierarchical social order. By contrast, alone among the Eurasian civilizations, the Semitic ones (though least so the Jewish) emphasized the equality of men's souls in the eyes of their monotheistic deities. Dumont has rightly characterized the resulting profound divide between the societies of *Homo aequalis*, which believe all men are born equal (as the *philosophes* and the American Constitution proclaim), and those of *Homo hierarchicus*, which believe no such thing.[22] The so-called universal values promoted by the West are no more than the culture-specific, proselytizing ethic of what remains at the heart Western Christendom.

Nor is there a necessary connection, as the West claims, between democracy and development.[23] If democracy is to be the preferred form of government, it is not because of its instrumental value in promoting prosperity—at times it may well not—but because it promotes a different Western value—liberty. Again, many civilizations have placed social order above this value, and again it would be imperialistic for the West to ask them to change their ways.

If no universal claims for cherished Western cosmological beliefs are valid, it is unlikely that they will be found acceptable by "the Rest." If the West ties its moral crusade too closely to the emerging processes of globalization, there is a danger that there will also be a backlash against the process of globalization. This potential cultural imperialism poses a greater danger to the acceptance of the new LIEO in developing countries than the unfounded fears of the cultural nationalists discussed below.

But even this backlash would not matter, or could be fought off, if like the homogenizing Chinese imperialists the United States would be willing to ruthlessly impose its will. But to do this, or even to maintain the Pax in multi-ethnic empires, every imperial power in the past knew it needed to expend its own men and materiel. Partly due to the quagmire of Vietnam, there is no stomach left in the U.S. for any similar sacrifice.[24] The fatality rate in a job with the U.S. postal service is now higher than in the U.S. armed services! No United States president is now willing to accept more than ten body bags from an armed conflict. Nor does the U.S. Constitution allow the alternative of hiring mercenaries, the backbone of past empires. This has hobbled the potential imperial giant in imposing its Pax.[25]

But given the continuing resonance of "idealism" in its foreign policy, the United States will probably continue to rain missiles every now and then in an impotent rage at some hapless country or other whose domestic politics it does not like. These countries in turn are learning that the only deterrent may be to credibly threaten the American heartland.[26] As many Third World diplomats have observed, the lessons from the Gulf War and Kosovo are that to maintain one's sovereignty one needs nuclear weapons. But all attempts to create some balance of power are roads to instability.[27]

With a reluctant hegemon unwilling to impose its Pax directly and with a balance of power infeasible and perhaps undesirable—because the prisoners' dilemma it creates will lead to arms races—the only remaining option to maintain global peace is some form of collective security. The United Nations, and in particular the Security Council, provides the requisite global institution. But, despite the end of the Cold War, which had effectively paralyzed the Security Council, and the success of the coalition it sponsored in the Iraq war, its subsequent record in preventing or ameliorating the deadly regional and intrastate ethnic conflicts can only be described as dismal. It only succeeded when the current hegemon led the coalition, as in Iraq. The body bags coming back from the U.S. intervention in Somalia have turned domestic opinion against even the indirect form of imperialism (much favored by the British during their period of hegemony), which it could exercise through the Security Council.

Thus I am led to conclude that the prospects of a sustained provision of the public good of peace remain clouded in the New World Order, unless domestic United States politics and its Western allies are willing to accept the associated costs *and* also emulate the sage Queen Elizabeth I. When her kingdom was being torn by different groups trying to get her to impose their "habits of the heart" on others, the Queen pronounced that she did not wish to "make windows into men's souls."[28]

Modernization and Westernization

With the worldwide movement from the Plan to the market, there seems to be a worldwide acceptance of the processes of modernization associated with globalization, underwritten by an acceptance of the West's material beliefs underwritten by Gregory VII's legal papal revolution. But the cultural nationalists in the non-Western world are afraid that this modernization will also lead to the Westernization promoted by Gregory the Great's family revolution. The ultimate fear of the cultural nationalists is that modernization will undermine traditional mores concerning marriage and the family. But is this justified?

Since Marx and Engels there has been the view that with modernization the traditional extended family identified with preindustrial societies is doomed. Modern families will become more and more like Western families: with love marriages, nuclear families, and a cold-hearted attitude toward the old. There are others who maintain that since the Western style of family seems to go back at least to the Middle Ages in Northern Europe, this modern family pattern was not merely the consequence of the Western industrial revolution, it was the cause. Research by Cambridge anthropologist Jack Goody casts serious doubts on both positions.[29]

First, the historical evidence shows that the Western family revolution predated the Industrial Revolution, so clearly the latter could not have caused the former. Second, as Goody shows at length, the purported advantages of the Western system, leading to a greater control of fertility, were to be found in many other Eurasian family systems, which, however, did not deliver industrial revolutions.

But it seems undeniable that the Western Christian world, particularly its Northwestern outpost, deviated from what had been the traditional family pattern in Eurasia from the late sixth century. The major difference was that in the West the Church came to support the independence of the young: in choosing marriage partners, in setting up their households, and in entering into contractual rather than affective relationships with the old. They promoted love marriages rather than the arranged marriages common in Eurasia. Friar Lawrence in *Romeo and Juliet,* who egged on the young lovers against their families' wishes, is emblematic of this trend. But why did the Church promote love marriages?

Since its inception, the Church has been in the business of seeking bequests, particularly from rich widows. The Church acquired so much wealth in this way that in July AD 370, Emperor Valentinian issued a decree to the Pope saying that male clerics should not hang around the houses of women and widows and worm themselves, and their churches, into the women's bequests at the expense of their blood relations. That the Church extolled virginity and discouraged second marriages also helped to increase the number of single women who would leave bequests to the Church.

This process of alienating property in favor of the Church was accelerated by Pope Gregory the Great's answers to questions posed by Augustine, the first Archbishop of Canterbury, in AD 597. Four of the nine questions concerned sex and marriage. Gregory's answers overturned the traditional Mediterranean and Eurasian pattern of legal and customary practices in the domestic domain whose aim was to provide an heir to inherit family property. It allowed marriage to close kin; marriages to close affines or widows of close kin; the transfer of children by adoption; and concubinage, a form of secondary union. Gregory banned all four practices. The net effect of these prohibitions was to leave 4 percent of families without a male heir. The Church became the main beneficiary of the resulting bequests and it accumulated vast wealth. Thus one-third of the productive land in France was in the Church's hands by the end of the seventh century.[30]

The promotion of "love marriages" and the independence of the young was part of the Church's strategy of wealth creation. It has been thought that romantic love is far from being a universal emotion, and that it was a Western social construct from the age of chivalry in the Middle Ages. Recent anthropological and psychological research, however, confirms that this is erroneous: Romantic love is a universal emotion.[31] Moreover it has a biological basis. Neuropsychologists have shown that it is associated with increased levels of phenylethylamine, an amphetamine-related compound. Interestingly, the same distinct biochemicals are also found in other animal species such as birds, which also evince this emotion. However, it appears that the emotion is ephemeral. After a period of attachment, the brain's receptor sites for the essential neurochemicals become desensitized or overloaded and the infatuation ends, setting up both the body and brain for separation-divorce. This period of infatuation has been shown to last for about three years. A cross-cultural study in sixty-two societies between 1947 to 1989 found that divorces tend to occur around the fourth year of marriage!

A universal emotion with a biological basis calls for an explanation. Sociobiologists maintain that in the primordial environment it was vital for males and females to be attracted to each other in order to have sex and reproduce; it was also important that the males be attached enough to the females to look after their young until they were old enough to move into a peer group and be looked after by the hunting-gathering band. The traditional period between successive human births is four years, which is also the modal period for those marriages that end in divorce today. Darwin strikes again! It seems that the biochemistry of love evolved as an "inclusive fitness" strategy of our species.

The capacity to love may be universal, but its public expression is culturally controlled. As everyone's personal experience will confirm, it is an explosive emotion. Its relatively rapid decay—the evolved instinct for mates to stay together for about four years and then move on to new partners to conceive and rear new young—would have been dysfunctional for settled agricultural societies. Settled agriculture requires settled households. Not surprisingly, most agrarian civilizations sought to curb the explosive primordial emotion that would have destroyed their way of life. They have used cultural constraints to curb this dangerous hominid tendency by relying on arranged marriages, infant betrothal, and the like, restricting romantic passion to relationships outside marriage. The West stands alone in using this dangerous biological universal as the bastion of its marriages. As it says in a popular song, "love and marriage go together like a horse and carriage."

As we have seen, the reason for this Western exceptionalism goes back to the earliest period of the Christian Church. But the Church also had to find a way to prevent the social chaos that would have ensued if romantic passion as the basis for marriage had been allowed to run its course in a settled agrarian civilization. First it separated love and sex, and then it created a fierce guilt culture based on Original Sin. Its pervasive teaching against sex and the guilt it engendered provided the necessary antidote to the "animal passions" that would otherwise have been unleashed by the Church's self-interested overthrow of the traditional Eurasian system of marriage. But once the Christian God died with the scientific and Darwinian revolutions, the restraints built on Original Sin were finally removed. The family became sick in the West, as Western humanoids reverted to the "family" practices of their hunter-gatherer ancestors.

Within Western cosmologies there was, however, another way to deal with the death of the Christian God, other than rely on these continuing secular variations on Augustine's "City" to provide the moral cement of society. These were the views associated with the Scottish Enlightenment, in particular those of its most eminent sages —David Hume and Adam Smith.

Hume, unlike the *philosophes*, saw clearly that Reason could not provide an adequate grounding for morality.[32] As Nietzsche later said so trenchantly about utilitarianism, any such attempt would be unsuccessful because "moral sensibilities are nowadays at such cross purposes that to one man a morality is proved by its utility, while to another its utility refutes it."[33] Kant's attempt to ground a rational morality on his principle of universalizability—harking back to the Biblical injunction "therefore all things whatsoever ye do would that men should do to you, do even so to them"—founders on Hegel's two objections. It is merely a principle of logical consistency without any specific moral content, and worse as a result it is powerless to prevent any immoral conduct that takes our fancy.[34] The subsequent ink spilt by Western moral philosophers has merely clothed their particular prejudices in rational form.

By contrast Hume clearly saw the role of morality in maintaining the social cement of society and that it depended on a society's traditions and forms of socialization. Neither God nor Reason needs to be evoked (or can be) to justify these conditioned and necessary habits. This is very much the view of ethics taken by the older non-Semitic Eurasian civilizations whose socialization processes are based on shame.

However, as this account shows, there is no reason whatsoever for the rest of the world to follow this peculiar and particular Western trajectory. It is not modernization but the unintended consequences of Pope Gregory I's family revolution that have led to the death in the West of the Eurasian family values the Rest rightly continues to cherish. The Rest do not have to embrace this cosmology. Moreover, even their Westernized elites can heal their fractured souls by embracing the Scottish sages: Hume's morality based on tradition and Smith's material beliefs based on the market. This classical liberalism provides a means of modernizing without succumbing to the moral emptiness of the current Western cosmology.

As the example of a modernized but non-Westernized Japan shows, there is no need for the non-Western world to accept the cosmology promoted by Gregory the Great's family revolution. The Rest can modernize without losing their souls.

Conclusions

Although an Imperium is useful in maintaining the global Pax that aids globalization, a homogenizing empire—such as the United States—can cause a backlash against the process by attempting to legislate its "habits of the heart" worldwide. Second, there is no ideal polity required, in its form, size, or ethnic composition, for the benign processes of globalization to work. Third, the fear of non-Western cultural nationalists that globalization will destroy cherished cultural forms, in particular traditional Eurasian family values, is unfounded. It is possible to modernize without Westernizing.

Notes

This essay is based on Lal (1998), (1999), (1999a), 2000, and (2000a).

[1]The reason we, unlike in the nineteenth century, no longer see free movement of people, particularly to the developed world, is because of the welfare states. These states have created property rights in "citizenship," and

the citizens have access to the purse of their fellow citizens, who are then naturally concerned about who can have such rights.

[2]Kaul et al. (1999).

[3]Lal (1998).

[4]See my model of the predatory state in Lal (1988) and Lal (1998).

[5]Kindleberger (1986) has argued that the interwar collapse of the world economy was due to the decline of the British Empire and the failure of the United States to assume its emerging imperial responsibilities. But Sally (1998) has cogently argued that it was not the lack of a hegemon but the failure to adhere to the classical liberal principles underlying the nineteenth-century LIEO by the emerging economic powers—the United States and Germany—which led to its dismantlement.

[6]Lal (1999).

[7]McNeill (1983).

[8]Jenner (1992).

[9]Toulmin (1990), Douglas and Wildavsky (1983), and Lal (1998).

[10]Mendez (1999).

[11]Thus Mendez (1999, p. 395) estimates that there were more than 22 million refugees and displaced persons worldwide in 1997, excluding economic migrants.

[12]Collier and Hoeffler (1998).

[13]Skidelsky (2000), volume 3, chapter 5, p. 38.

[14]Trivers (1985); Tooby and Cosmides (1989); Barkow, Cosmides, and Tooby (1992).

[15]Some natural experiments conducted by Francisco Gil Diaz of the department of anthropology at UCLA, and reported at a conference on "Norms," Center for International Relations, UCLA (1999), provide empirical support.

[16]Huntington (1993).

[17]Colinvaux (1983). This was the definition adopted in Lal (1988) and in Lal (1998).

[18]Hahn (1973).

[19]Lal (1998a).

[20]Lal (1998b).

[21]Lal (1998).

[22]Dumont (1970).

[23]Lal and Myint (1996).

[24]Rosecrance (1999).

[25]September 11, 2001, and its aftermath might suggest that this reluctance to behave in an imperial manner has changed. We shall have to wait to see if this happens.

[26]The action taken to root out the Taliban and Al Qaeda will hopefully show that no such credible threat can be made against the U.S. But will the U.S. be willing to maintain its Pax? This question remains.

[27]Jervis (1976).
[28]Elton (1955).
[29]Goody (1990).
[30]Goody (1983)
[31]Jankowiak (1995) and Fisher (1992).
[32]Hume (1740/1985).
[33]Nietzsche (1881/1982).
[34]Kant (1788/1958).

References

J. H. Barkow, L. Cosmides, and J. Tooby. 1992. *The Adapted Mind: Evolutionary Psychology and the Generation of Culture.* New York: Oxford University Press.

P. Colinvaux. 1983. *The Fates of Nations.* London: Penguin.

P. Collier and A. Hoeffler. "On Economic Causes of Civil War." *Oxford Economic Papers* 50 (4): 563–73.

J. Delumeau. 1990. *Sin and Fear: The Emergence of a Western Quilt Culture 13–18th Centuries.* New York: St. Martin's Press.

M. Douglas and A. Wildavsky. 1983. *Risk and Culture.* Berkeley: University of California Press.

L. Dumont. 1970. *Homo Hierarchicus.* London: Weidenfeld and Nicholson.

G. R. Elton. 1955. *England Under the Tudors.* London: Methuen.

H. Fisher. 1992. *Anatomy of Love.* New York: W. W. Norton.

J. Goody. 1983. *The Development of the Family and Marriage in Europe.* Cambridge: Cambridge University Press.

__________. 1990. *The Oriental, the Ancient, and the Primitive.* Cambridge: Cambridge University Press.

F. Hahn. 1973. *On the Notion of Equilibrium in Economics.* Cambridge: Cambridge University Press.

D. Hume. 1740/1985. *A Treatise on Human Nature.* London: Penguin Classics.

S. Huntington. "The Clash of Civilizations." *Foreign Affairs* 72 (3): 22–49.

W. Jankowiak, Ed. 1995. *Romantic Passion.* New York: Columbia University Press.

W. J. F. Jenner. 1992. *The Tyranny of History.* London: Penguin.

R. Jervis. 1976. *Perception and Misperception in International Politics.* Princeton, NJ: Princeton University Press.

I. Kant. 1788/1958. *Critique of Practical Reasoning.* London: Penguin Classics.

I. Kaul, I. Grunberg, and M. A. Stern. 1999. *Global Public Goods.* New York: Oxford University Press.

C. Kindleberger. 1986. *The World in Depression.* Berkeley: University of California Press.

D. Lal. 1988. *The Hindu Equilibrium,* Volume 1. Oxford: Clarendon Press.

__________. 1998a. *Unintended Consequences.* Cambridge, MA: MIT Press.

_________. 1998b. "The Communications Revolution and Economic Performance," paper prepared for Nemetria's VIth conference on "Ethics and Economics," Foligno, Italy. Reprinted in Lal (1999a).

_________. 1999a. *Unfinished Business.* New Delhi: Oxford University Press.

_________. 1999b. "Globalization: What Does It Mean for Developing and Developed Countries." In H. Siebert, Ed., *Globalization and Labour.* Hamburg: Mohr Siebeck.

__________. "The World Economy at the End of the Millennium." In J. Mueller, Ed. *Peace, Prosperity and Politics.* Boulder, CO: Westview Press. Reprinted in Lal 1999a.

_________. 2000a. "Does Modernization Require Westernization?" *Independent Review* 5(1) (Summer 2000).

_________. 2000b. "Globalisation, Imperialism and Regulation." *Cambridge Review of International Affairs* xiv(1) (July 2000).

D. Lal and H. Myint. 1996. *The Political Economy of Poverty, Equity and Growth.* Oxford: Clarendon Press.

W. H. McNeill. 1983. *The Great Frontier.* Princeton, NJ: Princeton University Press.

R. P. Mendez. "Peace as a Global Public Good." In Kaul et al. (1999).

F. Nietzsche. 1881/1982. *Daybreak: Thought on the Prejudices of Morality.* Cambridge: Cambridge University Press.

R. Rosecrance. 1999. *The Rise of the Virtual State.* New York: Basic Books.

R. Sally. 1998. *Classical Liberalism and International Economic Order.* London: Routledge.

R. Skidelsky. 2000. *John Maynard Keynes, 1937–1946: Fighting for Britain.* London: Macmillan.

J. Tooby and L. Cosmides. "Evolutionary Psychology and the Generation of Culture, Part 1." *Ethology and Sociobiology* 10: 29–49.

S. Toulmin. 1990. *Cosmopolis.* Chicago: University of Chicago Press.

R. Trivers. 1985. *Social Evolution.* Menlo Park, CA: Benjamin Cummings.

Lawrence H. White

Globalization and the Gold Standard

If national governments had never interfered, today we would have a unified global monetary system based on silver or gold. But the twentieth century was an era of monetary nationalism.[1] In countries where private banks had been issuing the currency (including the United States, Canada, and Australia, albeit with various degrees of national regulation), national governments monopolized the issue of banknotes and created national central banks. Central banks abrogated their contractual obligations to redeem their notes in gold and substituted national fiat monies for the international gold standard. The classical gold standard, which had approached the cosmopolitan ideal of a single nonpolitical worldwide money, gave way to a system approaching the opposite ideal of one fiat money per nation.[2] Every new nation–state, born as colonial empires broke up, created its own national fiat money. Many governments instituted exchange controls to restrict their citizens' access to monies issued in other nations.

Over the last dozen years or so, monetary nationalism has finally begun to wane. Driven by technological and ideological change, the global marketplace has begun to re-emerge as a major ordering force for both bank-issued money and basic money. New information-processing and communications technologies—for example, banking by fax and internet—are increasingly eroding exchange controls, geographic restrictions on banks, and other nationalistic impediments to financial markets. The process of erosion began decades ago with the emergence of the "offshore" banking market (once known as the "Eurodollar" market), which allows large-dollar lenders and borrowers to bypass an inefficiently restricted domestic banking market. With the price of remote access to offshore banking services now falling toward zero, increasingly small depositors and lenders are able to cheaply route their money around hampered domestic banks. Banking services are being globalized for the small as well as for the large.

The control of basic money—once gold, now fiat money—remains for now in the hands of national central banks. But trade and technology are making it increasingly easy for transactors to switch currencies, eroding the monopoly power that each central bank once had in supplying fiat money within its own territory. Around the world, and particularly in the former Soviet bloc and Latin America, nations with weak currencies are undergoing unofficial "dollarization" as their citizens switch their savings and even their transactions balances into U.S. dollars from weak domestic currencies.

National governments are responding to the erosion of their monetary monopolies in different ways. Eleven European nations, seemingly to form a cartel against currency substitution, have combined their currencies to create the Euro, a supranational fiat money issued by a supranational central bank. Several nations with previously weak currencies (Argentina, Lithuania, Estonia, Bulgaria) have in recent years partially conceded their monetary independence by fixing the domestic monetary unit to the dollar or the Euro through a currency-board-like arrangement. A currency board emulates adherence to the gold standard by re-establishing the redeemability of domestic currency for an international money at a fixed rate. Contrary to skeptics who dismiss the possibility that any government will ever again submit to the discipline of currency redemption in gold, these governments have submitted to the equally strict discipline of redemption in U.S. dollars or Euros. Last year the government of Ecuador abolished its domestic currency unit and adopted the U.S. dollar outright as the official currency, following the long-standing example of Panama. In doing so the government of Ecuador bowed to the marketplace, and adopted the currency that the country's private sector had already adopted.[3]

As a consequence of supranationalization, currency boards, and dollarization, the number of distinct fiat currencies in the world is shrinking. The emerging pattern recalls medieval arrangements in which silver and gold were international monetary standards, with respected large-value coins circulating across political borders. The fiscal appetite of nation–states for greater "seigniorage" revenues from money creation eventually led governments to insist upon exclusive national monopolies in money production.[4] This appetite has not disappeared, especially in those developing countries where 10 to 20 percent of the government's budget comes from printing money. But with trade and technology making it easier for citizens to acquire and use a stronger foreign currency, a government can no longer derive as much real revenue by exploiting holders of its domestic currency. The liberation of currency choice in all nations points toward a world of fewer monetary standards. Much as Carl Menger described prehistoric barterers discarding idiosyncratic media of exchange and spontaneously converging on a single suitable commodity as *the* commonly accepted medium of exchange, unrestricted money-users around the world will abandon weaker fiat monies in favor of the more widely accepted and more trusted monies.[5]

The Fiat U.S. Dollar as Global Money

Voluntary convergence on a single global monetary standard is a good thing, *provided* that the voluntarily selected standard is at least as trustworthy as any other potential standard. That is, it is a good thing to allow a single common money, freely chosen by money-users, to supplant a variety of monies of equal or lesser strength. The emergence of the international silver standard in ancient times is an example of such convergence; dollarization today is another. I judge it a "good thing," not according to some transcendent ethical norm nor according to my own subjective taste, but in the sense that it better satisfies the historically demonstrated preference of money-users for money of wider acceptance. With a medium of exchange, wider is better. With a single money accepted in region A and region B, cross-border spot transactions are relieved of money-changing expenses, and cross-border investments are freed from exchange-rate risk.[6]

But the proviso just mentioned, "that the voluntarily selected standard is at least as trustworthy as any other potential standard," is important. The disadvantages of having a low-quality money can more than outweigh the advantages of having a single money. This point bears emphasis because there is a danger in global adoption of the U.S. dollar that has not been widely appreciated: It changes the incentives of the Federal Reserve system in a way that reduces the trustworthiness of the dollar. The very popularity of dollarization can be the dollar standard's undoing.

When other countries circulate Federal Reserve notes, they provide the Fed with seigniorage, the profit from issuing any money that exchanges for a value greater than its cost of production. By printing up fiat dollars (aka "expanding the monetary base") that are exported in exchange for real goods and services or financial assets, the Fed gains a transfer from foreigners. Printing dollars faster means a greater profit, at least until the market begins to anticipate high dollar inflation and to abandon the dollar.[7] The more popular the global use of the U.S. dollar, the greater the potential profit and hence the greater the temptation to inflate. The temptation to inflate a globally held dollar is not merely hypothetical: The Fed succumbed to it during the Bretton Woods era, when foreign central banks held dollar reserves. During the early years of the Bretton Woods system, in the decade from 1952 to 1961, the Fed expanded the U.S. monetary base "only" 19 percent. In the following decade, the Fed expanded the monetary base 75 percent, precipitating the breakdown of the system in 1971 by creating a dollar glut that made it impossible for the Fed to continue honoring its pledge to redeem the dollars presented by foreign central banks at one ounce of gold per $35.[8] Under Bretton Woods, the transfer from foreigners was moderated by the fact that a foreign central bank could hold most of its dollar reserves in Treasury securities paying a competitive interest rate. When Federal Reserve notes are held abroad, as under Panama-style dollarization, the temptation is unmoderated.

To reduce the seigniorage they surrender to the Fed, countries adopting the U.S. dollar as a unit of account can allow their domestic banks to issue dollar-denominated currency (as U.S. banks did until the 1930s). To place and keep its notes in circulation, in competition against other banks and against Federal Reserve notes, a domestic commercial bank must endow its notes with properties that its clientele finds desirable. A system of this sort prevails today in Scotland and Northern Ireland, where local banks of issue (two in Scotland, four in Northern Ireland) circulate their own notes. The local notes, denominated in pounds sterling and redeemable for Bank of England notes, displace Bank of England notes from common circulation and thereby retain locally what would otherwise be seigniorage for the Bank of England.[9] The notes enter circulation in the usual ways: For example, the Ulster Bank's ATMs (or "cash dispensers") dispense Ulster Bank notes. With rivalry among the domestic issuing banks, the would-be seigniorage on currency is distributed to the banks' customers through price and nonprice competition.

With private domestic note issues filling the need for currency, the quantity of Federal Reserve notes held in dollarized economies will be limited to the much smaller quantity needed as bank reserves. With the globe holding a smaller real stock of Federal Reserve notes, the Fed's real profit from any given rate of monetary expansion is reduced, and more of the burden falls on U.S. citizens rather than on foreigners.

The temptation to inflate is not unique to the Federal Reserve and the fiat U.S. dollar. It faces the issuer of any fiat money and it is stronger on any issuer to the extent that the fiat money is held globally.

Gold as a Nonpolitical Global Money

Fortunately, there is a well-known alternative to fiat money that can provide a global monetary standard without creating a temptation to inflate: a commodity money standard. It should be clear that fiat money, produced by a stroke of the central banker's pen in any nominal quantity that central banker pleases, is prone to inflation in a way that gold or silver, produced by the efforts of miners, is not. Even a self-described socialist like George Bernard Shaw, in a volume of otherwise naïve commentary on economic policy, understood the point:

> To sum up, the most important thing about money is to maintain its stability, so that a pound will buy as much a year hence or ten years hence or fifty years hence as today, and no more. With paper money this stability has to be maintained by the

> Government. With a gold currency it tends to maintain itself. ...You have to choose (as a voter) between trusting to the natural stability of gold and the natural stability of the honesty and intelligence of the members of the Government. And, with due respect for these gentlemen, I advise you, as long as the Capitalist system lasts, to vote for gold.[10]

The greater stability of gold is evident both in theory and in the historical record. Supply and demand forces automatically keep the purchasing power of gold from drifting far off its long-run path: a fall in the purchasing power of gold (e.g., due to a drop in monetary demand for gold) discourages mining and encourages industrial consumption, both of which restrict the supply of monetary gold, and so bring the purchasing power back up. And vice-versa: A rise in the purchasing power of gold (e.g., due to growing demand for monetary gold) stimulates mining and discourages consumption, so that the monetary gold stock grows, and the purchasing power of gold is pushed back down.[11] No such constraint operates on a fiat money. Fiat money systems exhibit substantially higher price level inflation rates on average,[12] and less predictable inflation rates over long horizons. Evidence of the market's greater trust in the long-term stability of gold can be seen in the shorter maturity of corporate bonds issued under fiat money regimes. Bond buyers are naturally more reluctant to take on 30-year bonds when they have a far less reliable basis for projecting the purchasing power of the monetary unit 30 years hence. Benjamin Klein found that the average maturity of new U.S. corporate debt issues was 29 years from 1900 to 15 under the classical gold standard, but only 21 years from 1956 to 1972 under Bretton Woods. Guedes and Opler have found that the mean maturity was only 12 years during the period 1983 to 1993.[13]

A variety of commodity standards can be imagined, but gold and silver were the two that won out historically in a "survival of the fittest" contest among commodity monies.[14] Classical economists emphasized at least five desired features that coined gold and silver have in greater measure than other commodities, making gold and silver coins more suitable in the public's eyes as hand-to-hand media of exchange: *durability* (when suitably alloyed), *uniformity* (or easily recognizable quality), *divisibility* (pieces can be sized appropriately for even small purchases), *portability* (high value per unit of bulk), and *stability of purchasing power* (by contrast, for example, with seasonal food crops). The first three of these features were not fully realized in uncoined metal, so it was important to the adoption of gold and silver that merchants learned to fashion bits of precious metal and alloy into standardized marked pieces or coins.

A few advocates seem to want to freeze the gold standard at the stage of its evolution where gold coins are the predominant medium of exchange. A purely metallic monetary system, however, has serious practical shortcomings.

1. Full-bodied gold coins in circulation *lack durability* because they are subject to considerable wear and tear as they pass from hand to hand.
2. Coins *lack uniformity* or *easily recognizable quality* when they are variously worn or deliberately lightened by users (I assume honest mints, and leave aside the historically important problem of debasement by sovereign mints). Medieval bankers were so often compelled to weigh and assay the coins they received that the symbol of a medieval banker was a balance scale.
3. Silver coins serve well for ordinary retail transactions, but are bulky or *lack portability* for large-value payments. Medieval economies based on silver coins found it practically necessary to have a concurrent gold coinage for international trade. On the other hand, the greater preciousness of gold is a problem for small-value transactions. Gold coins *lack sufficient divisibility* in that they cannot practically be made tiny enough for small purchases. (Imagine how miniscule a pure gold coin would have to be to have the purchasing power of a present-day U.S. dollar.) To be practical, a monetary system based on gold coins requires a subsidiary currency for small-value transactions.

To ameliorate these problems, entrepreneurs centuries ago developed bank-issued forms of money: banknotes, transferable deposits, and tokens redeemable in gold. Bankers have continued to innovate, and newer forms include the electronic equivalent of banknotes, namely "smart" currency cards, as well as electronically transferable deposits, and redeemable "tokens" transferable over the internet. In a future gold standard, as they did in the most developed stage of the classical gold standard era that ended in 1914, people would presumably make most money payments with banknotes (or their electronic equivalent) and transferable deposits. Occasions for removing gold coins from banking system vaults would be rare. Even payment from one bank to another within a single clearing system would be made by transferring claims to gold deposited at the clearinghouse, not by physically transferring gold coins. Physical gold shipments would ordinarily be limited to net settlements between clearinghouses. Such a system remains a gold *standard* because bank-issued monies are denominated in gold and derive their value from their redeemability for specified quantities of gold, even if the redemption option is seldom directly exercised.

A system of fractional reserves for bank-issued money economizes on the real quantity of gold tied up in monetary use. It thus usefully economizes on the resource costs associated with maintaining a gold standard.[15] Banks can finance a volume of business loans equal to the volume of "fiduciary media," that is, the difference between the public's holding of bank-issued money and the banks' gold reserves. A corresponding stock of productive capital goods, purchased by the banks' borrowers, takes the place of gold coins on the economy's balance sheet. As Ludwig von Mises wrote: "Fiduciary media tap a lucrative source of revenue for their issuer; they enrich both the person that issues them and the community that employs them."[16]

Bank-issued money brings with it other problems, of course, associated with the fallibility of commercial banks operating on fractional metallic reserves. But historical evidence indicates that these problems are relatively mild in the absence of legal restrictions that weaken banks. In a laissez-faire system where nobody is compelled to use bank-issued money, a bank must behave very cautiously and conservatively to gain a clientele's trust, and the trust of other bankers (essential for gaining widespread acceptance for its liabilities). Money-users in a free banking system are free to insist on 100 percent reserves, but in practice (perhaps because of the storage fees required) they do not find it better, individually or collectively, to shun fiduciary media in favor of using only coins or warehouse receipts for coins.[17]

Gold and silver are not perfectly stable in purchasing power. Growth in trade can make the demand for metallic money sometimes grow ahead of supply, raising its purchasing power until mine output can catch up. Dramatic discoveries of new mining sources (such as California and Australia in the nineteenth century), although unlikely in the future now that the entire globe has been explored, can make supply surge ahead of demand, pushing the purchasing power down. A plan for a fiat standard with greater price-level stability can be designed on paper. Gold and silver standards are merely more stable *in practice* than the fiat standards the world has actually seen or is ever likely to see.

How Do We Get There from Here?

Some writers hope that removing legal obstacles would be enough to have the market spontaneously return to silver and gold standards. If metallic standards really are more trustworthy, and were chosen by the market once before, why not again? The reason why not is that today, unlike in the days of barter, we already have established monetary standards. It is in no individual's interest to be the first to switch from a prevailing money to a novel standard—with whom would he buy and sell?—unless the prevailing money is very unstable. (We have seen spontaneous dollarization in unstable peso and ruble regimes.) New technologies may be making it easier to switch, and thus lower the threshhold level of inflation at which spontaneous switching occurs. But the fiat dollar still has a substantial advantage of incumbency in the United States. As Menger's account of the origin of money teaches us, any seller prefers to be paid in the medium of exchange that he expects to be the most popular with other sellers. When the monetary unit that everyone uses is the fiat dollar, sellers of goods want to receive dollars, not gold, because they know they can turn around and respend dollars.

The example of a Kansas City firm called the Gold Standard Corporation illustrates this point.[19] In the 1980s, GSC sold gold pieces, notes denominated in units of gold, and even transferable deposit accounts denominated in gold. Its advertising slogan was "put yourself on the gold standard." But the marketplace did not move to embrace the gold-denominated media of exchange. The first Gold Standard Corporation customers who tried to spend gold-denominated notes would have discovered that almost no stores were willing to accept them in payment. The same problem faces customers of E-gold (<http://www.e-gold.com>), a firm currently offering gold-denominated accounts transferable through the internet, and of NORFED, an organization offering silver-backed notes.

The problem is one of achieving critical mass. Unless an alternative currency is regarded as a much more stable store of value, people will be reluctant to accept it knowing that it isn't as spendable as the incumbent currency. A critical mass for using gold does not exist until the network of traders willing to accept payments denominated in gold is large enough to make paying in gold about as convenient as paying in dollars, which therefore makes the network self-sustaining.

I conclude that to return to a gold standard without the duress of very high inflation, it will be necessary to persuade the U.S. government to redefine the dollar as a fixed amount of gold. For gold to be the definitive money, the U.S. dollar as an independent monetary unit must disappear. A gold standard is not a "gold price target" in dollars, nor a "gold price rule" fastened on the Federal Reserve, as some supply-side economists have proposed. It is a monetary system in which the monetary unit, whether a "dollar" or an "ounce" or a "gram," is nothing but a specified mass of gold.

With gold as the monetary standard, there is no need to have a central bank provide currency or clearinghouse services.[20] In fact, having a central bank is counterproductive. The classical gold standard of 1900 was needlessly fragile, subject as it was to manipulation and suspension by central banks like the Bank of England that monopolized the issue of currency and centralized the system's gold reserves. An issuer's commitment to redeem for gold is never fully credible when the issuer is a sovereign central bank. Only when banks of issue are private institutions can a note-holder sue a bank that fails to redeem its notes. Only when banks of issue face open competition do reputational forces strongly deter suspension.[21] To be more durable than the gold standard of the nineteenth century, a gold standard of the twenty-first century should operate with competing private mints, competing private banks of issue, and private clearinghouses.

Notes

[1]This phrase is due to F. A. Hayek (1937). These introductory paragraphs are drawn from Selgin and White (2002).

[2]Benjamin J. Cohen (1998) discusses the rise and current breakdown of this pattern.

[3]On currency boards, see Kurt Schuler (2000); on dollarization, see Bogetic.

[4]See Selgin and White (1999).

[5]Carl Menger (1892).

[6]In contrast to the standard macroeconomic or central planner approach to defining "optimal currency areas," I am suggesting a consumer-sovereignty approach.

[7]For a technical analysis of seigniorage, see White (1999, chapter 7).

[8]The U.S. consumer price index rose 13 percent the first decade, 37 percent in the second. Rates calculated from 1952.01, 1961.12, 1962.01, and 1971.12 adjusted monetary base and CPI data in the Federal Reserve Bank of St. Louis FRED® time series database. <http://www.stls.frb.org/fred/>

[9]Local seigniorage is inframarginal. At the margin, because of a 100% marginal reserve requirement beyond a specified circulation volume, all of the seigniorage goes to the Bank of England.

[10]George B. Shaw (1928, p. 263).

[11]See White (1999, chapter 2) for a stock-flow analysis of gold standard dynamics.

[12]See Rolnick and Weber (1994).

[13]Their sampling method may not be strictly comparable to Klein's, however.

[14]In this and the following two paragraphs I draw on White (2000).

[15]Resource costs are among the leading objections to a gold standard by mainstream economists. Milton Friedman (1953) famously estimated the resource cost of a gold standard at 2.5 percent of national income, but he was assuming 100 percent gold reserves behind all bank liabilities, even time deposits(!) Assuming a reasonable fractional reserve ratio produces an estimate about one-fiftieth the size of Friedman's, which is less than standard estimates of the "deadweight cost" of an average fiat money inflation rate. See White (1999, pp. 42–48).

[16]Mises (1980, p. 359). For an extended discussion of Mises's defense of fractional-reserve banking, see White (1992). For a defense of fiduciary media

against contemporary advocates of mandatory 100 percent reserves, see Selgin and White (1996).

[17]See White (1995, 1999); Selgin and White (1994, 1996).

[18]Menger (1892).

[19]This and next paragraph draw on White (2000b).

[20]See White (2001).

[21]See Selgin and White (2001b).

References

Bogetic, Zeljko. "Official Dollarization: Current Experiences and Issues," *Cato Journal* 20 (Fall): 179–213.

Friedman, Milton. 1953. "Commodity-Reserve Currency." In Friedman, *Essays in Positive Economics.* Chicago: University of Chicago Press.

Guedes, Jose, and Tim Opler. 1996. "The Determinants of the Maturity Structure of Corporate Debt Issues." *Journal of Finance* 51 (December 1996): 1809–33.

Menger, Carl. 1892. "On the Origin of Money." *Economic Journal* 2 (June): 239–55.

Rolnick, Arthur J., and Warren E. Weber. 1994. "Inflation and Money Growth under Alternative Monetary Standards." Working Paper 528, Federal Reserve Bank of Minneapolis.

Schuler, Kurt. 2000. "Introduction to Currency Boards." <http://users.erols.com/kurrency/intro.htm>

Selgin, George, and Lawrence H. White. 1994. "How Would the Invisible Hand Handle Money?" *Journal of Economic Literature* 32 (December 1994): 1718–49.

__________. 1996. "In Defense of Fiduciary Media." *Review of Austrian Economics* 9 (2): 83–107.

__________. 2001. "Credible Currency: The Commitment Problem in Commercial and Central Banking." Unpublished ms.

__________. 2002. "Mengerian Perspectives on the Future of Money." In Michael Latzer and Stefan W. Schmitz, eds. *Carl Menger and the Evolution of Payments Systems: From Barter to Electronic Money.* Cheltenham, UK: Edward Elgar.

Shaw, George Bernard. 1928. *The Intelligent Woman's Guide to Capitalism and Socialism.* New York: Brentano's.

Lawrence H. White. 1992 "Mises on Free Banking and Fractional Reserves." In John W. Robbins and Mark Spangler, eds. *A Man of Principle: Essays in Honor of Hans F. Sennholz.* Grove City, PA: Grove City College Press.

__________. 1995. *Free Banking in Britain: Theory, Experience, and Debate, 1800–1845*, 2nd ed., revised & enlarged. London: Institute of Economic Affairs.

__________. 1999. *The Theory of Monetary Institutions.* Oxford: Basil Blackwell.

__________. 2000a. "Introduction." In Lawrence H. White, ed. *The History of Gold and Silver*, vol. 1. London: Pickering and Chatto.

__________. 2000b. "A Competitor for the Fed?" *Ideas on Liberty* (July 2000).

__________. 2001. "In What Respects Will the Information Age Make Central Banks Obsolete?" *Cato Journal* 21 (Fall): 219–26.

Bryan-Paul Frost

Is a Global Liberal Democratic Order Inevitable?

The topic which I have been asked to address is an exceedingly difficult one, and many might say impossible. In the first place, I am asked to engage in historical prediction or speculation, and this sort of futuristic exercise often elicits, at best, bemused but skeptical smiles. One only has to look at the 2000 presidential election to see how difficult it is to predict the outcome of an event in the near future, let alone the possibility of something occurring many decades or centuries ahead. In the second place, I am asked to pronounce on the fate of my own country; for even if the United States is not the best example of a harmonious, liberal democratic regime, it is certainly the most powerful one in the world today, and as such it may very well be that the global fate of liberal democracy is inextricably yoked to the success or failure of the American polity. But to speak cogently about one's own country requires a nonpartisan insight into and appreciation of its genuine strengths and weaknesses, and this, in turn, requires a detachment and objectivity that is as demanding as it is rare. Taken together, these two difficulties present imposing obstacles for the would-be writer. Anyone who wishes to speak cogently on the global inevitability of a liberal democratic order would have to be, it seems, part prophet and part philosopher.

Fortunately there is someone to whom we can turn in order to begin to achieve clarity on this subject—namely, the French Hegelian philosopher Alexandre Kojève. Kojève articulated, perhaps better than anyone else in the last century, the philosophical foundation for the eventual triumph of a liberal democratic world order. Kojève elaborated a systematic understanding of world history which demonstrated that human beings could only be fully satisfied in such a political or social order, and in particular, he concentrated on its inherently superior concept of justice and right. It is Kojève's understanding of justice and right that I would like to focus on in this essay.

Since Kojève may not be a figure familiar to many people, it might be useful to start by saying a little about the man himself, and then to offer a brief sketch of his overall philosophic position.[1] Alexandre Kojève was born in Moscow in 1902, into a well-to-do bourgeois family. He escaped from Russia in 1920 and spent the first half of the decade in Germany, where he completed his dissertation on the religious philosophy of Vladimir Soloviev. Toward the end of 1926, Kojève traveled to Paris where he continued his studies; and in 1933, he began to teach a seminar on Hegel's *Phenomenology of Spirit*, lecturing on this one book until 1939. Kojève's seminar on Hegel achieved an exceptional notoriety: Not only was Kojève's interpretation of the *Phenomenology* recognized as compelling (albeit controversial), but the list of those who attended and were subsequently influenced by his lectures reads like a veritable who's who of future French intellectuals. Raymond Aron, Georges Bataille, André Breton, Gaston Fessard, Jacques Lacan, Maurice Merleau-Ponty, Eric Weil, and others attended Kojève's seminar at various times, and many of them attested to the power of his interpretation.[2] In 1940, Kojève was drafted into the French army, but he did not see combat. Unable to leave France the following year, he spent the course of the war in Marseilles, during which time he wrote and worked for the Resistance in various capacities. After the war, Kojève secured a job in the Direction des relations économiques extérieures; and for the next twenty years, he was, according to everyone who worked with him, the *éminence grise* of French economic policy, instrumental in promoting the European Union, the GATT negotiations, and fairer north–south trade relations.[3] He died of a heart attack in 1968 while giving a speech in Brussels before a meeting of the Common Market.

Kojève's lectures on Hegel's *Phenomenology of Spirit* were published after the war,[4] and it was during these lectures that Kojève coined what is certainly one of the most worn-out and misunderstood phrases of our time: "the end of history" and the "end state." By the end of history, Kojève did not mean that wars and revolutions would be eliminated in the foreseeable future; nor did he mean that newspapers would lack sundry material to fill their pages. By the end of history, Kojève meant first and foremost the end of the history of the development of politics. The most satisfying and fully rational political or social order would be one which embodied the principles of the French Revolution, namely liberty, equality, and fraternity. Kojève called this final social order the universal and homogenous state (often referred to as the "end state"). The state was universal (i.e., encompassed all of humanity) because Kojève saw no reason why people should be disadvantaged simply because of where they were born; and it was homogenous because he believed that everyone should enjoy equal rights and duties. In addition, Kojève argued that modern science and technology would continue to exploit with ever greater efficiency and ingenuity the power of nature, and this, in turn, would secure the material prosperity of all citizens. In the universal and homogenous state, wealth would be fairly distributed, people would live long and healthy lives, and everyone would have the opportunity to pursue those activities they found most fulfilling.

If all of this sounds like heaven on earth, it is—but Kojève emphasized that it was heaven *on earth,* without the crutch of religion. Kojève found in Hegel's *Phenomenology of Spirit* a convincing and wholly atheistic account of human history and progress, an account which demonstrated that human beings and human beings alone determine their future and that this is the future human beings wanted above all else. Phenomena such as nationalism, Islamic fundamentalism, neo-nazism, and radical environmentalism are nothing more than rear-guard actions by recalcitrant groups and states in response to the global expansion of technology and the ideals of the French Revolution. *But when the push of history comes to shove,* people will be persuaded that a Kojèvean future is the best and brightest of all, and no one will seriously advocate returning to some premodern form of government. Inevitably, nation–states will give way to ever larger trading blocks, and these, in turn, will slowly consolidate as humanity unites under a single form of government. It is not an exaggeration to say that Kojève understood, and worked toward, globalization a full half century before it became both a buzz word and a subject of contention.[5]

Except for scholars working primarily in the area of French Hegelian studies, Kojève remained a rather obscure figure; but this all changed in 1989 when Francis Fukuyama catapulted himself to global fame by publishing an article in the *National Interest* titled "The End of History?" Returning to the writings of Kojève and Hegel, Fukuyama wondered whether the collapse of the Soviet Union and the end of the Cold War did not herald an event of much greater global significance: the "unabashed victory of economic and political liberalism."[6] In remarkably blunt but bold language, Fukuyama offered the following explanation of the triumph of the political and economic ideals of the West over those of the Eastern Bloc:

> What we may be witnessing is not just the end of the Cold War, or the passing of a particular period of postwar history, but the end of history as such: that is, the end point of mankind's ideological evolution and the universalization of Western liberal democracy as the final form of human government. This is not to say that there will no longer be events to fill the pages of *Foreign Affairs*'s yearly summaries of international relations, for the victory of liberalism has occurred primarily in the realm of ideas or consciousness and is as yet incomplete in the real or material world. But there are powerful reasons for believing that it is the ideal that will govern the material world *in the long run.*[7]

Three years later Fukuyama fleshed out these ideas in greater detail in his best-seller, *The End of History and the Last Man.*[8] In a nutshell, Fukuyama argued that there are two mechanisms which have given an overall direction to history and which have driven us to see capitalistic, liberal democracy as the final and most satisfying form of government: modern natural science and the desire for recognition. Modern natural science is critical in two important ways: first, states that want to survive as independent entities must engage in it wholeheartedly if they hope to possess the latest military technology; and second, modern science yields great economic wealth that satisfies our appetitive desires.[9] But while modern natural science often flourishes in a *capitalistic* system, we do not choose *liberal democracy* for economic reasons; rather, we choose democracy because of the way in which it satisfies our pride (or Platonic *thymos*)—

because of the way in which this regime and no other recognizes us as free and equal individuals.[10] Now if liberal democracy overcomes the most fundamental social tensions within a state, then Fukuyama argued, the spread of liberal democracy should overcome tensions between states as well: If no individual has any rational reason to dominate another within a state, then one liberal democracy should have no fear of being dominated by another in the international system.[11] The end of history, then, heralds the universal reign of peace between all states: There will simply no longer be any reason for states to go to war.

> What will produce peace in the post-historical world will not be the fact that the major states share a common principle of legitimacy. This state of affairs existed at times in the past, for example, when all the nations of Europe were monarchies or empires. Peace will arise instead out of the specific nature of democratic legitimacy, and its ability to satisfy the human longing for recognition. . . . The post-historical world is one in which the desire for comfortable self-preservation has been elevated over the desire to risk one's life in a battle for pure prestige, and in which universal and rational recognition has replaced the struggle for domination.[12]

According to Fukuyama, however, very few individuals have grasped what Kojève understood some fifty years ago.

To say that Fukuyama's article, and the book that followed, created anything less than an academic and public firestorm would be an understatement. Journals as different as *Technology Review*, the *American Journal of Sociology*, and the *Journal of Communication* reviewed Fukuyama's article and book,[13] and the controversy surrounding his thesis became known as *Fukuyamismo* in Argentina.[14] Given such a voluminous response, it is not surprising to find that certain reactions were shared by more than one person.[15] While some critics more or less dismissed Fukuyama out of hand, others offered psychological and/or sociological reasons for the reappearance of the end of history thesis and the immense interest it generated. Still others argued that liberal democracies are not only threatened internally (e.g., by drugs, homelessness, and poverty) and externally (e.g., by nationalism, communism, and Islamic fundamentalism), but also that some unknown "X-factor" might arise and challenge liberal democracies in the future. And finally, some reviewers pointed to a contradiction in Fukuyama's claim that liberal democracy is the final and most satisfying political order and his fears expressed in the last part of the book that liberal democrats are nothing other than Nietzsche's last man. But looking beyond these critical responses to Fukuyama's thesis, one fact must not be forgotten: that so many persons bothered to respond to him at all. It seems that Fukuyama "touched a sensitive nerve," that he raised new and possibly disturbing questions about the meaning or spirit of our historical epoch.[16] That so many individuals felt it necessary to respond to Fukuyama—that even those who vehemently disagreed with his thesis could not silently dismiss it—strongly suggests that the issues Fukuyama raises, and *a fortiori* the issues with which Kojève wrestled all his life, are still relevant for contemporary students of politics.

Fukuyama, by his own admission, did not set himself the task of interpreting and critically assessing Kojève's political philosophy;[17] consequently, Fukuyama more or less ignored what I consider to be Kojève's most political work—the *Outline of a Phenomenology of Right.*[18] In this magisterial essay, Kojève lays out his understanding of right, law, and justice, and why these ideas or concepts can only be fully realized or achieved in a universal and homogeneous state. Let me now begin to articulate in more detail Kojève's overall understanding of right and justice, and the relationship between these concepts and politics.[19]

Kojève spends the first pages of the *Outline* laying out a "phenomenological" or "behaviorist" definition of right. There is right, or a juridical situation, when an impartial and disinterested third person, C, intervenes in the interaction between two subjects of right, A and B, in order to annul an act of one who has suppressed the act of the other. We know that A had a right to do the act in question, and B had a duty to let him do that act without suppressing it, only because the intervention to annul B's act is of a specific character—it is the intervention of one who is "impartial and disinterested." Without the intervention of an "impartial and disinterested third person C"—in other words, without the intervention of someone who is indifferent to A and B and who has nothing personal to gain by the intervention—it would be impossible *phenomenologically* to distinguish a juridical situation from one in which someone simply had the desire (without necessarily the right) to do or suppress the act in question.[20] The presence of a third person C is all the more crucial given that any interaction can provoke the intervention of C; therefore, only the intervention of C, and not the interaction per se, allows the phenomenologist to distinguish an authentic from an unauthentic juridical situation.[21] Kojève concludes that the essence of right is revealed or manifested "in and by the interaction between two human beings, A and B, which necessarily provokes the intervention of an impartial and disinterested third, C, whose intervention annuls the reaction of B opposed to the action of A."[22]

Kojève spends the next hundred pages or so clarifying the eight elements that make up his definition.[23] What is of most interest for the purpose of understanding the inevitability of a global democratic order is Kojève's discussion of the two defining characteristics of C: impartiality and disinterestedness. By impartiality, Kojève has nothing more in mind than that the third person C would intervene regardless of whether A was the plaintiff or defendant;[24] the real difficulty, Kojève reveals, comes in trying to find a satisfactory definition of "disinterestedness." The difficulty of coming up with such a definition should not come as too much of a surprise—for after all, in what sense can the third person C be genuinely disinterested given the fact that this person intervened in an interaction in the first place?

Strictly speaking, C cannot be disinterested precisely because his intervention is a voluntary, purposive act. Kojève therefore takes disinterestedness in a narrower sense: C is disinterested if the intervention results from a "*sui generis* 'interest,' a '*juridical* interest.'" Phenomenologically, this means that if C is not affected in any material or practical way by the intervention, but intervenes for "purely 'moral' or 'theoretical' reasons, in order to cause the reign of Justice," then the intervention can be considered disinterested. The difficulty with this formulation, however, is that C's intervention is an action, and as such it will affect the state or society to which C belongs. Thus, Kojève points out that C might profit "directly or indirectly" from the intervention, if only to the extent of helping his state survive by enforcing the rule of law. Kojève then argues that C is disinterested only if he intervenes *as if* he is willing to lose everything, including his own life. But the problem with this "as if" definition is that disinterestedness comes to depend upon C's subjective intentions, and Kojève agrees with Kant that such intentions can never be known phenomenologically with certitude. Kojève's third attempt is to suggest that C will be disinterested if he could be anyone at all *and* the same intervention would occur. Because the intentions for and consequences of intervening may vary from individual to individual, if everyone would intervene in a given interaction, then it would be highly unlikely that the intervention was the result of strictly self-interested motives.[25]

But no sooner does Kojève offer this definition of disinterestedness than he begins to reveal its deficiencies. Since C's intervention is influenced by the state or society to which he belongs, the juridical intervention will vary according to "epochs and peoples," and this means that C can never really be anyone at all. Furthermore, Kojève argues that C is always chosen from some exclusive or elite group within a state. This group (which Kojève identifies with those who govern a state) is defined by its ability to suppress or to exclude other competing groups who want to govern without destroying that state. Given these two mitigating conditions, Kojève is compelled to admit that C is disinterested only in the sense that he is "supposed to be able to be anyone at all within an exclusive group of a given Society at a given moment."[26]

Kojève is aware that all of the above difficulties have implications that go far beyond the viability of his own phenomenological approach: These are difficulties for anyone who does not want right and justice to be reduced to or to serve as camouflage for essentially utilitarian or mercenary motivations. For example, if C intervenes for the sake of material rewards, then C could be bribed, and this means that justice would be available to the highest bidder. Or again, if C is not willing to sacrifice everything when he intervenes—including his own life—then justice would, in the final analysis, have a price beyond which it would not be profitable to be just. Finally, if C is always chosen from within an exclusive group in society, then justice and right would more than likely serve the interests of this elite group rather than the common good of the society as a whole. The reader should no doubt be disappointed at this point in the discussion that C's disinterestedness—certainly one of the most fundamental aspects of our understanding of justice and right—is never pure in reality but is always sullied or compromised in some fashion. It is not surprising, then, that at the moment when the reader believes that right and justice are forever going to fall short of his ideal of them that Kojève briefly reveals how things would be in a universal and homogeneous state.

Kojève observes that if a society were universal and encompassed all of humanity, then the words "of a given Society" could be deleted from the above definition of C's disinterestedness; and if the state were homogeneous, with no group of persons having interests essentially hostile to any other, then the phrase "within an exclusive group" could be removed as well. And since a universal and homogeneous state would not "perish" or even change—it being threatened neither by external enemies nor undermined by internal cabals—the state would always be "in identity with itself," and this means that the phrase "at a given moment" could be erased as well. C can only be genuinely disinterested, and therefore truly just, in a universal and homogeneous state: Only in such a state, Kojève reveals, will the third person C genuinely be capable of being anyone at all.[27]

Although Kojève only briefly elaborates upon the implications of this claim, these implications are nothing less than extraordinary. If C could be anyone at all only at the end of history, then each and every individual would agree with the juridical principles which determined what specific actions were considered criminal, and the end state (and the end state alone) would give expression to a universally accepted and fully satisfying system of right. All previous understandings of right and justice which were relative to a particular epoch or nation would be dialectically integrated into a final and absolute system, and it could be explained why certain aspects of these understandings were rejected by or incorporated into that system. Moreover, universal agreement on the final system of right would preclude the possibility that C's intervention only served the narrow interests of an elite economic or social class. If C could be anyone at all, then no one person or group could claim to possess some unique or special knowledge of the law, or to represent some privileged interest, that conferred upon them an exclusive or exalted status in respect to judging criminal cases. But if the end state is not yet at hand, and if we must freely choose to enter into it, then Kojève has provided us with powerful incentives to bring this state into existence as soon as possible. By doing so, we would have achieved through our own efforts here on earth what we had always hoped and imagined right and justice to be. Only at the end of history, then, will a fully satisfying idea of justice be articulated by a universally accepted system of right. The *telos* or end of right is the universal and homogenous state; and the achievement of the universal and homogenous state requires the triumph of a single concept of justice.[28]

One of the most intriguing, and in some sense most puzzling and even disturbing, implications of this understanding of right and justice is what this all means for the state and politics, or more generally, for all things political. According to Kojève, a state possesses two characteristics: first, it is a "Society, of which all the members are 'friends,' and which treats as an 'enemy' all non-members, whoever they are"; and second, within this Society "a group of 'governors' must be clearly distinguished from the other members, who constitute the group of the 'governed.'"[29] Kojève appropriates the friend–enemy distinction directly from Carl Schmitt, and he assumes that his readers are familiar with and accept these two fundamental political categories.[30] The distinction between governor and governed, by contrast, corresponds to the exclusive or elite group which Kojève spoke about above—namely, that group which can suppress other competing groups who want to govern without destroying the state. For Kojève, politics or the political is defined by the existence of these two characteristics, and should both of them disappear, the state, politics, and even political history would cease to exist. And this is precisely what will occur in a universal and homogenous state! Because the state is universal, there will be no nations or national borders, and therefore no national enemies: States and nations as we know them today will simply no longer exist. And because the state is homogenous, no longer will one exclusive or select group of individuals rule or govern over others in an oppressive manner. Force and fraud as a tool of government will cease to exist because no one group can claim to have any privileged status in respect to another that means that it and it alone should rule or govern. What we arrive at is the rather shocking claim that politics is not necessary for the administration of justice but an impediment to it. In order for C to be genuinely disinterested, and therefore truly just, politics or the political as we know it must fundamentally cease to exist. Kojève firmly believes that the government of men can be replaced by the administration of things—that coercive government can be eliminated and that universal and willing obedience can be instilled in all citizens. The final system of right can stabilize a conception of justice such that what largely remains of "politics" is a set of second-order, administrative, or regulatory tasks that do not imply or entail a fundamental struggle between competing conceptions of justice or of the good.

At first blush, such a claim seems too preposterous and fanciful to merit serious attention—but I would claim that we do in fact have incipient proof of the possibility of this very thing occurring. For is not the European Union (which Kojève spent a considerable part of his life promoting) in many ways an adumbration of what Kojève had in mind? Although the European Union began as a set of economic treaties between sovereign nations, as the jurisprudence of the European Community evolved, the European Court of Justice came to understand the treaties as containing legally enforceable rights and obligations against member states; in other words, the Court invalidates any purported state act that does not conform to the specifics of the constitutional framework. Thus, member states are no longer completely sovereign, and European law is something more than international law. This displays exactly the logical sequence proposed by Kojève: *Political* unification occurs through the creation of a *juridical* union. As people and states begin to agree on what right and justice properly are, political differences and distinctions begin to evaporate.[31] Simply put, there is no foundation in human need for opposition between or within states; the uniting of individuals against one another on the purported grounds of race, language, sex, class, culture, and so on is purely conventional, a function of the inability to achieve so far the universal and homogenous state. Kojève would thus agree with Marx that the "withering away" of the state or of politics is something both good and possible, and that the coordination of production in order to provide for the satisfaction of human needs would become a purely technical problem at the end of history.[32]

Kojève is aware that if the universalization of the principles of justice and right is going to lead to the overcoming of politics, there will have to be agreement on a particular concept of justice, and on the application of that concept in and by right—for it is through the realization and application of a particular idea of justice that the universal and homogenous state will be able to provide for the spiritual satisfaction of all citizens. The concept of justice and right animating the end state is what Kojève calls the justice of equity and civic right, which themselves are a synthesis of two previous historical understandings: the justice of equality and aristocratic right, on the one hand, and the justice of equivalence and bourgeois right, on the other hand. Let me briefly describe each, and the synthesis that Kojève sees will be achieved in the end state.[33]

The justice of equality and aristocratic right is more or less what prevailed in the ancient city (e.g., the Greek *polis)* between members of the citizen class. Its goal is to foster formal and substantive equality between those individuals, and/or to reestablish such equality if it has been violated or disturbed. Because the goal of aristocratic right is to support the existence of formal and substantive equality, it tends to suppress or to discourage interactions between individuals: Not only are interactions between equals somewhat unnecessary, but such interactions may result in inequalities between the individuals concerned. Consequently, aristocratic right is rather static, and the justice of equality is generally the guiding principle of those practices which either perpetuate the status quo (e.g., forbidding the buying and selling of landed estates or property) or which attempt to reestablish a state of equality once it has been shattered (e.g., *lex talionis,* or an eye for an eye). But the justice of equality and aristocratic right are much more expansive than this. Kojève also points out that the justice of equality is the principle which underlies such egalitarian practices as universal suffrage, equality before the law, and the equality of everyone's vote—or more generally, any practice or policy which attempts to equalize wealth, living conditions, and opportunities. Although it may sound strange, Kojève argues that it is in fact the justice of equality in aristocratic societies that legitimates and in some sense stimulates modern egalitarianism and egalitarian revolutions over the long run.[34]

By contrast, the justice of equivalence and bourgeois right has prevailed in the postclassical period. As opposed to the justice of equality, the justice of equivalence and bourgeois right tolerates "inequalities" or "differences" between the rights and privileges of individuals—but only as long as those individuals are willing to fulfill corresponding duties. Because what is considered to be a commensurate amount of rights and duties is continually in flux, bourgeois right is dynamic, and it allows and encourages a multitudinous array of interactions, exchanges, and contracts between individuals. Thus, the justice of equivalence and bourgeois right justifies such practices as different salaries (those whose work is more difficult ought to earn more); progressive taxation (those who earn more ought to be taxed more); or more generally, any practice where individuals are assessed or related according to their needs or merits.[35] In comparing these two principles of justice, Kojève argues that their fundamental difference is that while the justice of equivalence strives to make every right correspond to an equivalent duty, the justice of equality attributes an equal array of rights and freedoms to those who are recognized as juridical persons.[36]

Kojève argues that the historical confrontation of these two competing conceptions of justice and right will eventually be synthesized in the justice of equity and civic right. The justice of equality and aristocratic right will seek to eliminate substantive and formal inequalities which are tolerated by the justice of equivalence and bourgeois right, while the latter will introduce the possibility of equivalent relationships which are discouraged by the former. At the end of the historical evolution of justice and right, everyone will have an equal share of rights and duties; and where irreducible differences exist between individuals, equivalent relations will be established between them. Kojève offers the following example to explain the process by and through which the principles of equality and equivalence are synthesized in the justice of equity:

> Let us assume in a general way that the Justice of equity is applied within a given Society which is still not absolutely conforming to the ideal of this Justice. And let us assume that

> at a given moment a being acting in a certain way is considered a human being: a warrior, for example, idle in time of peace. By relying on the principle of equality, one will consider human all the beings who act in the same way, and them only. But by relying on the principle of equivalence, one could observe that an action different from the action in question can be equivalent to it, and that there will then be good reason to consider human the being who carries it out. Thus, for example, the fact of working for Society can be equivalent, from the social and political point of view, to the fact of defending Society with weapons in hand, and the act of providing children to Society, i.e., future citizens, can be equivalent to the act of working or waging war. One will therefore recognize workers and women as human beings in the same way as warriors. But by taking into account the difference of their actions, one will assign different "statuses" to them. But placed in the midst of recognized human beings, one will, in accepting the principle of equality, try to equalize them—that is, to equalize their actions. One will require, for example, that warriors work in time of peace and that workers take part in wars. But in the case of women, one comes up against an irreducible difference: men cannot have children. One is thus forced to keep the principle of equivalence while trying to overcome as much as possible the human ("social") consequences of irreducible biological differences. Practically speaking, one will try to establish a perfect equivalence between maternity and military service, while putting men and women on an equal footing everywhere else.[37]

One might say that the synthesis achieved in the justice of equity and civic right is possible through making chances or opportunities equal, such that different conditions and rewards are just in their equivalence. Absent equal entitlements to secure equality of opportunity, however, there will always remain a more or less severe tension between equality and equivalence.

Kojève offers the reader very few specific examples of the justice of equity and civic right: indeed, throughout the *Outline,* his overall emphasis is on describing the form or formal conditions of right and justice rather than their concrete content. Given that the justice of equity and civic right is the result of a dynamic or synthetic process, Kojève freely admits that he cannot articulate in advance what the positive legal code of the end state will look like; what he can do, however, is delineate certain logical necessities or properties inherent in the very concepts of right and justice, and their historical evolution.[38] Consequently, Kojève does allow us to see the overarching goal at which this final and most satisfying form of justice and right aim. In the words of George Grant, this goal is nothing short of the aspirations of modernity itself: "the drive to the universal and homogeneous state remains the dominant ethical 'ideal' to which our contemporary society appeals for meaning in its activity. In its terms our society legitimises itself to itself."[39] Let me once again quote from Kojève at some length (leaving the French *droit* [right or law] untranslated throughout):

> Now the *Droit* of the citizen (i.e., all real *Droit* in general), being based upon the Justice of equity, which synthesizes equality and equivalence, must be by definition a synthesis of aristocratic and bourgeois *Droits*. In its pure state (not yet realized, moreover), this *Droit* must therefore combine in a perfect equilibrium the equality of *droits* and duties of all juridical persons with the equivalence of *droits* and duties in each of these persons. . . . [From this comes] a community of *droits* and duties, the *droits* and duties of one also being the *droits* and duties of all, and conversely, the *droits* and duties of the community also being the *droits* and duties of each of its members. . . .
>
> Here as well, then, there will be a synthesis of the universalism (or collectivism) of aristocratic *Droit* and the particularism (or individualism) of bourgeois *Droit*. Just like the Master, the Citizen will have *universal droits* (and duties). The *droits* of all being equal, they will follow from the membership of each one to the whole, to Society as such or to the State. And the duties will be duties toward all—that is, toward the Society taken as a whole or toward the State. But seeing that the State is universal and Society homogenous, the *droits* and duties will belong not only to groups but to each one taken individually. It is not as a citizen of such and such a national State, or as a member of

> such and such a family (aristocratic, for example), or of such and such a social group (class) that a man will have *droits* and duties, but as an individual.

Kojève continues by claiming that:

> Juridical *liberty*, therefore, will consist in the possibility of each one doing everything that he wants, provided that he remains in agreement with the equality of *droits* and duties, and their respective equivalence. And juridical *equality* will be guaranteed by the fact that the juridical value of an interaction will not be altered if one changes the places of the members interacting.[40]

Kojève's end state will be nothing less than a universal society of free and equal men and women: every citizen will recognize and be recognized by every other citizen as an autonomous and dignified individual, and all arbitrary juridical distinctions between human beings based on race, class, or sex will be eradicated. According to Kojève, the elimination of these and other unjust distinctions will have additional positive social and economic effects as well: Once we see that it is unjust not to extend rights and duties to women and minorities, for example, we will also realize the injustice of their social or economic inequality and seek to overcome it. In other words, it is only when the principle of equity has permeated every aspect of our lives that a stable and satisfying political or social order will emerge and establish itself, a social order which heralds the end or culmination of our development as human beings. Thus, the free development of each will be the condition for the free development of all, and one individual's pursuit of his own goals or interests will not be in fundamental tension with another's, nor will either of their pursuits conflict with the public good as a whole. We will freely create and abide by our own set of laws, laws which confirm that the reconciliation of the public and the private has been made manifest in the here and now. We might say that at the end of history, the common good will be both genuinely good and in common because the increasing homogeneity and self-consciousness of all citizens will prevent them from having serious disagreements over the legal principles governing their conduct. The principle of equity is that principle which Kojève saw guiding all contemporary European understandings of right and justice, and it is this principle, which both includes and is respectful of difference, that will emancipate and enfranchise humanity as a whole.[41] So far, however, no stable synthesis has yet been achieved between equality and equivalence within any state; but once such a synthesis was achieved, it would represent the final form of the concept of justice. For the argument of Kojève's *Outline* to be compelling, it is not necessary to show how fast the tendency in question is spreading—it is sufficient to identify the possibility of this occurring, and why its occurrence is driven by the logic of justice itself.

In conclusion, let me identify at least one challenge that Kojève's position offers to both the right and the left today in respect to the modern regulatory welfare state and globalization. Being a dynamic process, the achievement of the justice of equity and civic right cannot occur without some elements of inequality or inequivalence tending to be exacerbated in the short run. Pointing to these very disturbances, conservatives and liberals are often highly dissatisfied with the policies and practices of the modern state. In the equality policies of most liberal democracies, conservatives see excessive levelling, where unequals are being treated equally; but conservatives often do not see that the end result could in fact be a synthesis that allows differences in condition and result to be considered just. Likewise, liberals tend to decry the extent to which unequal market outcomes are now tolerated; however, they often do not recognize that in many cases a stable and just solution cannot be obtained by manipulating the outcomes of the market, but only by equalizing the chances or opportunities that individuals bring to the market. As the right and left look over the same evolving social welfare and regulatory state, they claim to see more of the inequalities and inequivalences that each of them does not like. The typical prognostication is that of increasing fragmentation, social division, and blatant injustice—or even an impasse in the project of liberal democratic politics altogether. But for both the right and the left, it is worthwhile at least to consider and address Kojève's challenge: The fundamental tendency, through these various disturbances and adjustments, is toward synthesis. Kojève simply accepts as a truth that political and economic society has an inherently global direction or universal character; what this means, however, is that a stable synthesis of equality and equivalence in human relations will never be achieved within the bounds of any individual state. There is nothing regressive, then, about the expansion of economic relations beyond the state, and the great intensification of such relations; and there is nothing surprising that the initial result of this expansion should be new inequalities and inequivalences both within a state and without that are disturbing to both conservatives and liberals. In short, there is nothing that has happened so far in the globalization debate that is inconsistent with, or that refutes, Kojève's understanding of the dynamics by which the synthesis of equality and equivalence proceeds and universalizes itself. At a minimum, Kojève's view is a powerful challenge to those on the left who have thrown in their chips with "culture" or the "nation" as supposed sources of a still viable resistance to the "injustices" of globalization, and to those on the right who have yet to acknowledge that success in the global marketplace not only brings with it a number of rewards and privileges, but also a corresponding set of "just" and "legitimate" duties.

Notes

[1]For a more complete description of Kojève's life, and the times in which he wrote, see Dominique Auffret, *Alexandre Kojève: La philosophie, l'État, la fin de l'Histoire* (Paris: Bernard Grasset, 1990).

[2]See, for example, Raymond Aron, *Mémoires: 50 ans de réflexion politique* (Paris: Julliard, 1983), pp. 94–100, 731–32; Georges Bataille, *Oeuvres complètes,* volume VI (Paris: Éditions Gallimard, 1973), p. 416; Raymond Queneau, "Premières confrontations avec Hegel," *Critique* 195–6 (August–September 1963): 699; Gaston Fessard, "Deux interprètes de la *Phénoménologie* de Hegel: Jean Hyppolite et Alexandre Kojève," *Études* 255 (1947): 372; and Elisabeth Roudinesco, *Jacques Lacan & Co.: A History of Psychoanalysis in France, 1925–1985,* trans. Jeffrey Mehlman (Chicago: The University of Chicago Press, 1990), pp. 134–42. In fact, according to Allan Bloom, both Leo Strauss and Raymond Aron admitted that Kojève was the most brilliant man they had ever met. See Allan Bloom, "Alexandre Kojève," in *Giants and Dwarfs: Essays 1960–1990* (New York: Simon and Schuster, 1990), p. 268n1. For a list of those who were registered for Kojève's seminar, see Michael S. Roth, *Know-*

ing and History: Appropriations of Hegel in Twentieth-Century France (Ithaca: Cornell University Press, 1988), pp. 225–27. Kojève's enormous influence on French intellectual life, from literature to philosophy, psychology to political science, is reflected in André Glucksmann's comment in *Le nouvel observateur*, No. 992 (November 11, 1983): 4, that "the big secret of French philosophy, behind Sartre, Merleau-Ponty, Aron, as well as Lacan, behind the thought which dominates France between '45 and '70, is the presence of Kojève, who formulates from 1936 to 1938 the leftist intellectual theory of *engagement*. ... [T]hanks to Kojève, an incalculable number of intellectuals and militants have seen the World Spirit pass by, in parades from Republique to Bastille, in various struggles of the Third World, or in the miracle of the Soviet economy."

[3]Indeed, Kojève's influence on French economic policy as a high-ranking civil servant was, according to many, nearly as profound as his influence on postwar French intellectuals. See Raymond Aron, "Interview with Raymond Aron," *Encounter* 41 (No. 6, 1973): 82; Olivier Wormser, "Mon ami Alexandre Kojève," *Commentaire* 3 (No. 9, 1980): 120–21; Robert Marjolin, *Le travail d'une vie: mémoires 1911–1986* (Paris: Éditions Robert Laffont, 1986), pp. 57–58; and Stanley Rosen, *Hermeneutics as Politics* (New York: Oxford University Press, 1987), p. 92. Auffret, *Alexandre Kojève*, discusses Kojève's career as a civil servant, and he emphasizes the unity between this life and his life as a philosopher.

[4]Alexandre Kojève, *Introduction à la lecture de Hegel*, ed. Raymond Queneau, 2nd ed. (Paris: Gallimard, 1947). An abridged English translation was published as *Introduction to the Reading of Hegel*, trans. James H. Nichols, Jr., ed., Allan Bloom (New York: Basic Books, 1969).

[5]Consequently, it should come as little surprise that Kojève would likely take issue with the very phrasing of the present Ludwig von Mises Lecture Series: to state the matter bluntly, for Kojève the question is not whether freedom *or* world government will dominate the international marketplace; rather, the question is whether genuine freedom can ever fully exist without an international social and economic order.

[6]Francis Fukuyama, "The End of History?" *The National Interest* 16 (1989): 3. See also his "A Reply to My Critics," *The National Interest* 18 (1989–1990): 21–28.

[7]Ibid., 4, emphasis in the original.

[8]Francis Fukuyama, *The End of History and the Last Man* (New York: The Free Press, 1992).

[9]Ibid., pp. xiv–xv, 71–81.

[10]Ibid., pp. 122–25, 131–39, 143–207.

[11]Ibid., pp. 245–65.

[12]Ibid., pp. 279 & 283.

[13]Samuel C. Florman, "The End of History?" *Technology Review* 93 (April 1990): 70; John A. Hall, "Review of *The End of History and the Last Man*,"

American Journal of Sociology 98 (1993): 1523–524; and Michael Cornfield, "What is Historic about Television?" *Journal of Communication* 44 (1994): 106–16.

[14]Michael Novak, "Beyond the End of History?" *Fortune* 125 (February 24, 1992): 112.

[15]I do not here engage in a review of the hundreds—if not thousands—of responses to Fukuyama's thesis. For those interested in wading through the critical literature, the best discussions (in general) were to be found in *The National Interest* and the French journal *Commentaire*. See also the fine collection of essays in *After History? Francis Fukuyama and His Critics*, ed. Timothy Burns (Lanham, MD: Rowman & Littlefield, 1994). On the tenth anniversary of the publication of the original article, Fukuyama revisited the end of history thesis and the controversy surrounding it: See "Second Thoughts: The Last Man in a Bottle," *The National Interest* 56 (Summer 1999): 16–33.

[16]Peter Foster, "A Whole Lotta History Goin' On," *Canadian Business* 65 (May 1992): 78.

[17]Fukuyama, *End of History*, pp. 144, 192n3.

[18]Alexandre Kojève, *Outline of a Phenomenology of Right*, trans. Bryan-Paul Frost and Robert Howse, ed. Bryan-Paul Frost (Lanham, MD: Rowman and Littlefield, 2000). All quotations from Kojève are from this edition, and all italics and capital letters within the quotations are contained in the original.

[19]It should go without saying that I cannot do justice to the richness and complexity of Kojève's argument in the space of this essay, but at best can only touch upon some of the high points of his analysis.

[20]For example, if one person (A) gives another (B) some money, it is impossible to know phenomenologically whether this is an act of charity, of extortion, or whether someone actually has a right to that money. Similarly, unless the third person (C) intervenes on behalf of either A or B in an impartial and disinterested fashion, then it would be uncertain phenomenologically whether C was assisting in an act of charity, of extortion, or whether C was participating in an authentic juridical situation.

[21]Even the killing of one person by another might not necessarily provoke the intervention of C; the interaction in question could be between a master and his slave in ancient Rome.

[22]*Outline*, pp. 35–42.

[23]These eight elements are: that A and B are human beings (pp. 42–66); that there are two of them (pp. 66–69); that there is an interaction (pp. 69–74); an intervention (pp. 74–77); a third person C (pp. 77–79); that C is impartial and disinterested (pp. 79–94); that the intervention is necessarily provoked (pp. 94–98); and that the reaction of B is annulled (pp. 98–105). It should also be mentioned that Kojève's understanding of C encompasses not only the judge or arbiter who renders a legal decision but also the police who execute the judge's sentence and the legislator who crystallizes

an idea of justice into law. This understanding of C as judge, legislator, and police also correlates to the ways in which B's reaction to A can be annulled. The judge annuls B's will to act; the legislator, his intention; and the police annuls the act itself.

[24]Ibid., p. 79.

[25]Ibid., pp. 79–82.

[26]Ibid., pp. 82–91.

[27]Ibid., p. 91.

[28]Ibid., pp. 91–94.

[29]Ibid., p. 134.

[30]Carl Schmitt, *The Concept of the Political*, trans. George Schwab (New Brunswick, NJ: Rutgers University Press, 1976).

[31]Perhaps the most illustrative passage describing this process comes at the end of Kojève's discussion titled "International Law, Domestic Law, and the Plurality of National Juridical Systems," *Outline*, p. 327. It is worth quoting in full (the French word *droit*, which can mean both right and law depending on the context, is left untranslated throughout):

> As a political entity, the State tends to propagate itself by conquest; it tries to absorb purely and simply foreign States. But as a juridical entity, the State limits itself to imposing abroad its domestic *Droit*. In other words, it tends to create a *Federation* of States or a federal State by becoming itself one of the federated States, the Federation having for a base and for a result the existence of a unique *Droit*, common to all the federated States, and implying—in its "public *Droit*" aspect—an element of "federal *Droit*," regulating the relations of the federated States among themselves, [and] in particular the federal organization of justice. If the Federation is not universal, if it has enemies–States outside, it will have to organize itself into a (federal) State properly so-called. Its integral elements—the federated States—will also have enemies; they will therefore be *States*. But they will always have common enemies and will only be able to be reconciled with them in common: they will therefore not be sovereign States but federated States. However, the Federation will have a tendency to propagate itself as much as possible. At the limit, it will encompass the whole of humanity. Then it will cease being a State in the proper sense of the word, no longer having enemies outside. And the federated States as well will consequently cease to be genuine States. The Federation will then become a simple, worldwide juridical Union (at least in its juridical aspect, which is not the only one).
>
> We thus see that one is led to the same result either by starting from (public) international *Droit* or by taking for a point of departure domestic *Droit*. By *actualizing itself* fully and completely, the two *Droits* lead to federal *Droit*—that is, to the *domestic Droit* of a federal State or a worldwide Federation. Domestic *Droit* existing in actuality implies in its "pub-

lic" aspect a federal *Droit,* which is nothing other than actualized (public) "international *Droit.*" Conversely, actualized international *Droit* is a federal *Droit,* which is necessarily part of a complete system of domestic *droit.* "Public international *Droit,*" therefore, is not a *sui generis Droit.* There is only a single *Droit,* which is domestic *Droit,* for *Droit* only exists *in actuality* as domestic *Droit* (the Society which realizes it being, at the limit, Humanity).

[32]Although the European Union is perhaps the most well-known example of what Kojève is talking about, it is not the only example. Generally speaking, Kojève would argue that the historical record unequivocally reveals how political units have progressively increased in size—from the small cities of antiquity to the Soviet and Anglo-Saxon empires of the Cold War—and he would certainly point to continental trading blocks such as the North American Free Trade Agreement as confirmation of this tendency today. In an important way, therefore, Kojève is much closer to Kant's suggestions in *Perpetual Peace* about achieving peace through a federation of republics than to Hegel's insistence in *Elements of the Philosophy of Right* (sec. 324) that war is necessary for the "ethical health of nations." If the end state is going to give expression to a coherent, just, and fully actualized system of right, then it must overcome the opposition between friends and enemies in foreign affairs (as well as the internal antagonism between governors and the governed).

[33]Kojève admits that no historical legal or political system has been "purely" egalitarian or equivalent; nonetheless, one of these two principles of justice has tended to predominate in every historical epoch (*Outline,* pp. 213–14, 224–25, 237–38, 242–43).

[34]Ibid., pp. 233–34, 238–51, 266–67, 437–45, 456–60.

[35]Ibid., pp. 236–37, 244–45, 251–62, 444–50, 459–70.

[36]Ibid., pp. 258, 272.

[37]Ibid., pp. 269–70.

[38]Ibid., p. 268.

[39]George Grant, *Technology and Empire* (Toronto: House of Anansi Press, 1969), pp. 88–89.

[40]*Outline,* pp. 272–73.

[41]Ibid., pp. 132–33, 216–17, 233–38, 263–76, 336–37, 470–71, 479. It is worth mentioning that Kojève's position does not imply that there will emerge a single positive law throughout the world: There will be differences in law that are due to different nonjuridical conditions in different places (e.g., climate, geography, and so on). But it does suggest that there will emerge a single concept of justice, since the remaining differences between laws will be understood as unrelated to a differing standard of justice, and thus as having nothing to do with right in the strict sense.

Mackubin Thomas Owens

Power, Sovereignty, and Freedom in a World of Globalization

> Few nations in the history of the world, if any, have ever enjoyed such a favorable situation, and the modern world has rarely enjoyed so extended a period of relative peace, prosperity and freedom. It stands to reason that the keystone of American strategy should be the effort to preserve and sustain these conditions as well and as long as possible. America's most vital interest, therefore, is the preservation of the general peace, for war has been the swiftest, most expensive and most devastating means of changing the balance of international power and destroy-ing prosperity and freedom.
>
> —Donald Kagan, Testimony before the House Armed Services Committee, Wednesday, June 20, 2001[1]

It is something of a cliché to observe that the world has changed immensely since the collapse of the Soviet Union. The great question of international politics continues to be, What ultimately will follow the bipolar system of the Cold War that pitted a liberal capitalist alignment against a communist one in a bid for global hegemony?

A consensus has emerged among political scientists and specialists in international relations that the victory of the West in the Cold War unleashed "globalization," the worldwide expansion of capitalist modes of production, consumption, and finance. Globalization has emerged as the most important force shaping today's international political system (IPS). The resulting liberal world order is characterized by the growing influence of international institutions. As G. John Ikenberry has noted, the current system bears all the earmarks of previous world orders created by victorious powers.[2]

Some have expressed optimism about the prospects for a world shaped by globalization, others pessimism. One of the earliest to advance the optimistic view was Francis Fukuyama, who argued that the collapse of communism leaves no major ideological competitor to liberal democracy and that therefore the great wars that characterized the twentieth century may be a thing of the past.[3] Joseph Nye also posited a fundamentally optimistic view of the future, which he called "multilevel interdependence."[4]

Most realists rejected the optimism of Fukuyama, Nye, and those who contended that international institutions would help keep a globalized world at peace. For instance, John Mearsheimer argued that the future will resemble the past. He contended that the bipolar structure of the Cold War world coupled with nuclear weapons created a certain stability that prevented great-power war. Therefore, the collapse of bipolarity means "we shall soon miss the Cold War."[5] In what can be seen as an explicit reply to Fukuyama, Samuel Huntington claimed not only that history and conflict survived the end of the Cold War, but also that future conflict will increasingly take on the character of "a clash of civilizations."[6]

Robert Kaplan also took issue with Fukuyama's optimism. He predicted that, far from being peaceful, the future will look like the Balkans, a region as far from the end of history as one can get, writ large. Indeed as one wag has put it, the problem with such regions as the Balkans is that there is too much history in too little space: ethnic and religious strife, the brutality and savagery of which is often shaped by events long past (although some would say that in such places the past is not really past).[7]

Other proposed future global environments have included "unipolar hegemony,"[8] a world system dominated by a United States at the pinnacle of its power; a return to bipolarity, in which Russia, China, or another "large peer competitor" arises to challenge the dominant position of the United States; a multipolar system similar to the Concert of Europe that dominated European politics after the defeat of Napoleon and the Congress of Vienna; or the emergence of economic blocs that eventually harden into alignments or even alliances.[9]

One thing is certain: The international system is extremely complex. To sort out this complexity, it is useful to examine the character and nature of international politics, to understand how it differs from domestic politics, and to consider the impact of globalization upon this system and its institutions.

The Nature of the International Political System

Domestic Politics vs. International Politics

International politics differs substantially from domestic politics. The most obvious difference is that in international politics, the actors have no common sovereign to establish and enforce norms of behavior. This lack of a common sovereign has legal, political, and social implications.

Domestic law is established by the sovereign power. If this established law is not obeyed, the police and courts enforce sanctions against the lawbreaker. In contrast, international law rests on competing legal systems and, because there is no international police, lacks the means of common enforcement.

In a well-ordered domestic political system, the government maintains a monopoly on the legitimate use of force. In the international system, no one actor has such a monopoly. Individual actors are the arbiters of their own interests and the need to use force on behalf of those interests.

In a well-ordered domestic system, politics and society exist hand-in-hand, giving rise to a sense of community. Consequences of such a sense of community include common loyalties, standards of justice, and agreement on legitimate authority. Accordingly, there is a tendency for two great political values, justice and order, to converge. In the international system, common loyalties and agreement as to what is just and legitimate may be absent. Thus only rarely has a sense of community arisen in the international realm.[10]

Historical Context

International politics since the seventeenth century can be characterized as an anarchical state system.[11] This is one of three basic forms of world politics that can be identified over the centuries.

The others are a *world imperial system,* in which one government dominates most of the world with which the empire has contact, and the *feudal system,* in which political obligations are not determined primarily by territorial boundaries but by personal fealty. Rome is, of course, the exemplar of world *imperium* in the West. Others have attempted to achieve such *imperium,* for example, Napoleonic France, Nazi Germany, and the Soviet Union, but all have fallen short.

The collapse of the Roman Empire led to the emergence in Europe of a feudal system, with its crosscutting, nonterritorial loyalties and conflicts,. In turn, European feudalism began to give way to dynastic territorial states such as Spain and France around 1500. The character of the modern state system was cemented by the Peace of Westphalia that ended the Thirty Years' War, the last great European war of religion, in 1648. The Peace of Westphalia formalized the principle of *cuius regio, eius religio*: "whose country, his religion." No longer, for example, would the religion of the monarch and people of England be a matter of concern to the Kings of Spain or France.

Secularized, *"cuius regio, eius religio"* becomes the basis for sovereignty, the idea that a *state* is absolutely *dominant* within its boundaries. Some have argued that because of the phenomenon of globalization, the state is losing its position of dominance in the international political system, that traditional concepts of sovereignty have been displaced, and that these developments have important consequences for international politics. Before we can adequately assess this claim, it is useful to examine the various building blocks of the international political system.

Building Blocks of the International Political System

The building blocks of the IPS can be categorized as actors, goals, instruments, and rules. Actors in the IPS include states, nations, and nongovernmental organizations, and intergovernmental organizations. Goals include security, prosperity, national self-determination, order, justice, respect for human rights, and the achievement of some form of international society. Instruments of power include diplomacy, economic statecraft, and the threat and use of force. Rules are codified by usage and international law and include respect for sovereignty and the legal equality of states.

Actors

States

States remain important and influential actors in international politics. The origin of the term state is the Latin *status*, a neutral word meaning condition or way of existence. While *status* is first used in a political sense during medieval times, its modern meaning as an organization endowed with the capacity of exerting and controlling the use of force over certain people and within a given territory first appears in the works of Niccolo Machiavelli (*lo stato*).[12]

In Western political thought, the state has been viewed in two ways. In a negative sense, the state is the means of removing man from the *state of nature*, which according to political writers like Thomas Hobbes, is the same thing as the *state of war*. In this condition, Hobbes observed, "the life of man is solitary, poor, nasty, brutish, and short."[13] The goal of the negative state is accordingly to protect the life, liberty, and property of its citizens.

The state has also been viewed in a positive sense. For instance German idealism portrayed the state as the very manifestation of human reason. Indeed, for G. W. F. Hegel, the state takes on a moral character, becoming an end in itself, the bearer of the highest human values and the supreme embodiment of justice.[14]

Anglo-American political thought has tended to stress the negative idea of the state, while the continental European tradition has emphasized the state as a positive means of human progress. With the collapse of fascism and communism, the great state-centric ideologies of the twentieth century, the positive view of the state has fallen on bad times.

No matter one's view of its purpose, all agree that the modern state possesses certain defining characteristics: (1) it is a geographically bounded entity with an identifiable population; (2) it possesses a recognized authority structure that makes and enforces laws, rules, and decisions for those within its boundaries; (3) it constitutes a territorial association of people recognized by international law and diplomacy as a legally equal member of the international system. This is *sovereignty*, the defining characteristic of the modern state.

Is the influence of the state in the IPS declining? Both optimists and pessimists have made this claim. The former point to the fact that many global transactions now often bypass governments, the latter to the disorder and anarchy that characterize much of the world. Both have a point. But do the challenges raised by globalization to the traditional state necessarily mean that it is on its way out?

The optimists observe that although many interactions within the IPS are initiated and sustained by states, an increasing number are not. Communications, transportation, finance, and travel are increasingly influenced by transnational organizations that essentially bypass governments.[15] Others argue that the rise of these organizations, instead of portending the obsolescence of the state may instead be evidence of the adaptability, flexibility, and survivability of the institution.

The pessimists believe they have identified a dangerous situation:[16] the increasing number of weak and "failed" states, and the consequent return of large numbers of people to the "state of nature." While states may be *legally* equal, they are not equal in fact. After all, states have proliferated during the twentieth century. At the outbreak of World War I, there were only 62 independent countries in the world. In 1946, there were 74. But during the last half-century, the number of states has exploded to 193.[17] Some states are strong, in that they are able to defend their sovereignty and enforce internal law, but many are weak.

Many of these weak states have collapsed. (Even some strong states, e.g., the Soviet Union, turn out to have been large but inefficient, collapsing under their own weight.) But weak states in the international system have always been a threat to stability and peace, since they are ever the potential victim of aggression by strong states. Poland was partitioned among Austria, Russia, and Prussia between 1772 and 1795. It was reconstituted after World War I, but divided again by Nazi Germany and the USSR in 1939, precipitating World War II. And weak states can "entrap" stronger allies, plunging an entire region, and even the world into war, viz. Austria–Hungary and Serbia in 1914.

Failed states are a more recent phenomenon, leading some to predict the end of the Westphalian system. Others argue that the Westphalian system will survive because although some states will collapse, creating a burden on the stronger members of the IPS, many others will adapt to the changing environment. They conclude that states, at least competent ones, will remain the most efficient and effective means of distributing political benefits within the IPS.[18]

Nations

The word "nation" comes from the Latin *natio*, a noun derived from a form of the verb *nasci*, "to be born." "Nation" has traditionally referred to a grouping having a common identity based on blood or language. What we now think of as national identity has manifest itself periodically throughout history. The ancient Greeks certainly saw themselves as different from Persians, Scythians, and Egyptians, and China's description of itself as the "Middle Kingdom" and others as barbarians indicates that the Chinese perceived themselves to possess a separate identity.

Nations have been described as "imagined political communities."[19] In some cases (e.g., France and Britain, and the United States), it was the creation of a territorial state that gave rise to a national tradition.[20] In other cases, the nationalism that culminated in an imagined political community predated the creation of a state. For example, Machiavelli ends *The Prince* with an "exhortation to seize Italy from the barbarians [mainly the French] and vindicate her liberty."[21]

Modern nationalism represents the confluence of two intellectual traditions: Rousseau's idea of a "general will" and the German romantic anthropological nationalism that arose in response to the French Revolution and the cosmopolitan form of civilization that it portended. The father of this romantic notion of nationalism is Johann Gottfried Herder, who popularized the idea of the *Volksseele* or *Volksgeist*, the "soul" or "spirit" unique to each people. Although Herder's nationalism was liberal in spirit and intent, it contained the seeds of racialism and anti-Semitism that helped to make the twentieth century the bloodiest in history.[22]

Modern nationalism is characterized by the beliefs: (1) that mankind is naturally divided into nations; (2) that there are determinate criteria for identifying a nation and recognizing its members; (3) that each nation is entitled to an independent government of its own and that states are legitimate only if constituted in accordance with this principle; and (4) that the world will be rightly formed, politically speaking, only when every nation forms a single state and every state consists exclusively of the whole of one nation. As the nineteenth-century Italian nationalist Giuseppe Mazzini put it, the political unity and independence of every nation within its boundaries is ordained by God.[23]

Much of the conflict in the post-Cold War era is nationalist and ethnic in character. Because nationalism is often highly suspicious, resentful, and fearful of other national groups (xenophobia), it frequently results in tension and bloodshed. This tendency of nationalism is visible in the wave of nationalist conflict that has erupted in the Balkans, the Trans-Caucasus, and elsewhere.

The distinction between a state and a nation is important because it helps to explain much of the chaos that has afflicted the world since the end of the Cold War, and which may portend even greater disorder in the future. There are five basic reasons for making this distinction.

First, many states contain several national or ethnic groups within their territorial boundaries, for example, the former Soviet Union and Yugoslavia. A group convinced that it is being treated unfairly by the leaders of the governing state is a certain source of real or potential regional insecurity.

Second, in many cases a national group overlaps several state boundaries, for example, Kurds in Iraq, Turkey, and Iran; Serbs in Croatia and Bosnia; and Russians in the Baltic States and Ukraine. The lack of a "fit" between a national group and a state is a continuing source of international conflict.

Third, some national groups, for example, Kurds and Palestinians, are "stateless," giving rise to enormous tensions with those who are perceived to be preventing the creation of a national homeland. The goal of every national movement since the nineteenth century has been the creation of a territorial state encompassing those possessing the common identity.

Fourth, the desire for national "self-determination" may lead a national group to attempt to break away from a ruling state in order to create its own state. Slovene, Croat, and Bosnian separation from Serb-dominated Yugoslavia in 1990–1991 illustrate the potential consequences of self-determination.

Fifth, self-determination often leads to the desire of one state to incorporate an ethnically related group under the political control of another state, creating the danger of *irredentism.*[24] Perhaps the most destructive example of irredentism in recent history resulted from the 1919 Versailles Treaty, which placed 3 million Germans in the newly created state of Czechoslovakia, more than 1 million in the reconstituted state of Poland, and hundreds of thousands more in "linguistic islands" scattered throughout Romania and northern Yugoslavia. From the establishment of the Weimar Republic through the Nazi reign of Adolf Hitler, Germany sought to overturn the Versailles settlements, claiming that they did not take into account the right of the German people to national self-determination.

But the threat of irredentism did not end with World War II. In Central Europe, every state contains substantial national minorities that constitute the seeds of a potential *irredenta.* Thus a place such as Kosovo, an autonomous region absorbed by Serbia after World War I, remains a powder keg because its 90 percent Albanian population desires union with Albania.

Nongovernmental Organizations (NGOs)

One of the most important changes to the IPS over the past few decades has been the proliferation of NGOs and transnational organizations (TNOs). NGOs and TNOs include, *inter alia,* multinational corporations (MNCs), national liberation movements, the Roman Catholic Church, Greenpeace, Amnesty International, drug cartels and other examples of what Ralph Peters calls "para-states" and "criminal enterprise armies," and some labor and industrial organizations.[25]

MNCs long have been important players in the IPS. While MNCs lack such types of power as military force, their economic power is substantial. For example, 12 MNCs have annual sales that are larger than the GDP of more than half the states of the world. Royal Dutch Shell and Exxon would rank after just eight states.

Since MNCs distribute output in accordance with strategies designed to enhance corporate profits, a multinational corporation based in a given state may pursue policies that have the effect of undermining the sovereignty and policy interests of that same state. This is only the most obvious challenge to the authority of the state in the IPS.[26]

International Institutions

International institutions include such governmentally supported international institutions as the United Nations and its associated agencies. In the broadest sense, they represent an attempt to achieve international security through collective and cooperative means. The goal of the League of Nations was to prevent another Great War. In the view of the League's advocates, World War I had been an accidental and unnecessary war caused by attempts to balance power. Such wars, they claimed, could be prevented if all states combined to punish aggression by one or more members against others. This attempt at collective security ultimately foundered on sovereignty and the perceptions of individual states that the League was not meeting their security needs.

The United Nations was an attempt to correct the flaws of the League, but the early hopes of its creators were frustrated by the Cold War. The ideological cleavage of this struggle made it impossible to agree on what constituted aggression and the legitimate use of force, leading to clear problems with the UN collective security system. However, in the absence of a workable UN system of collective security, there arose the concept of preventive diplomacy, later expanded to cooperative security.

While the UN has fallen far short of the hopes of its founders and most ardent advocates, it has helped to modify the world's view of both instruments of power and the goals of international politics.[27] We will examine the role of the UN more fully later.

Instruments of Power

Actors in the IPS have a variety of tools available to them. The include, *inter alia,* diplomacy, economic instruments, information programs, clandestine operations, and the threat and use of force.

Diplomacy

Diplomacy is by far the most common form of interaction in the IPS. It runs the gamut from "preventive" diplomacy, designed to identify potential problems and defuse them before they erupt in crisis, to "coercive" diplomacy, in which one actor employs the threat of force to influence the actions of another actor in the IPS.[28]

Diplomacy involves negotiations, settlement of disputes, and policy discussions. Diplomatic norms are the result of long practice. On the one hand, diplomats must observe strict rules of protocol and must not become involved in the domestic affairs of the host state. On the other, they are protected from prosecution by the host state by the long-established tradition of diplomatic immunity.

Diplomacy cannot be separated from the other tools of national power. Preventive and day-to-day diplomacy is usually carried out in conjunction with the economic instrument. Coercive diplomacy often employs economic sanctions and shades rapidly into the use of force. Indeed, Frederick the Great observed that diplomacy without force is like music without instruments.

Economic Statecraft

The economic instrument can be used both as a carrot and a stick in international relations. As a carrot, the economic instrument manifests itself as *aid, trade, and investment.* During the Cold War, economic and security assistance were used by both the United States and the Soviet Union to influence actors. Critics of foreign aid contended that private investment and liberalization of trade were much more effective in helping developing countries become prosperous.

Advocates of liberalized trade believe that economic nationalism and protectionism not only retard prosperity, but create conditions that may lead to conflict and war. They point to the role of protectionist policies between the wars in contributing to the worldwide Great Depression and World War II. The United States has been instrumental in the global trend toward liberalized trade. The World Trade Organization is the successor to the General Agreement on Tariffs and Trade, a series of negotiations dating from World War II designed to lower barriers to trade.

Investment is the infusion of capital that increases labor productivity and raises the standard of living. The major debate here is between those who advocate private investment as the engine of development and those who stress government's role. Investment is frequently more sensitive to domestic factors than to international ones. These include the quality of the labor force and interest rates. But the most important domestic factor for a potential investor is the internal stability of the state in which the investment is to be made. If the investor perceives that the risk exceeds the probable rate of return, the investment will not be made.

The economic instrument as a stick manifests itself in a number of ways. Economic power has taken the form of the *coercive use of financial and macroeconomics tools* (intervention in exchange rate markets, capital controls, i.e., controls over loans and investments); *punitive trade policy* (e.g., not granting or withdrawing "most-favored nation"—MFN—status); and *economic sanctions.*

During the Cold War, financial and macroeconomic tools were used in part to deny resources to the communist world (e.g., strict limits on loans to the USSR) and in part to push allies (e.g., financial leverage over Great Britain and France to force an end to their invasion of Egypt during the Suez crisis of 1956). Because of increasing interdependence, economists have become highly skeptical of the ability of financial and macroeconomic instruments to achieve foreign policy aims. For instance, raising short-term interest rates and imposing capital controls are now less effective than they once were because of greater capital mobility, the sheer volume of private international capital flows, and the ability of traders to circumvent national economic regulations.[29]

During the Cold War, trade policy was subordinated to military and diplomatic concerns. While MFN status was withheld from the USSR and other communist countries and controls were imposed on high-technology exports with potential for military use, the executive branch usually resisted pressure in Congress to employ trade sanctions in retaliation against what were seen as unfair trade practices on the part of allies (e.g., Japan). While this subordination is no longer in force, the United States continues to avoid using trade as a tool to influence the behavior of other actors, for instance to force China to improve its record on human rights. As in the case of financial and macroeconomic tools, a changing, more flexible and interdependent global economy has made it more difficult to use trade policy to coerce other actors.[30]

Economic sanctions constitute a form of coercive diplomacy. Sanctions are often popular with policymakers who see them as an alternative to the use of force. But there is considerable argument as to their effectiveness. They take time, perhaps longer than the diplomatic timetable allows. They require widespread commitment, without which they are difficult to enforce and maintain. Even the world's greatest economic power has been unable to enforce sanctions against Iran and Iraq. Finally, there is growing concern about the morality of sanctions. Critics contend that sanctions have little impact on the government whose behavior we are attempting to influence, but a great deal on the target state's population, especially the weakest.[31]

The Threat and Use of Force

Many commentators claim that the role of force in international affairs has diminished, and that particularly for large states such as the United States, it is much more costly to use force to achieve their goals than it once was.[32] Several reasons are offered for this situation: (1) the existence of nuclear weapons; (2) the apparent change in attitude toward the use of force (for instance, the United Nations Charter has codified the view that only defensive war is acceptable); (3) the rise of internal constraints, especially in liberal industrial democracies (these include domestic opposition to the use of force and the apparent fact that industrialized nations seem to have become averse to casualties); and (4) the apparent fact that many issues in the international arena do not lend themselves to the use of force.

Nonetheless, war and conflict continue to be staples of the IPS. In the five years before the Gulf War, there were 36 wars that killed between 3 and 5 million people. With slaughter in Bosnia, Rwanda, and Algeria, this trend only grows stronger. As the response of the United States to the terror attack of September 11, 2001, indicates, force still plays an important role in the international arena.

Additionally, there may be some global trends running counter to the view of the optimists. These may in fact make the use of force more, rather than less, likely in the future. These include a putative "revolution in military affairs" that may allow a great power to limit collateral damage if it chooses to use military force—and the conduct of the war against the Taliban and al Qaeda terrorism is a case in point; scarcity arising from population growth; and threats to environmental security arising from the spread of industrialism throughout the developing world.[33]

When should force be threatened or used? "National interests" are usually invoked to decide this question. But as policymakers attempt to flesh out the abstract concept of national interests, they often discover that, absent a defining moment like the terror attack in the United States, a domestic consensus is still difficult to achieve.[34] The U.S. debate preceding the Gulf War is a case in point.

As Clausewitz observed, the decision to use force requires policymakers continuously to calculate costs and benefits. They must consider not only economic factors, but political and psychological factors as well. And they must make these calculations within a realm of chance and uncertainty. What will be the eventual political outcome? What are the consequences of failure? Such calculations can prove daunting to even the most forceful and self-confident leaders.

Rules

Optimists argue that the IPS is evolving toward a more liberal, interdependent world order. They contend that the destructiveness of modern war, the gobalization of the economy, and more rapid communication among the actors in the IPS will tend to move the world toward increasing peace and prosperity. They argue that international society—that is, general agreement among the players in the IPS about rules and norms of international behavior, including the fundamentals of international law—is possible even in an anarchic state system.[35]

Pessimists disagree. They argue that power is still the coin of the realm in international affairs, that competition among states will continue unabated, that states will do whatever is necessary to advance their position in the IPS, and that modern international relations are merely a footnote to Thucydides. For them conflict, not cooperation, will continue to be the essence of the IPS.

Sovereignty

As discussed previously, sovereignty is the key characteristic of the Westphalian system: The concept is understood to mean that a state controls a specified territory, has an identifiable citizenry, and operates under a generally recognized authority. States jealously guard their sovereignty. They will go to war to protect it. They will execute saboteurs, spies, and sometimes political opponents who threaten it. Yet states will also willingly, even eagerly, surrender or limit their own sovereignty to achieve what they perceive to be some cooperative good (for example, they will join NATO or the WTO).

Armed attack traditionally has constituted the clearest threat to sovereignty. But in the current environment, there are other, more subtle threats to the concept. One, previously mentioned, is "self-determination." Sovereignty is understood to apply to states, self-determination to "nations," some of which do not possess a state. Self-determination, manifest as either the quest for a national state or irredentism, may threaten the territorial integrity of existing states. A Kurdish or Palestinian state would come at the expense of other states.

Another emerging threat to sovereignty is the idea that it should be subordinated to humanitarian concerns or a "higher" principle such as human rights. A number of recent interventions have been justified on the basis of this claim.[36] Does a violation of sovereignty, even for the best of reasons, undermine the concept itself? The answer may depend on whether one believes that sovereignty resides in the people or in a reified "state." In any event, there is a danger that the door is being opened to the pre-Westphalian system in which something like the religion of the people of a state constitutes a *casus belli.*

It seems to be the case that sovereignty is a function of power. Strong states can defend their sovereignty; weak states cannot. This does not mean that strong states have nothing to worry about. As the events of September 11 illustrate, the threat of terrorism is very real, even in a secure state like the United States. And weak states are not completely at the mercy of strong ones. Saddam Hussein has been able to raise the cost of what some might claim is a post-Gulf War, U.S.-led violation of Iraqi sovereignty: no-fly zones, safe zones, and the UN-sanctioned inspection of Iraqi installations to uncover weapons of mass destruction.

Legal Equality of States

Through most of history, the distinction between strong states and weak states was the law of necessity in international relations. Strong states did what they wished at the expense of weak states. A weak state's only recourse was to place itself under the protection of another strong state. However, the dismantling of colonial empires in the wake of World War II and the resulting proliferation of new small states led to the establishment of the liberal principle that all sovereign states are to be treated as equals in the IPS, a principle embedded in Article 2 of the UN Charter.

This principle rules in some respects but not all. The ambassador from Chad is rendered the same formal courtesies in Washington, D.C., as the ambassador from Russia or China. In the UN General Assembly, the representative from Burkina Faso has the same voting power as the representative from the United States. And the sovereignty of small states presumably has the same legal status as that of large states, although as suggested above, in reality a state possesses as much sovereignty as it can defend

But even the UN makes a distinction between the "great powers" and others. The Security Council clearly has more clout than the General Assembly. The real argument here is whether the permanent members of the Security Council reflect the current realities of global power distribution or that of 1945.

International Law

Just as international politics differs from domestic politics, international law differs from domestic law. The main differences between the two are the provisions for enforcement, adjudication, and orderly revision by legislation. Although public international law provides for revision, adjudication differs between the two, and enforcement of international law is difficult if not impossible.

International law consists of treaties, which are agreement among states, and custom, the generally accepted practice of states in the international system. Thus in terms of revision, international law resembles domestic law. But in international law, adjudication is by states, not individuals, and the resolutions that constitute much of international law are often ambiguous. Such resolutions do not have the character of binding legislation as is the case with domestic law. And enforcement of international law is difficult because there is no common superior to force a sovereign state to accept a ruling of an international court.

Although international law lacks the character of domestic law, it nonetheless seems to be a manifestation of what Hedley Bull calls "international society." International society exists "when a group of states, conscious of certain common interests and common values, form a society in the sense that they conceive themselves to be bound by a common set of rules in their relations with one another, and share in the working of common institutions."[37] Indeed, what we now think of as international law grew out of the Christian Natural Law doctrine common to Europe in the medieval period. This common tradition united such writers as Hugo Grotius, Francisco Suarez, Samuel Pufendorf, and Emmerich de Vattel.[38]

Since international politics is a self-help system, it usually devolves upon a hegemonic power to enforce international law. But who enforces the law if it is violated by the hegemonic power? As Joseph Nye observes, enforcement in self-help systems is a one-way street. International law as it is understood in the Westphalian system enshrines sovereignty and nonintervention. One of the great questions is whether or not the world is moving toward a post-Westphalian system that places more emphasis on principles such as human rights than on nonintervention. As suggested before, there is some indication that this is, in fact, the case. But as Joseph Nye says, "the absence of a common executive with a monopoly on the legitimate use of force means that sovereign states are in the realm of self-help and in the realm of force and survival. And when matters of survival come up, law usually takes second place."[39]

An American Grand Strategy of Primacy

What is the best hope for establishing and maintaining freedom in a complex world characterized by globalization? To answer this, we must first answer two other questions. First, what is the greatest obstacle to freedom and economic liberalism? Second, what conditions lead states and other actors in the IPS to forego a certain amount of relative power and status in order to achieve mutually beneficial cooperation?

The answer to the first is the threat of war and aggression. The greatest threat of course arises from the enemies of freedom, for example, future Hitlers and Stalins, as well as international terrorists such as Osama bin Laden and the al Qaeda network. Unless such regimes are reined in or destroyed, they disrupt the IPS and divert resources to war.

But even in the absence of a major aggressor, the threat of conflict can undermine mutually beneficial cooperation and economic liberalism. As noted above, the IPS can be characterized as international anarchy, in which each player is the arbiter of his own security. International anarchy is a self-help system. Depending on one's assessment of the security environment, one seeks to improve one's security by increasing armaments and forming alliances.

A consequence of this self-help system is the *security dilemma.* State A takes the minimum steps it believes necessary to increase its security. State B interprets State A's buildup as aggressive and increases its own defense expenditure. State A then reacts against the perceived threat from State B. The logic of the security dilemma leads to arms racing and even preemptive war.

To achieve cooperation among states and to maintain peace and prosperity in a liberal world order, it is necessary somehow to counter the security dilemma. Some entity must keep the peace by underwriting security. How can this be done?

The traditional answer has been to create organizations for collective and cooperative security such as the League of Nations and the United Nations. But ultimately, goes the argument, the achievement of lasting peace will require the establishment of some sort of world government. Indeed, in Bryan-Paul Frost's essay, Alexander Kojève described what a universal homogenous state might look like.[40] Leo Strauss rejected such an arrangement as the foundation of tyranny.[41]

But there is an alternative. It is described with elegant simplicity by the magnificent Yale historian and classicist Donald Kagan. What seems to work best for keeping the peace, he writes, "is the possession by those states who wish to preserve peace of the preponderant power and of the will to accept the burdens and responsibilities required to achieve that power."[42] This is called primacy.

Primacy holds that the key to future peace and prosperity is for the United States to maintain the power position it held at the end of the Cold War. The central purpose of primacy is preventing the emergence of a potential new rival along the lines of the former

Soviet Union. In the words of a draft of the George H. W. Bush administration's Defense Planning Guidance—a document that was subjected to much ridicule after it was leaked to the press in March 1992—the U.S. must "endeavor to prevent any hostile power from dominating a region whose resources would, under consolidated control, be sufficient to generate global power. . . . Our strategy must now refocus on precluding the emergence of any potential future global competitor."[43]

Primacy is based on hegemonic stability theory, which argues

> fundamental . . . international trade based on the liberal principles of comparative advantage and the division of labor does not just occur through the actions of a global "invisible hand." Instead, economic openness only arises in the presence of a hegemonic power, a state willing and able to provide the world with the collective goods of economic stability and international security. A state will only adopt the leadership role of hegemon when it is in its national interest to do so. In short, the theory of hegemonic stability rests on two propositions: (1) order in world politics is typically created by a single dominant power, and (2) the maintenance of order requires continued hegemony.[44]

By underwriting security in various parts of the world, including Europe and Asia, American preponderance has obviated tensions by reducing the perceived need to take unilateral steps on behalf of security.

The cornerstone of hegemonic stability is the idea that the liberal world order so many people take for granted does not just arise spontaneously. The conditions for peace and prosperity must be created and maintained by hegemonic power. The "invisible hand" works, but only after the "state of nature," both domestic and international, has been overcome.

During the Cold War, the benefits of economic liberalism were limited to the North Atlantic region and Japan, the areas in which the United States had created and sustained a maritime system of alliances tied together by transoceanic commerce. The collapse of the USSR and the socialist economic model means that a liberal world order can expand worldwide. This is the phenomenon we call globalization.[45]

If the United States were to reduce its commitment to keep the peace, other states would have an incentive to "renationalize" their foreign and security policies. As Alberto Coll argues, U.S. preponderance restrains "traditional rivalries" among regional powers "that otherwise could unravel into unrestrained military competition, conflict and aggression."[46]

According to the theory of hegemonic stability, a decline in relative U.S. power could create a more disorderly, less peaceful world. The precedent for the United States is the decay of *Pax Britannica*, which, many believe, created the necessary, if not sufficient conditions for the two world wars of the twentieth century. As British hegemony declined, smaller states that previously had incentives to cooperate with Britain "defected" to other powers, causing the international system to fragment. The outcome was depression and war.[47] The decline of American power could lead to a similar outcome. In the words of Sam Huntington,

> the maintenance of U.S. primacy matters for the world as well as for the United States. . . .
>
> A world without U.S. primacy will be a world with more violence and disorder and less democracy and economic growth than a world where the United States continues to have more influence than any other country in shaping global affairs. The sustained international primacy of the United States is central to the welfare and security of Americans and to the future of freedom, democracy, open economies, and international order in the world.[48]

Critics claim that it is futile for the United States to pursue primacy for several reasons.[49] First, the very economic system that the hegemonic power of the U.S. underwrites leads to the diffusion of the economic and technological instrument upon which the United States depends to maintain its preponderant power. Thus it is likely that, despite the best efforts of the U.S., other great powers will arise.

Second, despite the fact that U.S. hegemony is qualitatively different from the hegemonies of the past in that it eschews territorial conquest, U.S. power, benevolent as it may be, is likely to engender resentment on the part of other states or nonstate actors, such as international terrorists. One consequence will be increasing resistance to U.S. leadership, possibly undermining the various multilateral institutions that the U.S. requires in order to ensure that it does not bear the burden of international security alone. Another, more serious consequence might be that disaffected states will attempt to tip the balance against the U.S. Finally, some have argued that the terrorist attacks against the U.S. on September 11 were the consequences of anti-U.S. resentment.

Additionally, there is the temptation of what Paul Kennedy calls "imperial overstretch."[50] There may be a tendency to argue that if a certain level of power is good, more power is better. For primacy to be effective, it would be necessary for the United States to maintain such overwhelming power that others would not even think of challenging it. One consequence of this may be that at some point, commitments far outstrip the resources the public is willing to provide for defense. Another is that potential adversaries may employ asymmetric, cost-incurring strategies to increase the U.S. defense burden.

Kennedy contends that Great Britain was the victim of imperial overstretch. But one can make the argument that it was not imperial overstretch that led to the decline of Britain, but the onset of a war Britain could not prevent: It was World War I that doomed the British empire, not the expenditures to maintain the empire. In light of this observation, the burden of its defense posture on the U.S. is significant, but the benefits of the resulting world order far outweigh the costs.

One obvious benefit of bearing this burden is the prevention of war: 4.5 percent of GDP is a small price to pay when we consider the alternatives. During the peak years of World War II, U.S. defense spending was nearly ten times greater than what we propose. U.S. defense spending constituted 38.6 percent of GDP in 1943, 39.9 percent in 1944, and 40 percent in 1945—not to mention 280,000 dead over the course of the war. Clearly, the cost of preventing war is far less than the cost of fighting one, even if it results in victory. And prevention of war is the objective of a grand strategy of primacy.

This leads to the final objection to primacy: It requires a level of public commitment that may not be possible to achieve in a democratic society in the absence of an identifiable threat. Without such a commitment, it is impossible either to fund security needs or to use

U.S. power abroad. Obstacles to such a commitment include economic complacency and the erosion of a commonly accepted understanding of U.S. national interests.

Despite these very serious objections, primacy offers the best hope for achieving U.S. national interests in the world, both today and in the future. Without a grand strategic vision that seeks to shape the security environment as primacy does, policymakers are left in a reactive mode, rushing from one crisis to another.

What must the United States do to sustain the liberal world order? Most important, it must maintain its ability to reassure allies and friends by underwriting security. This will minimize the impact of the security dilemma. But there are other aspects of an effective grand strategy designed to foster a world environment in which the American system can survive and flourish.

The liberal democratic order created by U.S. leadership is based on the principles of economic openness, political reciprocity, and the management of conflict as much as possible through multilateral institutions. This brings us back to the role of international institutions such as the United Nations. Such institutions in principle support U.S. objectives because when states join, they are in effect agreeing to a process that shapes, constrains, and channels their actions.[51]

International institutions can help overcome and integrate diverse and competing interests. They help concentrate resources while spreading the burdens, habituate other states to American leadership, and help avert political backlashes that might otherwise be triggered by unilateral U.S. actions. The Gulf War illustrates the benefits of achieving U.S. interests within the framework of multilateral institutions.

International institutions create incentives for states to cooperate in mutually beneficial ways by reducing the "transaction costs" of making and enforcing agreements. Even the most powerful states have an incentive to follow the rules and conform to norms because of reciprocity: If we abide by the rules, we can expect others to abide as well, and as the hegemon, we can enforce the rules. This improves predictability in the international system.

The key point here is that the most successful international institutions are not above states or opposed to sovereignty, but constitute an international regime—international society—a more or less informal structure of rules and norms that create the conditions that must exist for states to cooperate.

But the system of international institutions will work only if the United States continues to exert leadership. Thus the "us vs. them" mindset with regard to the UN is wrong. The United Nations is not a "super-state" with the Secretary General as CEO of the world. The key to the UN is the Security Council, in which the United States wields great influence regarding the things that really matter. The United States can determine what the UN does or doesn't do. The UN can't do everything, but it should be permitted and encouraged to do what it can, reducing the burdens on the United States. We should embrace those institutions that work and ignore those that don't.

The quest for cooperation is a prudent part of a U.S. strategy of underwriting global security. On the one hand, only in such a system can economic liberalism fulfill its promise. On the other, we cannot afford to become complacent. The last long stretch of economic prosperity ended in 1914. It is useful to remember that the last time the world was as "interdependent" as it is now was on the eve of World War I. In his memoir *The World Crisis*, Winston Churchill mocked this sort of fatuous optimism as it manifested itself during the Agadir crisis of 1911, which although it was peacefully resolved, marked another milestone on the road to Armageddon:

> [War] is too foolish, too fantastic, to be thought of in the 20th Century. . . . Civilization has climbed above such perils. The interdependence of nations in trade and traffic, the sense of public law, the Hague Convention, liberal principles, the Labour Party, high finance, Christian charity, common sense have rendered such nightmares impossible. Are you quite sure? It would be a pity to be wrong.[52]

In that regard it is interesting to note the similarities between Norman Angell's *The Great Illusion* in 1911 and Fukuyama's essay "The End of History," written only a little over a decade ago.[53] But maintaining peace and prosperity takes a great deal of effort. This condition does not arise spontaneously. If a hegemonic power does not provide the international "public good" of security upon which global stability, interdependence, and ultimately peace and prosperity depend, the liberal world order desired by all will atrophy. World War I illustrates how rapidly an interdependent world order can collapse if the rise of aggressive powers is not checked. When the British began to believe that unarmed liberal ideas and "progress" leading to changes in human nature had created a world in which war was impossible, the system came crashing down.

There is no more reason to believe that the international security environment is naturally less competitive than it has been in the past. Anarchy still prevails in the international system, meaning that the realm of international politics is one of "self-help" in which each state is the arbiter of its own security requirements. Insofar as a cooperative international society exists, it is because the hegemonic power of the United States underwrites it.

Notes

[1]"For the Record," *Washington Post* (June 22, 2001): 24.

[2]G. John Ikenberry, *After Victory: Institutions, Strategic Restraint, and the Rebuilding of Order After Major Wars* (Princeton: Princeton University Press, 2001).

[3]Francis Fukuyama, "The End of History?" *The National Interest* 16 (Summer 1989), and "Reply to My Critics," *The National Interest* 18 (Winter 1989). Fukuyama tempers his optimism a bit in *The End of History and the Last Man* (New York: The Free Press, 1992), which raises the real possibility that the eventual outcome of a world characterized by peace and prosperity is the emergence of Nietzche's "last man."

[4]Joseph S. Nye, Jr., "What New World Order?" *Foreign Affairs* (Spring 1992); and "Interdependence and Power," chapter 7 of *Understanding International Conflicts: An Introduction to Theory and History* (New York: Harper Collins, 1993), pp. 160–79.

[5]John J. Mearsheimer, "Back to the Future: Instability in Europe After the Cold War," *International Security* 15 (1) (Summer 1990). Cf. also Colin S. Gray, "Villains, Victims, and Sheriffs: Strategic Studies and Security for an Interwar Period," *Comparative Strategy* 13(4) (1994).

[6]Samuel P. Huntington, "The Clash of Civilizations?" *Foreign Affairs* (Summer 1993); and *The Clash of Civilizations and the Remaking of World Order* (New York: Simon & Schuster, 1996).

[7]Robert D. Kaplan, "The Coming Anarchy," *Atlantic Monthly* (February 1994).

[8]Charles Krauthammer, "The Unipolar Moment," *Foreign Affairs: America and the World* 70 (1) (1990/91).

[9]Nye, *Understanding International Conflict*, pp. 190–92.

[10]But on the possibility of "international society," see Hedley Bull, *The Anarchical Society: A Study of Order in World Politics*, 2nd ed. (New York: Columbia University Press, 1995).

[11]Nye op. cit., p. 2. Cf. also Hans Morgenthau, *Politics Among Nations* (New York: Knopf, 1955), chapter 1; Kenneth N. Waltz, *Man, the State and War* (New York: Columbia University Press, 1959); and *Theory of International Politics* (New York: McGraw-Hill, 1979), pp. 79–128; and Bull, op. cit.

[12]Alexander Passerin d'Entreves, *The Notion of the State: An Introduction to Political Theory* (Oxford: At the Clarendon Press, 1967), pp. 30–33. For Machiavelli's innovative use of *lo stato*, see Leo Paul de Alvarez, "Introduction," in de Alvarez, trans., Niccolo Machiavelli, *The Prince* (Irving, TX: University of Dallas Press, 1980), pp. iv–x.

[13]Thomas Hobbes, *Leviathan*, Michael Oakshott, ed. (New York: Collier Books, 1962), p. 100.

[14]G. W. F. Hegel, *The Philosophy of Right*, T. M. Knox, ed. (Oxford: Oxford University Press, 1942). Cf. Shlomo Avineri, *Hegel's Theory of the Modern State* (Cambridge: Cambridge University Press, 1972).

[15]Jessica T. Mathews, "Power Shift," *Foreign Affairs* 76 (1) (January/February 1997), and Richard Rosecrance, "The Rise of the Virtual State," *Foreign Affairs* 75 (4) (July/August 1996).

[16]Kaplan, op. cit.; Martin van Creveld, *The Transformation of War* (New York: The Free Press, 1991), and "The Fate of the State," *Parameters* XXVI (1) (Spring 1996); John Keegan, *A History of Warfare* (New York: Knopf, 1993).

[17]Alberto Alesina and Enrico Spolate, "On the Number and the Size of Nations," *Quarterly Journal of Economics* (November 1997).

[18]Michael Desch, "War and Strong States, Peace and Weak States," *International Organization* 50 (2) (Spring 1996); Michael Porter, *War and the Rise of the State: Military Foundations of Modern Politics* (New York: The Free Press, 1994).

[19]Benedict Anderson, *Imagined Communities* (London: Verso, 1991). Cf. Hans Kohn, *The Idea of Nationalism: A Study of Its Origins and Background* (New York: Macmillan, 1944), p. 10: "Nationalism is first and foremost a state of mind, an act of consciousness, which since the French Revolution has become more and more common to mankind."

[20]Mikulas Teich and Roy Porter, eds., *The National Question in Europe in Historical Context* (Cambridge: Cambridge University Press, 1993); Liah Greenfeld, *Nationalism: Five Roads to Modernity* (Cambridge, MA: Harvard University Press, 1992).

[21]Machiavelli, op. cit., chapter XXVI, p. 151.

[22]Cf. Herder, *Ideas for the History of Mankind*, reprinted in Hans Kohn, ed. *Nationalism: Its Meaning and History* (New York: Van Nostrand Reinhold, 1956),

pp. 104–8; Isaiah Berlin, *Vico and Herder: Two Studies in the History of Ideas* (New York: Viking Press, 1976); and Lonnie R. Johnson, *Central Europe: Enemies, Neighbors, Friends* (Oxford: Oxford University Press, 1996), pp. 130–34.

[23]Giuseppe Mazzini, "Mazzini: On the Unity of Italy," in Kohn, *Nationalism*, pp. 118–21. Cf. "Europe: Its Conditions and Prospects," *Essays: Selected from the Writings, Literary, Political, and Religious of Giuseppe Mazzini*, William Clark, ed. (London: Walter Scott, 1880).

[24]From *Italia irredenta*, literally "unredeemed Italy."

[25]Robert O. Keohane and Joseph S. Nye, Jr. eds., *Transnational Relations and World Politics* (Cambridge, MA: Harvard University Press, 1970); Ralph Peters, "After the Revolution," *Parameters* XXV (2) (Summer 1995).

[26]Cf. e.g., Robert Gilpin, *US Power and the Multinational Corporation: The Political Economy of Foreign Direct Investment* (New York: Basic Books, 1975), and *The Political Economy of International Relations* (Princeton: Princeton University Press, 1987, pp. 231–62.

[27]On the debate over international institutions such as the UN, see *inter alia*, Robert Alexrod, *The Evolution of Cooperation* (New York: Basic Books, 1984); Robert O. Keohane and Joseph S. Nye, Jr., "International Interdependence and Integration," and "Realism and Complex Interdependence," in Viotti and Kauppi, op. cit., pp. 384–421; John J. Mearsheimer, "The False Promise of International Institutions," *International Security* 19 (3) (Winter 1994/95); and Robert O. Keohane and Lisa L. Martin, "The Promise of Institutionalist Theory," *International Security* 20 (1) (Summer 1995).

[28]Adam Watson, *Diplomacy: The Dialogue Between States* (New York: McGraw-Hill, 1983); Gordon A. Craig and Alexander L. George, *Force and Statecraft: Diplomatic Problems of Our Time*, 2nd ed. (New York: Oxford University Press, 1990); Stephen Stedman, "Alchemy for a New World Order: Overselling 'Preventive Diplomacy,'" *Foreign Affairs* (May/June 1995); Michael S. Lund, "Underrating Preventive Diplomacy," *Foreign Affairs* (July/August 1995); Alexander George and William Simons, eds., *The Limits of Coercive Diplomacy*, 2nd ed. (Boulder: Westview Press, 1994).

[29]Cf. e.g., Ethan B. Kapstein, *Governing the Global Economy: International Finance and the State* (Cambridge: Harvard University Press, 1994).

[30]Helen V. Milner and David A. Baldwin, *East-West Trade and the Atlantic Alliance* (New York: St. Martin's Press, 1990).

[31]Gary Hufbauer et al., *Economic Sanctions Reconsidered*, 2 volumes (Washington, D.C.: Institute for International Economics, 1990).

[32]Cf. e.g., John Mueller, *Retreat from Doomsday: The Obsolescence of Major War* (New York: Basic Books, 1989); Richard Rosecrance, *The Rise of the Trading State: Commerce and Conquest in the Modern World* (New York: Basic Books, 1986); and Evan Luard, *The Blunted Sword: The Erosion of Military Power in Modern World Politics* (New York: New Amsterdam, 1988); as well as Fukuyama, op. cit.

[33]John Orme, "The Utility of Force in a World of Scarcity," *International Security* 22 (3) (Winter 1997/98).

[34]Michael G. Roskin, "National Interest: From Abstraction to Strategy," *Parameters* XXIV (4) (Winter 1994–95).

[35]On the possibility that international society and an anarchical international system can coexist, see Bull, op. cit.

[36]Tony Blair, "Doctrine of the International Community," speech to the Economics Club of Chicago, April 22, 1999, from *NATO—50 Years: 1949–1999* website. Reprinted in *Strategy and Force Planning Faculty*, *Strategy and Force Planning*, 3rd ed. (Newport, RI: Naval War College Press, 2000), chapter 39, pp. 587–97.

[37]Bull, op. cit. p. 13.

[38]Hugo Grotius, *The Law of War and Peace* (Oxford: At the Clarendon Press, 1925 [first published 1625]); Richard Cox, "Hugo Grotius," in Leo Strauss and Joseph Cropsey, eds., *History of Political Philosophy*, 2nd ed. (Chicago: Rand McNalley, 1972); E. B. F. Midgley, *The Natural Law Tradition and the Theory of International Relations* (New York: Harper and Row, 1975); A. P. d'Entreves, *Natural Law* (London: Hutchinson University Library), 1970 [first published 1951]).

[39]Nye, *Understanding International Conflict*, p. 141.

[40]See Bryan-Paul Frost, "Is a Global Liberal Democractic Order Inevitable?" this volume.

[41]For the debate between Strauss and Kojève on the idea of a universal homogenous state, see Leo Strauss, *On Tyranny*, revised and expanded edition (Chicago: University of Chicago Press, 2000).

[42]Donald Kagan, *On the Origins of War* (New York: Doubleday, 1995), p. 570.

[43]Excerpts from "Pentagon's Plan: 'Prevent the Emergence of a New Rival,'" *New York Times* (March 8, 1992): 14.

[44]Ethan Barnaby Kapstein, *The Political Economy of National Security: A Global Perspective* (New York: McGraw-Hill, 1992), p. 3. Cf. Robert Gilpin, *Global Political Economy: Understanding the International Economic Order* (Princeton: Princeton University Press, 2001), pp. 93–97.

[45]See note 1 above.

[46]Alberto Coll, "Power, Principles, and Prospects for a Cooperative International Order," *The Washington Quarterly* (Winter 1993).

[47]Robert Gilpin, *War & Change in World Politics* (Cambridge: Cambridge University Press, 1981); Joseph Greico, *Cooperation Among Nations* (Ithaca: Cornell University Press, 1990); and Charles Kindleberger, *The World in Depression: 1929–1939* (Berkeley: University of California Press, 1973).

[48]Samuel Huntington, "Why International Primacy Matters," International Security 17 (4) (Spring 1993): 82–93. Cf. also William Kristol and Robert Kagan, "Toward a Neo-Reaganite Foreign Policy," *Foreign Affairs* 75(4) (July/

August 1996); Joshua Muravchik, *The Imperative of American Leadership: A Challenge to Neo-Isolationism* (Washington D.C.: AEI Press, 1996); Robert Kagan, "The Benevolent Empire," *Foreign Policy* (96) (Summer 1998); Robert Kagan, "The World and President Bush," *Survival* (Spring 2001); and Charles Krauthammer, "The Bush Doctrine: ABM, Kyoto, and the New American Unilateralism," *The Weekly Standard* (June 4, 2001).

[49]Critiques of primacy include Robert Jervis, "International Primacy: Is the Game Worth the Candle?" *International Security* 17 (4) (Spring 1993); Christopher Layne and Benjamin Schwarz, "American Hegemony—Without an Enemy," *Foreign Policy* (92) (Fall 1993); Chalmers Johnson, *Blowback: The Costs and Consequences of American Empire* (New York: Metropolitan Book, 2000); Patrick A. Buchanan, *A Republic, Not an Empire* (Chicago: Regnery, 1999). See also Richard N. Haass and Sydney Stein, Jr., "What to do With American Primacy," *Foreign Affairs* 78 (5) (September/October 1999).

[50]Paul Kennedy, *The Rise and Fall of the Great Powers* (New York: Random House, 1987).

[51]See, e.g., Robert O. Keohane, "International Institutions: Can Interdependence Work?" *Foreign Policy* 110 (Spring 1998); and G. John Ikenberry, "Why Export Democracy?" *The Wilson Quarterly* 23 (2) (Spring 1999).

[52]Winston Churchill, *The World Crisis*, Vol. 1 (New York: Scribners, 1923), p. 45.

[53]Note 3 above and Norman Angell, *The Great Illusion: A Study of the Relation of the Military Power in Nations to their Economic and Social Advantage* (New York and London: G.P. Putnam's Sons, 1911).

Jeremy A. Rabkin

The International Criminal Court: A Challenge to American Policy and American Principles

The proposed International Criminal Court (ICC) would be a major innovation in international affairs. Many advocates see it as the symbol of a new era, a major step toward "global governance." As such, it is partly silly, partly sinister, and partly quite serious.

Advocates insist that the ICC is needed to deter genocide and comparable crimes against humanity. But there is no reason to believe that indictments from this Court would deter a future Pol Pot. Any tyrant capable of mass murder is more than capable of flouting the claims of a far-off court. In this sense, the ICC is silly.

Since the Court has no police or army to back up its authority, it will only be able to assert its jurisdiction where states are willing to cooperate in its ventures. Actual states are likely to be guided in the future, as they have in the past, by unsentimental calculations about the best means of advancing their own interests and thwarting those of their rivals. Many, perhaps most, states will see the Court as a device for humbling the United States. In that sense, it is sinister.

Still, many countries not determinedly hostile to the United States are drawn to what the Court represents—the notion that supranational authorities can constrain sovereign states, even if they do not assert full governmental responsibility on their own. It should give us pause that such a notion now seems plausible to many governments we think of as Western democracies. Whatever its practical consequences, the Court represents a serious challenge at the level of ideas. It is, if you like, an ideological challenge. In that sense, it is not merely silly or sinister, but serious.

A Silly Response to Moral Challenges

Many advocates of the ICC depict it as fulfilling the promise or principle established by the postwar trials of Nazi leaders at Nuremberg. It is true that the Nuremberg trials were hailed by some at the time as a precedent for a new kind of international justice. While the trials were still ongoing, for example, the United Nations General Assembly adopted a resolution endorsing them as an example for the future.

For almost forty years thereafter, however, this precedent was not repeated. With the exception of the contemporaneous trials of Japanese leaders in Tokyo, there was no further effort to mount an international trial for war crimes or crimes against humanity. The Cold War was one reason. The United States and the Soviet Union were able to agree on the establishment of an international tribunal to judge their common enemies in World War II. They were not able to agree on much else thereafter.

But the larger reason there were no further international trials was that war criminals in subsequent wars were not available for trial. Since World War II, the United States has never fought a major war to the same sort of ultimate conclusion. Whatever the crimes of war leaders in Pyongyang, in Hanoi, or in Baghdad, those leaders were not in American custody when the United States agreed to stop fighting in Korea, Vietnam, and Iraq. By contrast, the Nazi leaders surrendered unconditionally to Allied armies after those armies had marched into the heart of Germany and imposed their will on every acre of German territory. The subsequent trials were not organized by the United Nations but by the four occupying powers in Germany—which were the only governing power of any kind there after the Nazi surrender. As the judges at Nuremberg declared on the first day of the trial, they were acting in the name of the new sovereign powers in that territory.

The end of the Cold War may have made international cooperation seem to be more feasible. It has not made national governments more willing to risk their own troops to enforce abstract notions of justice in the world. So the most recent precedents for international justice—of the kind that the ICC is supposed to deliver—are hardly impressive. We have not used force to end monstrous abuses and then established courts to try the monsters after the victory. Instead, international courts have been a substitute for force—that is, a substitute for serious action.

The first experiment was launched in response to ethnic violence in the Balkans. The break-up of Yugoslavia left an independent Serb state and an independent Croatian state and both sought to claw territory from the multi-ethnic Bosnian state in between. Under UN authorization, troops from several Western European states were actually dispatched to Bosnia in the early 1990s to keep the peace, but they failed miserably in this mission. The presence of these small Western military contingents actually deterred Western governments from contemplating serious reprisals against Serb forces, for fear of retaliation on Western troops. Despairing of protecting Bosnian Muslims in their homes, the UN peacekeepers announced at one point that they would establish a safe haven for refugees in the town of Srebrenica. The refugees streamed in and Serb militias followed them. Armed gangs killed almost 10,000 unarmed civilians—including women and children—while Dutch troops remained passive. UN forces, it turned out, were meant to "deter" attacks, but they were not actually prepared to repel them.

Instead of mounting a serious military operation, the UN Security Council decided to impose a war crimes tribunal. The special Tribunal for the Former Yugoslavia, established at the Hague in the Netherlands in 1993, was the first such venture since the end of World War II. The value of this gesture may be judged by the fact that the massacre in Srebrenica actually took place shortly after the establishment of the tribunal. After more than eight years in existence, this tribunal has indicted some one hundred "war criminals," but it has apprehended less than half of them and completed full trials for only a handful.

The main causes of this poor performance are readily explained. Until recently, Serbia consistently refused to hand over any of its nationals indicted by the tribunal. Even the NATO forces—which finally launched a sustained bombing campaign against Serbia on behalf of Albanian rebels in Kosovo in 1999—have not pressed very strongly for the extradition of Serbs accused by the tribunal. Serbian President Milosovic, indicted by the tribunal at the end of the Kosovo War in 1999, was finally turned over to the Hague tribunal in the spring of 2001—after he had already been overthrown and arrested by a new democratic coalition and after Western European leaders imposed intense pressure for Milosovic to be tried at the Hague rather than by his own people in Belgrade. But in return for this extradition, Western leaders agreed to lift economic sanctions and start delivering aid to the new Serb government. There has not been comparable pressure to find and extradite other individuals sought by the Hague tribunal. Similarly, in Croatia, a policy of noncooperation with the tribunal gave way after some years to a policy of grudging and partial accommodation and not much more was demanded. Even in Bosnia, where NATO troops are on the ground, they have not been willing to risk firefights with Serb warlords and have therefore not tried very hard to find or arrest those accused of war crimes.

The UN authorized a second venture in international justice in somewhat different circumstances in Rwanda. The experience reflects the same preference, however, for gestures over serious commitments. In Rwanda, a government controlled by ethnic Hutus launched an actual program of genocide against minority Tutsis in 1993. Nearly a million people were slaughtered, from grandmothers to babies, by government-organized killers operating for the most part with primitive weapons and proceeding in their grisly task for a period of several weeks.

The international community failed to take any action to protect the innocent. Indeed, the main focus of UN efforts was to protect outsiders. Several thousand UN forces, mostly Belgians and Canadians, were actually in Rwanda in response to previous border conflicts in the region. At the prompting of President Clinton, the UN ordered the bulk of these forces evacuated—to keep Western countries from getting embroiled. For the same reason, the remaining Belgian forces focused their efforts on rescuing white people (mostly Europeans) from the local violence. The carnage was finally brought to end when a Tutsi army, supported by neighboring governments, invaded Rwanda and overthrew the murderous Hutu government.

The United Nations responded by establishing a new war crimes tribunal—or to be more precise, by adding responsibilities for war crimes in this area to the legal machinery in the Hague that was already in place for Yugoslavia. With more than 800,000 murders, this tribunal has thus far prosecuted some two dozen Hutu officials. In effect, the UN has been shielding others from swifter justice.

The same bitter farce has recently been repeated in the West African nation of Sierra Leone. The so-called Revolutionary United Front, a guerrilla force with no clear political agenda apart from self-enrichment, had terrorized the countryside for much of the 1990s. Its horrifying tactic was to lop off arms and legs so that victims would be walking—or crawling—reminders of their ferocity. For this purpose, it made no difference to the RUF if the victims were innocent civilians, women, or children. When a democratically elected government managed to catch the rebel leader, Fouday Sanko, Britain and the U.S. tried to negotiate a general peace agreement. They sent, as chief negotiator, the Reverend Jesse Jackson, who proceeded to pressure the local authorities to release Fouday Sanko and take him into a new "coalition government." The RUF returned to its most savage practices and stopped any UN interference by capturing a lightly armed UN peace-keeping contingent and holding them hostage. The British government finally sent more capable forces which succeeded in freeing these hostages and recapturing Fouday Sanko. But the British did not want to maintain a permanent military presence in this former British colony, despite pleas for such a commitment. Instead, the UN established yet a third special war crimes tribunal.

In the midst of these episodes, the UN decided to sponsor a larger and more ambitious project in international justice. In the summer of 1998, a UN conference in Rome drew up a detailed plan for a permanent International Criminal Court. Based on the record of international action in the 1990s, one might guess that the new project did not reflect a very serious determination to stop mass atrocities. Certainly no such determination was in evidence in the 1990s. A glance at the ICC charter would confirm this suspicion. The Preamble to the "Statute for the International Criminal Court" reaffirms the "principle" that "all States shall refrain from the threat or use of force against the territorial integrity or political independence of any state...." The Statute then makes "aggression" into a criminal offense (Art. 5.1.d). The ICC proposes to punish extreme crimes after the fact. While they are going on, it actually discourages outside intervention to stop them.

It is hardly plausible that a government which is so depraved that it commits mass atrocities will, at the same time, be so sensitive to the rule of law as to cooperate with the new international court. If a murderous government is overthrown, the successor government may be willing to cooperate with the international court. But even here, the rationale for the ICC is hard to follow. If the new government does want to punish the crimes of its predecessors, it can do so without any international assistance—as new governments have done throughout history toward the governments they have overthrown. If the new government does not want to impose full justice, it has no clear reason to cooperate with the international court.

In the wake of the terror attacks on the United States of September 11, some advocates insisted that the ICC was more necessary than ever. Others urged that an interim international court should be established to deal with perpetrators of international terror. Such proposals got no serious attention in the U.S. for the same old reasons. An international authority would contribute nothing at all to the military measures requried to find and seize terrorists based in Afghanistan or elsewhere. The U.S. would have to supply this military muscle on its own. And no one had a convincing answer to why the U.S., which had exerted the force required to isolate and seize terrorists, would not have the moral authority to try them on its own (those, that is, who survived American military assaults).

It may be too charitable, then, to call the court "silly." As a response to the moral challenge of mass atrocities, it might better be described as pathetic. But as a propaganda forum, it may well be sinister.

Sinister Potential

The Clinton administration was one of the major sponsors of ad hoc tribunals for Yugoslavia, Rwanda, and Sierra Leone. These gestures were in keeping with a general policy that preferred generous gestures to serious commitments. The Clinton administration also supported the ICC, as a gesture. But the scheme that actually emerged from the Rome conference was unacceptable, even for the Clinton administration.

The Clinton administration had pressed for a criminal court beholden to the UN Security Council—where the United States is a permanent member (along with Russia, France, Britain, and China) and any permanent member can block action. Instead, the Rome conference produced a plan where initiative is in the hands of an independent prosecutor, neither appointed nor removable by the Security Council. The Security Council can "suspend" a particular prosecution for one year, but only if no permanent member vetoes the resolution for suspension. The U.S. has no assured means of protecting itself from being the target of prosecution.

In fact, the U.S. has many reasons to fear that it will be the target of a prosecution. Any state may refer a case to the prosecutor and the prosecutor is authorized to initiate investigations and prosecutions on his own initiative as well. So it will matter a great deal who serves as the prosecutor. Who will choose? The ICC Statute provides that the prosecutor will be elected by a simple majority of the states which adhere to the Court (Art. 42). Some 120 countries voted to support the ICC charter at the Rome conference. As in the General Assembly of the United Nations, the majority of these states may often feel hostile or jealous or resentful toward the United States. Approximately the same group of states that elected China, Cuba, Syria, and Sudan—that is, among the most repressive regimes on the planet—to sit on the UN Human Rights Commission will determine who gets to be the prosecutor.

Then the crimes which the prosecutor can go after will be subject to redefinition, or entirely new crimes can be added, by legislative determination of an assembly of the participating states (Art. 121). A seven-eighths majority is required, which might seem a formidable barrier to impulsive or controversial action. But the votes at the Rome conference itself left the United States in a minority much smaller than one-eighth The final vote on the draft was 120–7 (with the U.S. among the 7).

As it is, the draft defines many crimes in disturbingly broad or open-ended terms. To start with, the ICC is supposed to have jurisdiction over four categories of "international crimes": "aggression" and "war crimes," along with "genocide" and "crimes against humanity" (Art. 5). The crime of "aggression" is not defined at all but simply left up to future determinations by the assembly of ratifying states (Art. 9). The definition of "genocide" includes "causing mental harm to members of the group," which might mean almost anything (Art. 6.b). The actions defined as "crimes against humanity" include "persecution against any identifiable group... on political grounds" where "persecution" is then defined as "intentional and severe deprivation of fundamental rights" (Art. 7.h). Efforts to imprison the members of particular terrorist organizations could easily be described as "crimes against humanity" under this catchall definition.

Meanwhile, "war crimes" include "launching an attack in the knowledge that such attack will cause incidental loss of life... or damage to civilian objects... which would be clearly excessive in relation to the concrete and direct overall military advantage anticipated" (Art. 8.2.b.iv). In the air war against Serbia in the spring of 1999, American bombing targets included highway bridges, power plants, chemical factories, and water treatment facilities. These were meant to put pressure on the civilian population. Was the "damage to civilian objects" here "clearly excessive in relation to the military advantage anticipated"? Doubtless, the answer depends on who weighs the "damage" and then determines the "anticipated military advantage." Amnesty International and other outside observers concluded that NATO was, in fact, guilty of war crimes because of its choice of targets. The American-based advocacy group Human Rights Watch concluded that bombing tactics were often highly questionable but not quite in the category of "war crimes." That was the ultimate judgment of the prosecutor for the existing tribunal for war crimes in the former Yugoslavia, who interrogated top NATO commanders before reaching this conclusion. At the least, the existence of a permanent general ICC prosecutor invites similar close questioning of American tactics in future military operations. And the statute provides that the ICC gets the last word in determining whether "war crimes" have been committed.

The definition of "war crimes" also includes the "transfer, directly or indirectly, by the occupying power of parts of its own civilian population into the territory it occupies" (Art. 8.2.b.viii).

This definition was inserted at the insistence of Arab states at the Rome conference and it was clearly aimed at fastening the label of "war criminal" on Israeli officials. The Israeli ambassador pleaded against this propaganda maneuver, designed to equate controversial Israeli policy with Nazi atrocities. The plea was ignored.

The point of all this is to establish a forum in which definitive condemnations can be imposed. To the extent that the world has had anything of the sort up until now, it has been the Security Council, the one place in the UN system empowered to make "binding" determinations. But in the Security Council, the United States (along with Britain, France, Russia, and China) can block any resolution by unilateral veto. The United States has frequently exercised this veto to block one-sided condemnations of Israel—as well as of international actions by the U.S. itself. At heart, the ICC is a device for shifting authority away from the Security Council or, in other words, away from a forum in which the U.S. exercises a veto to one in which independent officials speak for the world.

In fact, the ICC Statute sets up a system in which the new Criminal Court would have jurisdiction over the U.S., even if the U.S. did not ratify the Statute. The Statute confers jurisdiction in cases where the perpetrator of crimes is a national of a signatory state but also in cases where the victims are nationals of a signatory state, even if the alleged perpetrators are not (Art. 12.2.b). In other words, if Iraq should ratify the Statute, it could demand prosecution of Americans for attacks on Iraqis, even if the U.S. does not accept the tribunal's jurisdiction. Of course, Iraq might not want to place itself under the jurisdiction of the ICC, but a separate provision allows even non-signatory states to authorize ICC action for particular cases (Art. 12.3). So Iraq could trigger an ICC prosecution against the U.S. without at all accepting ICC jurisdiction over its own internal offenses.

In a variety of other ways, the Statute seems designed to isolate the United States unless it submits in full to the ICC. When the U.S. ratified human rights conventions in the early 1990s, for example, it attached particular reservations, disclaiming any obligation to honor requirements that would conflict with American constitutional limitations at home. The ICC Statute stipulates that no party can ratify with reservations (Art. 120). While Iraq can trigger ICC action against foreign suspects, without committing itself at all, the U.S. is told that it must accept every aspect of the ICC's charter if it wants to endorse any of it.

In the 1970s, the U.S. withdrew from UN agencies it found to be intolerably politicized (notably UNESCO and the ILO). The ICC Statute carefully stipulates that a party that has ratified will still be subject to prosecution and obliged to cooperate with the Court for a full year after it has tried to withdraw its ratification of the Court's Statute. The U.S. has tried to exert leverage on UN agencies in the past by withholding dues. The ICC Statute authorizes the Court to accept private donations, in unlimited amounts and with no restrictions on the sources, to make up for shortfalls in dues payments by member states (Art. 116).

With all its potential for abuse, the ICC Statute does not even seek to limit international prosecutions within its own agreed procedures. To the contrary, it specifies that nothing in the Statute "shall affect the characterization of any conduct as criminal under international law independently of this Statute" (Art. 22.3). So, while the Statute purports to endorse the maxim that nothing can be criminal without a law which specifies it to be such (*Nullum crimen sine lege*, the Latin maxim placed at the head of Art. 22), the Statute actually provides the opposite: that individual countries are free to claim anything they might like as a crime under international law.

This is a recipe for "international justice" as a series of propaganda forums, directed at the U.S., at Israel, or at any other country that happens to run afoul of shifting coalitions in the UN. It is not so much building structure over the anarchy of world politics. It is rather empowering anarchy.

A Serious Philosophic Challenge

The Habsburg monarchy, according to the old joke, was hopeless but not serious. International trends can be dismaying or even threatening as a practical matter without raising any deeper question than how to make the right practical response in the circumstances. But in fact the ICC represents something deeper than another ill-considered propaganda blast from the UN. It reflects something more serious than resentment of American power or jealousy of American success. It reflects a current of opinion which has surprising strength even in Western countries. And in this sense, it is serious and deserves serious reflection.

Some of the strongest support for the ICC comes from countries in Western Europe. They had many reasons of their own to be skeptical toward this project. If the ICC is an end-run around the Security Council, for example, it devalues not only the American veto there, but also the vetoes of Britain and France. The British and French governments initially joined the Clinton administration in seeking to preserve some directing or restraining role for the Security Council. But they soon bowed to pressure from other European states and accepted the current arrangements in the ICC Statute. Constitutional courts in France and in Germany advised that there were constitutional objections to extraditing nationals of their own countries for international trial. Both France and Germany then amended their national constitutions to overcome these objections to their full participation.

From an American perspective, this level of enthusiasm may seem surprising. Among other things, the ICC claims the authority to retry defendants already tried and acquitted by national courts if the outcome was not satisfactory to the ICC Prosecutor. Even if a defendant had been pardoned by his own government, the ICC Statute authorizes the International Prosecutor to ignore the national pardon. A country that is trying to recover from wrenching upheaval may decide to seek peace through a general amnesty. This is what happened in former Communist states in Eastern Europe in the 1990s, as well as in Latin American countries during the same period that made a transition from military dictatorship to democracy. Even in Nelson Mandela's South Africa, the transition to black majority rule was accompanied by a general amnesty for the abuses of the old white supremacist government and the violence committed by its opponents. The ICC would authorize the International Prosecutor to ignore all such amnesties in order to pursue his own notions of justice (Art. 20.3).

What if an international prosecution upsets a fragile domestic balance and provokes a new round of violence and civil unrest? As the ICC has no army to enforce its judgments, it has no force to handle the consequences of its intervention. It claims the right to judge, without the power to enforce. It claims the right to intervene, without the power to protect.

Suppose, on the other hand, that a country experiences terrible repression and turmoil and a new government determines to prosecute perpetrators of abuses under the old government. The Statute provides that the new government may not act if the ICC has already judged that punishment, in any particular case, is improper (Art. 20.2). So, while the Statute authorizes the ICC to nullify a national government's (or national court's) decision in favor of leniency, it binds national governments to respect the ICC's own decision that a particular suspect is not guilty of "war crimes" or "crimes against humanity." In sum, the ICC is set up as a global supreme court for fundamental criminal cases, pre-empting the authority of national governments and national courts in accord with its own independent notions of true justice.

All this may look extremely presumptuous to Americans. Yet it looks much less strange to Europeans. After all, some of the most ancient states in Europe have ceded vast powers to the supranational authority of the European Union. The regulatory bureaucrats in the European Commission claim the authority to regulate everything from the accent marks on typewriters to the content of sausage and the proper brewing technique for beer. Meanwhile, the European Court of Justice claims authority to nullify parliamentary enactments of member states if they conflict with regulatory standards imposed by the Commission. The European Court of Justice even claims the authority to nullify rights protections in the constitutions of member states, if they conflict with the Court's interpretation of European law. Yet the EU does not have any army of its own to enforce its decrees. It does not even have a police force. European states submit to all this, however, in what politicians describe as a "pooling of sovereignty."

There is a directly elected European Parliament but it cannot choose the executive officials in the EU (who are appointed by governments) and it cannot initiate legislation. The scheme rests on a succession of treaties, and new treaties have continually expanded the power (and also the membership) of the European Union. But after decades of enlargement and deepening of its powers, the EU still does not have its own constitution to give definitive form—and definitive limits—to its powers. It has developed by a succession of improvised adjustments in an overall scheme which to American eyes (and by the standards of European states themselves in their domestic affairs) looks only partially democratic and only partially constitutional.

It is notable that with all the powers handed over to the European Union, there is still no common criminal code for Europe and no European criminal court. For centuries, the power to enforce criminal law in its own territory has been considered a unique attribute of a sovereign state. But Europeans are no longer very concerned about protecting attributes of state sovereignty. Indeed, Europeans are eager to affirm that sovereignty is an anachronistic principle in the modern world.

So Europeans are particularly receptive to arguments on behalf of "international justice." A global criminal court may be a remarkable innovation, it may tread on national pride, but general objections count for little if the Court can be "useful." And if it is too ambitious to be effective, it can register commitment to a great "moral principle." Such arguments have very considerable force in Europe.

In truth, appeals to what is "useful," or alternately, to what honors "moral principle," are powerful in most modern countries. Such appeals draw, after all, on the two most powerful currents in modern legal philosophy: on the one hand, a pragmatic utilitarianism, which judges every policy by the scale of benefits it can provide; on the other hand, Kantian moralism, which disdains to look at consequences and measures moral obligation by universal standards of right action.

These philosophies are not quite as opposed to each other as they may seem. They both find it difficult to recognize boundaries and to respect the need for brakes on their own momentum. Utilitarians, in seeking the greatest good for the greatest number, are hardpressed to explain whose benefit should count: All people in one place? All people in the world? All people living now or all who may ever live? Kantian moralists, entranced with universal (or "categorical") moral imperatives, cannot bring themselves to admit exceptions or acknowledge special circumstances. The utilitarian and the Kantian moralist are alike in their readiness to set themselves up as legislators for mankind, since nothing in their outlook tells them this is over-reaching or absurd.[1]

For Americans, talk of a "legislator for mankind" may sound like a mere metaphor in a philosophical exposition. But over the past decade, quite a lot of energy has been invested in building up institutions that might well be described as legislators for mankind. The Kyoto Protocol, for example, seeks to avert global warming by imposing limits on energy use around the world. To make good on this project, it would delegate vast powers to monitor and regulate industrial and agricultural practices throughout the world. And Kyoto is only the most ambitious of many global projects proposed in the name of environmental protection, economic development, human rights, and so on.

In this larger context, it is not, after all, so surprising that many people think countries should not be able to decide for themselves when to seek peace and reconciliation with general amnesties and when to insist on punitive justice. In this larger context, it is not so surprising that many people think such decisions should be referred to a global prosecutor and a global criminal court.

Wouldn't it be easier to leave such difficult decisions to each country to make for itself? For Americans, letting countries decide for themselves might almost be called the "natural" approach. It is, in fact, what our Declaration of Independence proclaims, that the "Laws of Nature and Nature's God entitle" each independent state to "a separate and equal Station among the Powers of the Earth." God is surely above all nations, but here on earth each nation has the equal right to go its separate way and decide for itself how to govern its own affairs. The Declaration goes on to explain why this is so: "all men are created equal, endowed by their Creator with certain inalienable rights" and "to secure these rights, governments are instituted among men, deriving their just powers from the consent of the governed." Individual rights can only be secured by a government which rests on the consent of the governed. A just government derives its powers from the consent of the political community which it governs. And consent implies a world of separate nations—as global consent is almost meaningless when there is no meaningful global political community (at the level of consenting individuals).

The American founding doctrine establishes firm brakes and boundaries on schemes of global governance. It raises the principle of individual rights as a brake on utilitarian calculations in government and stands by the principle of national sovereignty as a brake on globalist moralism. Individual countries must retain the right to decide for themselves, if individual human beings can retain any solid hope of securing their own personal liberty. At least the U.S. will want to go its own way, if that is what most Americans desire.

The International Criminal Court is finally worth taking seriously as a philosophic challenge. It is a monument to very different ways of thinking about political authority and "the course of human events" from those on which the U.S. is founded. Americans will be less effective in resisting this challenge—with its insistent moral rhetoric and its seductive appeals for pragmatic adaptation—if they do not understand why it is so contrary to our Founding doctrines.

But this is not just an immediate political challenge. There cannot be individual rights without individuals who understand them well enough to assert them. There cannot be government by consent if people do not have the understanding to insist on accountable government. Our whole system depends on a certain level of understanding among citizens.

Still, there is no better path to understanding than trying to apply an abstract principle to a concrete challenge. The International Criminal Court is not an academic question or a hypothetical problem for a student essay. It is a genuine challenge, but one which calls on us to exercise our highest calling as citizens—to understand the political duties that sustain our claims to our rights. It is well worth thinking about.

Note

[1]For a classic account of Kantian and utilitarian arguments in contemporary legal theory, emphasizing their strangely complementary tendencies to extremism, see Richard A. Posner, *The Economics of Justice* (Harvard University Press, 1983), chapter 3. For the latest effort to recruit both Kantian and utilitarian ethics in pursuit of "global justice," see Charles Jones, *Global Justice, Defending Cosmopolitanism* (Oxford University Press, 1999).

James K. Glassman

Free Trade: A Consumer Revolution

It was Ronald Reagan who made the wonderful statement that "economists are people who see something work in practice and wonder if it would work in theory." What is working in practice—or has been working for the last two decades—has been the U.S. economy. We have just been through the longest period ever in American history of sustained growth. Even though we may have entered a recession in the first quarter of this year, we have broken all records for growth over the last ten years. And if it is a recession, it will probably be a very shallow one.

Since 1982 we have had sustained growth with only one very shallow recession that lasted three-quarters of a year. Unfortunately, it was deep enough for George Bush, the elder, to lose his job. We had never had a period like that before in American history. In August 1982 the Dow Jones Industrial Average stood at 777. Today, it is hovering around 10,000. It is up by a factor of 13 in the last 18 years. Including reinvested dividends, which is something I recommend, the DJIA is now up by a factor of 20. If you had invested $10,000 into the broad market in 1982, you would have $200,000 today.

Although the economy is slowing down, why has it been so strong over the last ten years and the last two decades? I believe the answer is the supply side revolution that began in the early 1980s.

The Supply Side Revolution

When people talk about supply side, often they are referring to the tax cuts that were put in place during the early years of the Reagan administration. Those tax cuts certainly had a supply side effect. Until that point in the Reagan administration, however, most economists had concentrated on the demand side.

Although tax cuts were certainly part of it, this revolution meant more supply had to come on line. As a result, the business cycle changed.

The business cycle is really very simple. When there is prosperity and low unemployment, people begin to demand more goods—they have more money so they want to buy more things. The demand then bumps up against supply constraints and prices rise, which gives us inflation. Then the Federal Reserve comes in and raises interest rates because they have to maintain the value of the dollar, which causes the economy to slow down and go into recession—and the cycle starts up again.

We have had nine recessions since the end of World War II and most of them worked just that way. But over the last eighteen years, we have had only one, very shallow, recession—and it didn't work that way. The reason is that during this shallow recession, as demand rose, it didn't bump up against the same kind of supply constraints. In fact, more and more supply came on line and the prices didn't rise. This is basically the same model we are dealing with today.

Tax cuts are one way to keep supply flowing because they encourage investment, and to some extent, encourage an increase in the labor supply. The Federal Reserve has done a much better job maintaining a stable currency; it has done much better with monetary policy. Businesses are being run more efficiently and so are getting more output from the same amount of input.

The Role of Trade

A major reason that supply has increased over this period has been free trade. There has been a constant flow of goods, as well as a constant flow of people. Immigration is a form of trade, and it has added capital to our markets. While it started roughly after World War II, it has been accelerating in recent years.

Notice that I don't say trade creates markets for U.S. goods. It does, but that is not the point I want to convey. In recent years we have heard over and over again that freer trade creates jobs. The idea is that by lowering trade barriers to our goods, we can increase exports. Those exports increase the overall sales and profits of American companies, which then hire more workers. Trade does create jobs, on a net basis, but it really does not create more jobs overall. Instead it leads to more jobs in some sectors, fewer jobs in others. In the aggregate, the country trades good jobs for bad. Overall, trade creates wealth, which frankly is more important than jobs alone.

An anecdote will further explain this point. Jerry Jordan, the President of the Federal Reserve Bank of Cleveland, told me about an American businessman who went to China a few years ago. The businessman came upon a team of one hundred workers, armed with shovels, who were building a dam. The businessman commented to a local official that one single worker with an earth-moving machine could build the dam in an afternoon. The official replied, "That's true, but think of all the unemployment that that would create." "Oh," said the businessman, "I thought you were building a dam. If it's jobs you want, take away the shovels and give them all spoons."

Work is what we do in order to acquire the things that enable us to live well. Free trade helps us get those things more cheaply because it allows many more producers to sell to us, and because it frees us to concentrate on the work that we do best. That is why we trade with other countries.

Our Comparative Advantage

With all the din over trade, NAFTA, WTO, Fast Track, and the rest, the best arguments for trade have really not been heard. One very powerful argument has been made cogently by economists for more than two hundred years, but not so much by politicians. The other is a brief argument from principle. Neither argument has a thing to do with jobs nor exports. (The argument for exports has just one positive: It seems to carry a lot of political punch at the local level.)

Melvin Krauss of the Hoover Institution writes in *How Nations Grow Rich*, "free trade does not create jobs; instead it creates income for the community by reallocating jobs and capital from lower productivity to higher productivity sectors of the economy." In other words, trade allows us to concentrate on what we do best. Trade may kill jobs in the textile industry, which is labor intensive, but it breeds jobs in electronics, where ingenious Americans have a comparative advantage.

A famous example of this is the lawyer who is an excellent typist, better than his secretary. Should the lawyer split his valuable time between practicing law and typing? Or is it better for the lawyer to lawyer and for the typist—who might not be very good at lawyering—to type? Which approach makes the most sense for a sound economy? Obviously, it is the latter.

That is the idea behind comparative advantage. Why do we trade? We trade for imports. We don't trade for exports.

No one put it better than Adam Smith two hundred years ago, when he said, "It is the maxim of every prudent master of a family never to make at home what it will cost him more to make than to buy." If a foreign country can supply us with a commodity cheaper than we ourselves can make it, we should buy it from them. This is why most American families do not grow their own wheat or grind their own flour or bake their own bread. They have better things to do with their time.

Many years ago Milton and Rose Friedman wrote, "a fallacy seldom contradicted is that exports are good and imports are bad." We cannot eat, wear, or enjoy the goods that we send abroad. We eat bananas from Central America, we wear Italian shoes, we drive German automobiles, and we enjoy programs on our Japanese TV sets. Our gain from foreign trade is what we import. Exports are the price we pay to get imports. That is: We do not eat in order to work; we work in order to eat.

In exchange for imports, we offer other countries the things that we produce cheaper or better—computers, chickens, movies, power generators, or we just offer them dollars. In the words of my former colleague, Herb Stein, they send us cars; we send them little pieces of paper. Not a bad deal.

Those little pieces of paper are, in effect, noninterest-bearing IOUs that the people who send us imports have to spend in this country. If they aren't spent on goods then they are spent on investments, real estate, auto plants in Tennessee, or Treasury bonds.

That is quite a deal. We benefit from the lower prices imports give us, and we can use the money we save to buy things made at home—or better, we can invest it. It is at this point that imports have immense benefits. They do a great deal to throttle inflation, and U.S. businesses have been forced to become more productive. The Clinton administration failed to promote imports in their confused battle for Fast Track authority.

We must wait to see what happens in the current presidency. The Bush administration has a very experienced trade team. Whether they will use the import argument, which I think most Americans understand intuitively, remains to be seen. However, it is very promising that President Bush is cutting back in his budget on export promotion programs, such as the Export–Import Bank. Institutions such as this promote exports and basically give money or provide subsidies to corporations to export. I think there are special breaks for corporations that we should not have, but also they are oriented in the wrong direction.

Consumer-Friendly Policies

Adam Smith wrote that consumption is the sole purpose of production. Ralph Nader and others who say they are consumer advocates are in reality producer advocates. They favor certain kinds of producers over other kinds of producers.

When surveying a policy, ask this question: Does the policy help consumers? Free trade allows consumers to buy a cornucopia of higher quality goods from other countries at lower prices than they would be able to do were they restricted to domestic goods. Trade is obviously a huge benefit for consumers, or individual buyers, and as Adam Smith says, what's good for the consumer is good for the economy. Yet, consumer advocates like Nader want to stop consumers from enjoying the benefits of free trade. Why? To help others, to help producers—or to help trade unions which basically represent cartelized producers.

It is indeed true that some producers are hurt by free trade and we can expect producers such as the textile industry and tomato growers to kick and scream over free trade. Well, that's fine. But consumers—all 270 million of us in the United States—benefit mightily from free trade.

Taxation With Representation

Let me direct some outrage at so-called liberal Democrats, people like Representative David Bonior of Michigan or Nita Lowey of New York or any of the others who oppose Fast Track—that is to say, those who oppose giving the President increased trade negotiating authority—out of concern for "working" Americans.

Why do these people oppose Fast Track? It could be mere economic ignorance. More likely it is the desire to help preserve the interests of producers and unions, just as big business did in the Smoot-Hawley days of the 1920s and 1930s.

We have come full circle. In 1928, Republicans wanted high tariffs to protect their business supporters. Now the Democrats do. This is an amazing change. The 1928 Democratic platform proposed to "increase the purchasing power of wages by reducing the monopolistic and extortionate tariff rates." That was the Democratic platform, and it was right.

Tariffs, or even nontariff barriers, amount to a tax. Another word for tariff is tax. Tariffs raise the price of goods for consumers. Tariffs are, in fact, a discriminatory tax. They raise the price of a Japanese-made Toyota, but not the price of a U.S.-made Chevrolet. And as we know, the price of the U.S.-made Chevrolet will rise to meet, or maybe slightly undercut the price of the Toyota. That's the way it works. And who benefits? Certainly not the consumer.

I believe that the arguments for imports are simple and powerful. In fact, they carry a lot more political punch than most politicians understand. By some estimates, 13 percent of American jobs are export-dependent, that is, the jobs of some 18 million American workers. Counting their family members, that means an immediate impact on 40 million Americans. But all 270 million of us benefit from imports. But as one of President Clinton's economic reports correctly stated, imports of goods have kept inflation low, while imports of capital have kept interest rates low helping to sustain rapid income growth.

Another kind of import also helps us—the import of labor. Imported labor helps to keep prices low and technology humming. Jobs associated with exported goods tend to pay wages that are about 13 to 18 percent higher than other jobs.

Free Trade and Human Rights

Free trade is not merely an economic concept: It is a human right, a natural right. People should have the right to exchange the sweat of their brows, the product of their hands and their minds, with whomever they wish. I should be free to trade with my corner drycleaner, with a Balinese shirt maker, with a Cuban cigar roller—yes, even a Cuban cigar roller—a Japanese laptop manufacturer. The right to trade is one of our inalienable rights, along with life, liberty, and the pursuit of happiness.

The government should be able to stop trade between two people only if that trade threatens the interests of national security, if we are at war or close to it. Unfortunately, the Constitution itself is at odds with this sentiment. It specifically allows Congress to lay and post excises—that is to say, tariffs—and to regulate commerce with foreign nations. It is easy to understand that tariffs were far more important in the eighteenth century, when they were the main source of government revenue, than they are today. But it is hard to deny that there is some natural or human rights interest in trade.

No More Tit for Tat

What does all this mean in a policy sense? My conclusion is that it would be smart for the United States to abandon its current negotiating posture, which is, "we will take down our trade barriers, if you take down yours." This reciprocity-based argument is built on the very faulty premise that current protectionist measures are good for the United States, but we are willing to abandon them if other countries abandon theirs because we really want to get into their markets.

Brink Lindsey of the Cato Institute wrote in 1991 in an article for *Reason* magazine, "the reciprocity-based free trade strategy helps to frame the whole free trade debate in terms that favor the protectionist lobby." This is a very important point. The special interests that seek a protectionist bailout rarely admit that they are "out-competed" by their foreign rivals; rather they claim that they are the victims of unfair competition.

"A policy of trade negotiations lends credence to this ploy by focusing attention on the other country's import barrier and 'unfair' practices," Lindsey said. And this is exactly right. If our aim is to get imports into the United States, then the best way to do that is to take down our barriers no matter what anybody else does.

Unilateral free trade should be the United States' policy. Forget negotiations. The Friedmans wrote in 1980 that we could assume a consistent and principled stance. Americans could say to the rest of the world, We believe in freedom and we intend to practice it. We cannot force you to be free, but we can offer full cooperation on equal terms to all. Our market is open to you without tariffs or other restrictions. Sell here what you can and wish to, buy whatever you can and wish to, and that way cooperation among individuals can be worldwide and free.

Are unilateral free trade agreements still such a flaky idea? You rarely hear about them, but they aren't that flaky. A professor of economics at Columbia University points out that Hong Kong and Singapore are conspicuous unilateral free traders, as is New Zealand. Those countries have done exceptionally well economically. A large portion of the world's trade liberalization in the past quarter century has been unilateral, with beneficial effects to the countries that practice it. That Columbia professor writes, "The most potent force for the worldwide freeing of trade is unilateral U.S. action." If the U.S. continues to do away with tariffs and trade barriers, other countries will follow suit.

In general, nations will dismantle their obstacles to free trade only when they understand that it is in the best interest of their citizens, the consumers. That makes sense. More and more nations are realizing this. By unilaterally adopting free trade, the U.S. can show the way. With the demonstration effect, we will thrive. Taking down barriers has brought competition. It has made our auto industry better and our communications industry the best in the world. The demonstration effect is very powerful. Other nations will see the success of what we have done and they will rush to do it themselves. Eliminating trade barriers is quite simply the right thing to do.

Doug Bandow

The IMF and the World Bank: The Legacy of Global Institutions

As the Bush administration confronts the horrific challenge of terrorism, the need for global cooperation is ever more evident. Although terrorism is now at the forefront of America's international agenda, other issues, too, loom: poverty, instability, and war. How to confront them, and particularly how to best use global financial institutions in doing so, will be a critical concern for Washington in the years ahead.

The roles of the World Bank, International Monetary Fund (IMF), and other multilateral development banks (MDBs), in particular, and foreign aid in general, are not obvious in today's world, which is very different from the one in which these organizations were established. Today markets are global and capitalism has triumphed. Most people in the West live in a world of changing technology, expanding economies, and exploding opportunities. For them the future is bright. The great anomaly of this age is that in this world of plenty persists ethnic, racial, and religious divisions, along with grievous poverty.

It is easy for the prosperous to try to wall off the world's problems: they seem so far away and beyond our control. But as the terrorist attack of September 11 demonstrates, the world's problems often become America's problems.

We have an obligation to care as human beings. To have so much when others have so little should give us pause. We must also be concerned as a nation, one with cultural, economic, and political ties the world over.

But the desire to help is not enough. It requires thoughtful action, policies which will help the poor and dispossessed around the globe, and which will do so effectively and affordably.

The most common policy tool is foreign aid. But anyone seriously interested in helping the less fortunate must ask a basic question: foreign aid or hindrance? The answer matters, since it will determine whether we can achieve our goals as a humane people, and as citizens in the world's most dominant nation.

Foreign aid has often been presented as an ethical issue. The late Tanzanian dictator Julius Nyerere, for instance, long contended that foreign aid was due the Third World as a matter of moral right. But that is true only if less developed states are impoverished because wealthy industrialized nations are rich.

The evidence is overwhelming that this is not the case. As noted later, the most important factor in economic development is a country's own policies. This means that foreign aid should be viewed as an act of charity by a compassionate people, not the payment of a moral debt. Its provision therefore requires discernment and wisdom. That is, aid must actually aid; if it makes the underlying problems worse, it will be, in fact, a moral evil.

Concern over aid's ineffectiveness has led to the program's lack of public support, in contrast to many domestic wealth transfer programs. Yet foreign aid continues.

In part that reflects simple emotion. Supporters of foreign aid have long effectively used pitiful images of impoverished and starving refugees to shake money out of compassionate donors and skeptical legislators alike.

This was a constant theme of the Clinton administration, which mixed moral blackmail with political demagoguery: Then-Secretary of State Warren Christopher even warned of "a new isolationism" among GOP opponents of foreign aid. Republican paladins, such as former President George Bush, joined the chorus. And the newly Republican Congress ended up voting for spending increases for the first time in a decade. Although the George W. Bush administration seems skeptical of previous IMF and World Bank loans, it is also bound to use funding for those organizations as bargaining chips in its attempt to build an enduring coalition against terrorism.

Crumbling Intellectual Foundations

Support for foreign aid persists even as the program's intellectual foundations crumble. Since World War II, Washington has provided over one trillion dollars in foreign assistance (in current dollars).

U.S. economic assistance comes in various forms—grants and loans for bilateral projects, primarily through U.S. AID, as well as credit from multilateral agencies, including the IMF, the World Bank, and such regional agencies as the European Bank for Reconstruction and Development, to underwrite borrower development projects and provide aid for "structural" economic reforms. Other forms of foreign assistance include security programs, disaster relief, and subsidized crop shipments (primarily "Food for Peace").

Although there is no doubt that some individual development projects can do some good, and that humanitarian aid can help alleviate the effects of crises, there is little evidence, despite the presumption of the term "foreign assistance," that American cash transfers, whether bilateral or multilateral, actually do much to advance growth or stability throughout the developing world.

Even the Clinton administration admitted that the record of aid was not altogether good. An early task force reported that "despite decades of foreign assistance, most of Africa and parts of Latin America, Asia and the Middle East are economically worse off today than they were 20 years ago." As a result, the administration cut off funding for some 50 nations, mainly because they were, like the Democratic Republic of Congo (then Zaire), abject failures. The administration was even more critical of U.S. AID as an organization. Said AID administrator Brian Atwood: "We were an agency on the road to mediocrity, or worse."

Similarly, in 1989, under the previous administration, U.S. AID acknowledged: "only a handful of countries that started receiving U.S. assistance in the 1950s and 1960s has ever graduated from dependent status." The United Nations Development Programme reported in 1996 that 70 developing countries, aid recipients all, were poorer than they were in 1980; 43 were worse off than in 1970. Indeed, virtually every nation in crisis, from Burundi to Somalia, received billions of dollars from the West, to no avail.

International comparisons are obviously fraught with difficulty, but overall aid levels do not correlate positively with economic growth, and many of the biggest recipients of foreign assistance, such as Bangladesh, Egypt, India, Philippines, Sudan, and Tanzania, have been among the globe's worst economic performers. Of course, even correlation would not be enough to prove that aid actually aids. The real issue is causation, but there is no evidence that aid generates growth.

The Primacy of Policy

What does matter is policy. This is evident enough in the differences in prosperity between China and Taiwan, North and South Korea, or Asia and Latin America, as well as the broader experiences of poor nations. This fact suggests that it is time for a major change in U.S. strategy—to abandon so-called foreign aid as anything but a political tool to buy influence.

Today few development professionals dispute the necessity of markets for growth. People need economic freedom to prosper. Aid advocates also increasingly admit that aid cannot work in the absence of market reforms. In a bad policy environment, no government can use money well. There is even growing agreement that assistance cannot force market reforms. If there is no domestic political will, foreign cash won't buy needed changes.

The increasingly beleaguered band of aid defenders have been reduced to claiming that foreign assistance might be useful in promoting development if governments have already adopted good economic policies. But these are the nations that need aid the least. If they have the right policies, they will succeed without aid. It is worth considering these points in more detail, particularly on how the debate has changed over the last decade.

First is the importance of market policies. Perhaps the best broad-based international development study is *Economic Freedom of the World: 1975–1995* (updated regularly) by economists James Gwartney, Robert Lawson, and Robert Block. Although such international comparisons must be used with care, two important lessons emerge. First, economic policies matter. Second, changes in economic policy matter. In both cases, open markets yield higher growth rates.

Similar results are given in the *Index of Economic Freedom* (with annual editions) produced by the Heritage Foundation. It concludes that "economic freedom is the single most important factor in creating the conditions for economic growth and prosperity." Studies by numerous other analysts and organizations, including the World Bank, yield the same overall conclusion. Whether looking at the degree of regulation, openness to trade, levels of taxes and spending, you get the same result: Less intervention yields better economic results. Although one can debate the proper role of government, statism—with large government attempting to manage the economy—is no longer an intellectually serious option.

There is a similar consensus developing that foreign aid doesn't work when recipients follow *dirigiste* economic policies. That doesn't mean that no aid program has ever done any good. But overall, foreign assistance does not raise economic growth rates.

The Failure of Foreign Aid

For years economist P. T. Bauer was almost alone in criticizing the efficacy of so-called foreign assistance. His views are now mainstream. For example, Peter Boone of the London School of Economics assessed the experience of nearly one hundred nations, concluding that foreign transfers had no impact on recipient country investment levels. "Long-term aid is not a means to create growth," he reported. Why not? Boone explained: "Poverty is not caused by capital shortage, and it is not optimal for politicians to adjust distortionary policies when they receive aid flows."

Most poor countries have had access to capital. That is, after all, how they have amassed a $2 trillion international debt. Moreover, there are political reasons to maintain stupid policies—to enrich one's allies and thereby stay in power, for examplee. Economic inefficiency is often less important than other ends.

Boone's conclusion has been backed by that of World Bank economists Craig Burnside and David Dollar. Although they argue that assistance can work in a good policy environment, they note that foreign transfers tend to increase spending by recipient governments. This fact, they conclude, "provides some insight into why aid is not promoting growth in the average recipient." A similarly tepid assessment of foreign assistance comes from Michael O'Hanlon and Carol Graham of the liberal Brookings Institution in *A Half Penny on the Federal Dollar: The Future of Development Aid.* They conclude that "the negative relationship between aid flows and performance is clear at a general level." After endorsing limited assistance programs, they caution: "larger initiatives are unlikely to be effective unless recipients have sound economic and demographic policies."

Also skeptical of aid's efficacy were the congressionally created International Financial Institutions Advisory Commission, which reported in 2000, and the Task Force on the United States and the Multilateral Development Banks (created by the Center for Strategic and International Studies), which issued its conclusions in 1997. The former was highly critical of the performance of the many MDBs. In the latter's report, the Task Force concluded that "development cannot be induced by resource transfers alone, but depends heavily on appropriate policies, functioning institutions, and cohesive societies." A more recent Congressional Budget Office study termed the overall impact of aid at best "marginal" and "modest."

Further evidence comes from the fact that not only is there no positive correlation between assistance levels and economic growth, but most aid recipients remain dependent on foreign transfers. As U.S. AID acknowledged in 1989, "only a handful of countries . . . has ever graduated from dependent status." Similarly, some countries have been on IMF programs for literally decades—more than forty years in cases like India. Aid has kept them poor and made them dependent, rather than wealthy and independent.

Searching for New Justifications

As the aid lobby has encountered increasing resistance to its funding requests, organizations like the World Bank and U.S. AID have searched for new justifications for old aid programs. One of their most potent arguments has been the importance of promoting policy reform. That is, they say markets are necessary for growth, and then argue that they can help promote markets. All IMF loans are formally conditioned; the Bank offers what it calls Structural Adjustment Loans, among others.

Unfortunately, these incentives don't work in practice. A host of critical internal World Bank audits raise serious doubts about the efficacy of so-called adjustment lending. The details are tedious, and often buried in lengthy Bank evaluation reports, but in general the MDBs want to lend more than the borrowers want to borrow, which leads to lax conditions and more loans. One Bank report cited the institution's "culture of lending," and numerous evaluations have found little evidence that loans have achieved significant changes. The World Bank's own Burnside and Dollar go even further: "We find no systematic influence of aid on our index of fiscal, monetary, and trade policies." For each case where one can argue assistance advanced reform, "there is a Zambia, in which policy deteriorated continuously from 1970 until 1993, while aid receipts rose continuously."

In July 2001 Bank chief economist William Easterly reported that despite nearly one thousand conditional loans during the 1980s and 1990s, "with a few notable exceptions, government mismanagement usually continued in these countries. The growth rate of income per person of the typical member of this group during the past two decades was zero." (The Bank considered disciplining him for failing to seek permission to publish the offending article, which was adapted from his then-forthcoming book.) The CSIS Task Force points to "the limits of the MDBs' ability to exert leverage for policy changes." O'Hanlon and Graham also acknowledge serious deficiencies in conditionality, before endorsing its use on a more selective basis.

The basic problem is that many governments simply are not interested in policy reform. Some want to develop, but are unwilling to pay the political price of adopting the policies necessary to do so. Others treat ideological objectives as paramount. Still others are simply most interested in staying in power. One need not be a reflexive critic of government to recognize that such regimes are an impediment to development.

Writes Alan Carter of Heythrop College in London: Third World governments are "rational actors who will industrialise their economies when practicable, but who often find it in their interests to be accomplices in the dependent development or even underdevelopment of their own economies." In such cases, he warns, "aid primarily serves to prop up regimes that are complicit in the exploitation of their people and the destruction of their environment." Unfortunately, that has been the experience of the IMF and World Bank, which for years have supposedly been underwriting policy "reform" around the world. Yet most governments have simply taken the money and run, causing the financial institutions to... extend new loans.

For this reason, both CSIS and the Brookings Institution, though MDB supporters, acknowledge the limits in trying to promote policy reform. Cindy Williams of the Congressional Budget Office warns: "Without reform, however, aid can reinforce policies that do not further development." Thus, another argument for aid collapses.

It seems evident, then, that nations must allow free markets to grow economically. Aid cannot work without a economic freedom. Assistance does little to engender market reforms.

Helping Those Who Help Themselves

The last economic redoubt to which aid defenders repair is that financial contributions at least help countries that help themselves. If they have good policies they will put the money to good use.

Even here there is reason for skepticism. Nations with good policies don't need assistance. Today private capital flows dwarf all "aid" transfers. It is true that investment has been concentrated in a limited number of developing states, and can cause problems when it leaves—witness East Asia. But that merely demonstrates the power of the private marketplace to reward good policies. Investors easily fulfill the role being sought by aid bureaucrats. So one doesn't need aid (that is money, in contrast to advice, technical assistance, and the like) if the policy environment is positive.

Moreover, however well-intentioned, assistance to even the best governments risks reducing the incentive to reform. Moving toward a free market is a continuing process, but foreign transfers reduce the economic penalty otherwise naturally imposed on dumb economic policies.

Evidence of this problem comes from an October 2000 study by Alex Dreher and Roland Vaubel, two German economists. They found that monetary expansion and government spending increased as IMF loans rose. They did so despite conditionality that was supposed to achieve the opposite result.

That is, by masking the pain of economic failure, development assistance allows borrowers to delay reforms, worsening the underlying problem. "Scarcity of resources" in such cases "is good for reform," writes Dani Rodrik of Columbia University. Necessity, brought on by collectivist and populist economics, almost always drives the reform process. Observed U.S. AID: "Few people, least of all politicians, embark on a deliberate course of change without being motivated by some significant political or economic crisis. The simple fact behind most subsequently successful economic policy is the failure of the one that preceded it."

The Incentive of Economic Failure

Surely that is the lesson of Russia, where failure forced the Soviet Union to reform, and where aid—more than $22 billion from the IMF alone—acted as a simple subsidy of the Yeltsin government, irrespective of its economic policies at the time. If those payments could be justified, it was to keep Boris Yeltsin in power, not to promote capitalism. Similar was the experience of India, which maintained a disastrous collectivist economic strategy until the mid-1980s, despite huge international transfers. Failure, not aid, drove New Delhi to reform. In 1998, when the U.S. suspended assistance out of nonproliferation concerns, India responded by approving fifty private investment projects to bring in money.

So even where countries are well-governed, one cannot assume that aid equals aid. There is a dearth of success stories—where aid caused development rather than followed it.

Even if there are a few cases in which well-administered aid might speed up development that would otherwise occur, this is a dubious justification for tens of billions more in assistance every year. Harvard's Jeffrey Sachs calls for "a carefully designed" and "better focused foreign aid program," one "limited in duration" with "a plan to phase it out." But bureaucrats and legislators are no more likely to meet such conditions today than they were at any other time during the last fifty years. More selectively delivering aid would minimize the waste, not yield significant benefits.

With the collapse of the traditional arguments for aid, centered around promoting economic development, supporters of the program have looked for creative new ones. If there is no evidence that assistance generates economic growth or policy reform, then what? Perhaps the most important, and most superficially appealing, new justification is that assistance can forestall social collapse—the kind of disasters in Burundi, Somalia, Zaire, and even Yugoslavia, which in turn triggered expensive American rescue efforts.

For instance, Sadako Ogata, then-U.N. High Commissioner for Refugees, asked: "What might have happened in Rwanda if the estimated $2 billion spent on refugee relief during the first two weeks of the emergency had been devoted to keeping the peace, protecting human rights and promoting development in the period that preceded the exodus?"

It seems like a good question. Whether or not foreign aid can bring economic benefits, could it have prevented the human catastrophe that we see in so many countries?

The question is impossible to answer with certainty. But the answer is probably no. Sadly, this argument is no more convincing than any other. There is nothing in five decades of foreign aid experience to indicate that Washington or its allies have a unique ability to predict which nations are in the greatest danger of dissolving, let alone to use assistance to forestall such human catastrophes. To the contrary, most of the countries that have collapsed into chaos received significant amounts of aid over the years. Unfortunately, not only was that money used poorly. It often buttressed the very governments that were most responsible for the ensuing disasters.

Abundant Aid for All

Rwanda, for example, which did not go unaided before imploding. To the contrary, between 1971 and 1994 that nation received $4.7 billion in foreign assistance from America, the multilaterals, and European nations. In fact, most every country in crisis received abundant outside transfers from a variety of sources before disaster struck. Over the same period, Sierra Leone received $1.8 billion; Liberia,

$1.8 billion; Angola, $2.9 billion; Haiti, $3.1 billion; Chad, $3.3 billion; Burundi, $3.4 billion; Uganda, $5.8 billion; Somalia, $6.2 billion; Zaire, $8.4 billion; Sri Lanka, $9.8 billion; Mozambique, $10.5 billion; Ethiopia, $11.5 billion; and Sudan, $13.4 billion. Through 1991, Yugoslavia received $530 million; through 1994, the total territory had received $6.1 billion.

In none of these cases did foreign assistance forestall catastrophe. Indeed, few nations in Africa, irrespective of aid levels, have escaped social breakdown. Conflict and economic decline have resulted in tens of thousands of refugees fleeing Gambia, Mali, Mauritania, Niger, Senegal, Togo, and Western Sahara, as well as the dozen states listed above.

Obviously, there are numerous reasons that so many nations, including some in Southeast Asia and the Transcaucasus, suffer so. Angola has been brutalized by a long civil war, and military intervention by Cuba; only recently has the conflict moved toward resolution, only to flare again. Burundi and Rwanda were rent by cycles of tribal violence, the genesis of which reaches back to colonial policies that favored one tribe over another. Chad has endured civil war and outside intervention by Libya. Ethiopia has suffered through three scourges: Marxist revolution, war with Somalia, and a separatist campaign by Eritrea.

Haiti spent most of its history under repressive authoritarian rule. Liberia, Mozambique, and Sierra Leone underwent the ravages of particularly bitter civil wars. Somalia was victimized by a Western-backed strongman who proved unable to defeat either Ethiopia or indigenous guerrillas; when his rule collapsed so did central authority, as competing clans struggled for control. Sudan has been rent by conflict between Muslims, Christians, and animists for decades. Uganda disintegrated under the effects of misrule by the grotesque Idi Amin, followed by domestic insurgency and outside intervention. Zaire had the misfortune to be an artificial state created for Belgian colonial interests and born of civil strife. Rebellion, U.N. intervention, and authoritarian rule by the egregiously corrupt Mobutu Sese Seko and successor Laurent Kabila sent that country spiraling into chaos.

However similar the general causes of these and other examples of economic and political collapse, the individual circumstances varied greatly by country. Few of the problems were amenable to outside intervention; in none of these cases was inadequate international aid the determining factor. Of course, were these nations capable of better using capital, foreign transfers would be of more use. But precisely because they are not, past aid has been wasted, as would have any additional transfers as part of an "early warning system."

Creating Problems

Indeed, foreign aid almost certainly helped create and aggravate problems in Ethiopia, Somalia, Sudan, and Zaire, in particular, by subsidizing dictators whose rules proved to be especially disastrous. Among the most important causes of social division and catastrophe is Alan Carter's "overpoliticized state." Yet government-to-government aid only strengthens those very same overpoliticized states. Even the most humanitarian sounding aid—so-called Food for Peace shipments—can accelerate social breakdown. One-time relief worker Michael Maren criticizes a decade of assistance to Somalia. Of Western humanitarian personnel, he writes: "Separately we'd arrived at the conclusion that the relief program was probably killing as many people as it was saving, and the net result was that Somali soldiers were supplementing their income by selling food, while the WSLF [Western Somali Liberation Front]—often indistinguishable from the army—was using the food as rations to fuel their attacks into Ethiopia." At the same time, food assistance discouraged local production and enhanced the central government's control over its people. Then, after the regime finally collapsed, Western assistance worsened the chaos by enriching the local militias and discouraging local reconstruction efforts.

In short, past aid did not stop crises. We have tried this strategy too, and it has failed—abysmally.

At best, advocates of aid can argue that they would do better next time. And with the end of the Cold War, there is less pressure to use assistance as de facto bribes to assorted dictators. However, the bulk of aid to all of the failed states was always economic, not security-based. Between 1971 and 1994 the United States accounted for barely one-fifth of total aid received by Somalia. The rest was economic assistance from a variety of sources—the multilaterals (particularly World Bank and IMF) and Europeans, in particular.

During the same period Rwanda received more from the International Development Association (IDA), a World Bank affiliate, alone than from the United States; Burundi collected 3.6 times as much from IDA as from Washington. In short, the problem with past aid to failed societies is not that it was overly oriented toward political purposes. Rather, it is that international financial transfers turned out not to be aid at all.

Experience has demonstrated aid to be a failure. Unfortunately, outside assistance has only marginal effect for good, if that. Policymakers who want to be both compassionate and effective must realize that aid cannot generate economic growth. It cannot overcome the effects of bad policies. It cannot make poor states improve their policies. And it cannot hold failed nations together.

Whose Destinies?

This result should leave us both frustrated and liberated: frustrated that it is so hard to help those in need; liberated in being able to see both the problem and solution more clearly. Poor countries are largely responsible for their own destinies. Developing peoples have it within their own power to succeed.

As noted earlier, experience has demonstrated that sound domestic policies, not foreign aid, are what generate economic growth. This deserves further emphasis. The West's dramatic escape from poverty has always been a good place to start in attempting to understand development. The rapid economic and social progress of Europe, during which people first rose out of the dismal poverty that characterized most of human history, was largely limited to a specific kind of regime—classical liberalism. It generally allowed markets to operate, respected the rule of law, protected private property, and permitted economic competition. That experience has been repeated more quickly and spectacularly in East Asia, where it has taken but a generation or two for desperately poor nations to be included among the world's most successful economies. (This is not to say that the British or German, let alone the Japanese or South Korean, experiences were laissez faire. Rather, all broadly relied on market forces, despite varying degrees of government economic involvement.)

What was true of Great Britain, the United States, Japan, and South Korea is also evident with today's successful developing states. But this experience long has been obscured by ideology. Extensive state economic intervention has persisted around the world, including in the West, for political as well as philosophical reasons. Such policies have been especially evident throughout the twentieth century. In particular, the vast majority of Third World states traveled the socialist path as decolonization proceeded after World War II. Their decision was in part nationalistic; many new countries believed that true independence required indigenous control of economic resources. Ghana's Kwame Nkrumah, for instance, explained that his nation's "socialist transformation would eradicate completely the colonial structure" of the economy. Statism also tended to benefit, both economically and politically, the elites that gained power after independence.

The result, alas, has been economic catastrophe. Yet these sort of policies were exacerbated by the World Bank, IMF, and similar institutions. Stanley Please, a senior Bank official for two decades, wrote of arriving at the institution as "a committed socialist," yet being "surprised and shocked by the emphasis that the Bank at the time gave to the public sector in general and to the government in particular. Here was an institution which had the reputation of being ultra-free enterprise and market-oriented, yet had more confidence in the rationality, morality, and competence of governments than I ever had." He also cited growing lending programs in the very countries the Bank was criticizing for poor policy environments.

Similarly, the IMF made clear that borrower foolishness was no bar to aid. It discounted criticism that it was biased against collectivist systems: "In many instances, fund-supported programs have accommodated such nonmarket devices as production controls, administered prices, and subsidies." Loan after loan and project after project have continued to be thrust upon such countries, even as they followed development strategies destined to fail, and to fail disastrously.

Conclusion

For all of their new rhetoric about markets, the IMF and World Bank spent most of the last half century subsidizing statism and thereby inhibiting development. Statism has failed. Today the primary responsibility for development lies with Third World states themselves. Governments must create an economic environment in which people are free to be productive.

We in the industrialized nations can help. As individuals, we can support humanitarian groups which attempt to relieve the worst effects of poverty and disaster, and to foster the grassroots entrepreneurship necessary for self-sustaining economic growth. As citizens, we can push Western governments to do no harm. Washington should end government-to-government assistance, which has so often buttressed regimes dedicated to little more than maintaining power, and eased the economic pressure for needed reforms.

At the same time, the United States should allow poorer nations to participate more fully in the international marketplace. The Congressional Budget Office has observed that: "The broad economic policies of the major Western countries—trade policies, budget deficits, growth rates, and the like—generally exert greater influence on the economies of the developing countries than does aid." Access to the markets of wealthier nations is particularly important for poorer states. The World Bank's J. Michael Finger figures that Western protectionism reduces the Third World's GNP by a full three percentage points, twice the amount of foreign aid now provided by those same industrialized nations. It makes no sense to tell poor countries that we wish them well, but then to refuse to buy their goods.

Mass poverty, famine, and murder blight our globe. However, the understandable desire to do something should not become an excuse to maintain the failed policies of the past. Foreign aid has not delivered self-sustaining economic growth or prevented the collapse of numerous poor societies into chaos over the past five decades. If we are serious about helping the poor throughout the Third World, we must recognize that foreign aid will do no better in the future. Instead, we need to develop new solutions for a very old problem.

Mickey Craig

Human Nature and Politics: The Case for Constitutional Government

Will the future be characterized by freedom, free trade, and free markets, or will it be dominated by regulation and world government? There are three positions from which to examine these possibilities: the economic or free market position; the world state position; and the political or constitutional position.

The economic position looks to free markets and a system of free or voluntary exchange as the key to the expansion of liberty in the world. It sees the expansion of free markets as the key to the eventual disintegration of the state and sees the spread of the principle of free and voluntary exchange as the key to world peace. According to the economic position, the greatest impediment to the spread of free trade is the nation–state or national governments.

Although there is much in the free market position with which I agree, I disagree that national governments per se are impediments to freedom. National governments animated by classical liberal or constitutional principles are champions of liberty. National governments not animated by those constitutional principles, but rather by radical ideologies—such as a master race or a master class—or even by somewhat milder ideologies—such as progress or social justice, the welfare state, or the entitlement mentality—are what threaten liberty in the modern world.

The world state position looks to the establishment of the universal and homogenous state as the desirable end of history. According to the theory of the universal and homogenous state, genuine freedom has never existed in the world. Genuine freedom will only emerge with the establishment of the universal and homogenous state at the end of history. This world state position vests the authority to manage and plan the economic and social affairs of the world in a centralized bureaucracy. In the universal and homogenous state, economic liberty, civil liberty, and religious liberty, as we understand them in the American political tradition, disappear, and genuine freedom emerges in a new world order, establishing heaven on earth.

There is nothing in the world state position, or in the argument for the universal and homogenous state, with which I agree.

The constitutional position, while appreciative and supportive of free markets, does not envision that the state, politics, or government will ever wither away or that world peace will ever be established. Nor does it share the utopian expectations informing the idea of the universal and homogenous state. It is critical of international organizations such as the International Criminal Court, in part because the authority of that body is unaccountable; it does not derive its authority from the consent of the governed. The constitutional position looks rather to American primacy as a source of hegemonic stability in the world.

Understanding the original Constitution requires that we understand the principles which inform it. We find these principles articulated in what James Madison and Thomas Jefferson called the fundamental act of Union: the Declaration of Independence.[1] The Declaration does two things. First, as a practical matter, it explains to the world why it was necessary for the American colonies to break with Great Britain and form an independent nation. Second, and more important, it outlines the principles by which that break with Britain can be called legitimate or just.

What are the principles that justify this defiance and break with Great Britain? Or how can we say that one government is tyrannical and another legitimate? Can government ever be legitimate? Answering these questions is the chief burden of the Declaration of Independence.

What is interesting about the Declaration is that the rights that the Americans pointed to in justifying their break with Britain were rights they claimed not as Americans or as British subjects, but rights they claimed to possess in common with all men everywhere. The principles which justify the break with Great Britain are outlined in the following familiar phrases: "We hold these truths to be self-evident, that all men are created equal, that they are endowed by their Creator with certain unalienable rights, that among these are life, liberty and the pursuit of happiness. That to secure these rights, Governments are instituted among Men, deriving their just powers from the consent of the Governed."

From these principles, the Founding Fathers derived a theory of moral and political obligation that informs legitimate government. Of course, a legitimate government is a rare thing. Throughout history, most people have lived under tyranny of one form or another. Legitimate government is characterized as having constitutional limits. Its purpose is limited to securing the God-given rights shared by all human beings. Limited government understands and respects the classical liberal distinction between state and society.

Let us briefly examine three ideas from the Declaration of Independence: (1) Creator, (2) equality, and (3) consent.

The Declaration of Independence embodies a reflection on the whole of nature, including the nature of God and the nature of man. To understand the idea of equality at the heart of the Declaration, we have to understand not only what man is, but also what he is not. To begin to do so, let us start with the references to God in the Declaration. Aside from the reference to God as Creator, God is mentioned three other times: He is referred to in the first paragraph in the phrase the "Laws of Nature and Nature's God," and in the concluding paragraph in the phrases "appealing to the Supreme Judge of the world for the rectitude of our intentions" and "with a firm reliance on the protection of Divine Providence." God and the laws of nature, God as Supreme Judge, and God as protector—thus God in the Declaration is portrayed not only as Creator but also as Chief Legislator, Chief Justice, and Chief Executive. The implications are obvious. God is all-powerful. Yet still He remains just. Even though all-powerful, He can distribute justice impartially. There is no need for legal restrictions on God. There is no need to make Him follow the rule of law. Not so with man.

Given man's imperfect nature, it follows that when any man or group of men, including a majority, exercises power, he or they are potentially tyrannical. Man cannot exercise absolute power impartially or without corruption. Thus when men exercise power over other men through government, that power has to be limited. This sentiment was expressed most powerfully in the famous passage from *The Federalist Papers*: "It may be a reflection on human nature that such devices should be necessary to control the abuses of government. But what is government itself but the greatest of all reflections on human nature? If men were angels, no government would be necessary. If angels were to govern men, neither external nor internal controls on government would be necessary."[2] In the Founders' understanding, the purpose of government is derived from this understanding of the imperfection of human nature. Because man is imperfect, the legal authority of man over man must be limited by the impartial rule of law. That man is not a god must be coupled also with the observation that man is not simply a beast, governed by instinct. Man possesses reason. The law of human nature is the law of reason. Man's liberty and reason distinguish him from the beasts, just as his passion or selfishness distinguishes him from God. Man, then, is the in-between being. In order to live well, he must live under just government. Because men are men and not gods or beasts, there will always be a need for politics and government. This sentiment that government is a reflection on human nature is akin to Aristotle's understanding that man is by nature a political or a social animal, and that a man without a city must be either a god or a beast. To put it another way, it is unnatural or utopian for man to try to live an asocial or an apolitical life. What I mean to suggest is that politics reflects that man is concerned with more than self-preservation and safety; he is naturally concerned with justice.

The idea of human equality is, then, an assertion that all men share a common nature. Men are said to be equal in that God bestowed on mankind certain unalienable rights. The moral principle informing the Declaration is that all enlightened men will recognize each other as fellow human beings who possess rights that deserve respect. The purpose of government is to protect those rights. The idea of limited government is that government has no other purpose than to secure those rights. American constitutionalism is the prudent attempt to accomplish that end or purpose.

The Declaration of Independence is not simply an egalitarian document. The proposition that all men are created equal means that all human beings are the same in one respect, but not in every respect. Jefferson did not mean to suggest that men were equal in size, strength, beauty, intelligence, or talent. Men are equal simply in possessing certain unalienable rights: life, liberty, and the pursuit of happiness. Each man is equal in his right to judge how best to secure his life and liberty and his right to pursue happiness, which includes especially the right to acquire property. According to the Founders, the right to acquire property is understood to be a God-given right because man owns himself, his labor is an extension of himself, and property is an extension of his labor. The Founders expected that man's natural inequalities or talents would manifest themselves as men pursue happiness.[3] Jefferson speaks of a natural aristocracy emerging as the equal rights of all citizens are secured. As Madison put it in *Federalist 10*, it is the equal protection of the unequal faculties of acquisition or speculation that constitutes the principal aim of modern government. While property rights include man's external or material goods, the term property had a much wider meaning to the Founders. James Madison described it as follows:

> Property... in its larger and juster meaning, embraces every thing to which a man may attach a value and have a right; and which leaves to every one else the like advantage. In one sense, a man's land, or merchandise, or money is called his property. In another sense, a man has a property in his opinions and the free communication of them. He has a property of peculiar value in his religious opinions, and in the profession and practice dictated by them. He has a property very dear to him in the safety and liberty of his person. He has an equal property in the free use of his faculties and free choice of the objects on which to employ them. In a word, as a man is said to have a right to his property, he may be equally said to have a property in his rights.... Government is instituted to protect property of every sort... this being the end of government, that alone is a just government, which impartially secures to every man, whatever is his own.[4]

Madison's understanding of property rights extends from material or external goods to freedom of speech and the rights of conscience. We might say that Madison's understanding of property rights includes what we mean in our time when we speak of economic liberty, political or civil liberty, and religious liberty. Economic liberty is the right to acquire and create property; political or civil liberty includes the right to vote, the right to free speech, and the right to participate in making the laws under which one lives; religious liberty is the right to worship God as our conscience dictates. The protection of this broad sense of property is what informs the operation of constitutional government.

Politics is the common deliberation among citizens regarding how best to secure their safety, property rights, and happiness. Thus government arises in the first instance as people have a common desire or need to secure these things, and also the common desire to be ruled not by arbitrary whims or decrees but by the rule of impartial law. It is the violation or alienation of these common property rights that justifies opposition to any government. It is the protection of these rights that is the limited purpose of legitimate government. In the Founders' view, the right to property is just as sacred as the right to life.

The Declaration of Independence argues that governments are instituted to secure these rights. But is government really necessary for this end? Why is government instituted at all? Our Founders understood that because of man's imperfection, the natural liberty that each individual possesses cannot be well protected or secured by an individual in a state of nature. The insecurity thus experienced compels man to create an authority, a government, to secure those rights. How to constitute a government that secures our rights is a difficult, dangerous, and tricky business. Even after that is accomplished, keeping the government within its limited purpose requires the eternal vigilance of its citizens. According to America's Founders, the first step in so constituting a good and limited government is to recognize that the just powers of government are derived from the consent of the governed. The idea of consent is the idea of social contract or compact, a voluntary association in which each party recognizes reciprocal obligations that inform the operation of the government created by the contract. This idea of consent or compact as the basis of legitimate government is echoed in almost all state constitutions written following the adoption of the Declaration of Independence in 1776. To give a typical example, the Massachusetts Bill of Rights of 1780 reads as follows: "The body-politic is formed by a voluntary association of individuals; it is a social compact by which the whole people covenants with each citizen and each citizen with the whole people that all shall be governed by certain laws for the common good."

Consent, then, is a corollary principle to equality. Men are equal in their rights and subject to no earthly authority other than that to which they have consented. In other words, no human being is by nature the subject of any other human being. Alexander Hamilton put the idea this way: "The only distinction between freedom and slavery is this: in the state of freedom, a man is governed by the laws to which he has given his consent; in the state of slavery, he is governed by the will of another."[5] No human being is so low that he deserves to be treated like a beast; at the same time, no human being is so high that he should be regarded as a God. Thus the just powers of government derive not from wisdom, virtue, wealth, beauty, brute strength, hereditary office, the grace of god or divine right, but from the consent of the governed. The social contract is a contract between fellow citizens, not a covenant between God and a government. The operative mode of consent in American politics is through elections and majority rule. However, "it is not simply the will of the majority that is to be paramount in the government, but the enlightened and deliberative will formed in accordance with each individual man's God given rights. At the same time that the just powers of government are derived from the consent of the governed, those powers are defined and circumscribed by that same consent."[6] In other words, although the people are sovereign, they remain the legitimate authority only insofar as they respect the God-given rights of all citizens, including the rights of conscience and the rights of property. The majority must respect the rights of the minority. In its American version, consent as a political principle finds expression in the idea of a written constitution that, while deriving all legal authority from the majority, includes restraints on majorities, protections for individuals, elections, representation, the separation of powers, federalism, due process, trial by jury, and other legal niceties that reflect the idea that the law should be impartial or that the law should be reason unaffected by desire.

The great difficulty, of course, is to keep government within its limits once it has been founded. But in a republican form of government, if government becomes unlimited it is the fault of the people who return the scoundrels to office. Our Constitution gives us the opportunity, through elections and appointments, to keep the government true to its original limited purpose. Insofar as our government violates that purpose, it is our fault or our responsibility. Only active citizens can maintain limited government.

The word duty is used only once in the Declaration: We have a duty, it says, to defend our God-given freedom. Suffering under tyrannical circumstances, sacred honor requires men to risk their lives and fortunes for the sake of liberty. To put it another way, American citizenship requires citizens to govern themselves and to be jealous of their liberty. The only way to have limited government is to have citizens who are self-governing. This concern with duty and citizenship is an oft-neglected aspect of the Declaration.

In conclusion, then, let us compare the principles of the Declaration of Independence to the principles of the idea of the universal and homogenous state. First, the theology of the Declaration of Independence assumes that there is a living God. The theology of the universal and homogenous state is radically and dogmatically atheistic. According to Alexandre Kojève, following Hegel, the idea of the universal and homogenous state rejects the theistic conception of Truth (and of Being), and accepts the radical atheism according to which Being itself is essentially temporal and creates itself insofar as it is discursively or dialectically revealed in the course of History.[7]

What does it mean to say that Being creates itself and that Being is essentially temporal? Bryan-Paul Frost provided us with that answer when he explained Kojève's understanding of human nature. Professor Frost stated that Kojève believes that man doesn't have a nature or that man's being is infinitely malleable or perfectible. The theology of the Declaration of Independence and the U.S. Constitution assumes that man has a fixed nature, that man is what he always has been and always will be. Above all man is imperfect.[8] Kojève's understanding of human nature, on the other hand, is that man's nature is not fixed but completely changeable. The idea of perfectibility is illustrated most clearly in Frost's statement that at the end of history, the universal and homogenous state will create heaven on earth. The radically atheistic starting point of the universal and homogenous state, coupled with the notion of perfectibility, leads to a redefinition of the purpose and aims of the state. The state's purpose is no longer the constitutional purpose of securing God-given rights; its purpose is unlimited and the state becomes the vehicle for creating heaven on earth. In fact, the state becomes deified in this understanding. As Kojève asserts: "As a consistent atheist, one replaces God . . . by Society (the state) and History."[9] As Hegel argued: "As high as mind stands above nature, so high does the state stand above physical life. Man must therefore venerate the state as a secular deity."[10]

A second approach to comparing the principles of the Declaration of Independence and the principles of the universal and homogenous state is in terms of politics and freedom. According to Frost again, at the end of history, politics will disappear and be replaced with the administration of things. This follows from Kojève, for whom the disappearance of politics means the eradication of false notions of freedom entertained by men in bygone aristocratic and bourgeois eras. In other words, the idea of civil liberty and religious liberty that informed the Founding Fathers is fundamentally false: The freedom of a man or citizen who governs himself, or who participates in making the laws under which he lives, is rejected by Kojève as false freedom. Genuine freedom occurs only with the establishment of the universal and homogenous state, and consists of the satisfaction each individual receives in seeing himself recognized by that state as having equal autonomy and dignity. Frost gives a detailed and sophisticated account of how this notion of recognition operates in the world state, in his discussion of the synthesis that emerges from the justice of equity and the justice of equivalence. Man is somehow fully satisfied as a subject in this "New World Order." And one must admit, Kojève's account of recognition in the universal and homogenous state is compelling and consistent—if one accepts his radical starting point.

As Frost indicated, what characterizes the universal and homogenous state is the disappearance of politics and the emergence of the administration of things. This consists of a centralization of all legal, economic, and social authority in the hands of a bureaucracy manned by scientific experts or elites. The authority of the bureaucracy is derived from its alleged wisdom or scientific expertise. The authority of the state is not derived, as it is in constitutional government, from the consent of the governed or elections. Rather, the bureaucracy will negate—through the dialectics of history—the authority of all unequal traditional institutions such as elections, separation of powers, federalism, families, churches, and, yes, even voluntary associations (witness in our own domestic politics the attack on the Boy Scouts).

One of the most powerful critics of modern bureaucracy was the French philosopher Alexis de Tocqueville. He saw clearly that the consequence of this vast bureaucratization is the disappearance of political liberty and citizenship. According to Tocqueville, this centralized administrative state will relieve us of the burden of governing ourselves. The state will increasingly take on all public and private responsibilities and relieve us of the burden of citizenship. It will become our caretaker and our nanny. In Tocqueville's words, the power of the centralized state

> is absolute, minute, regular, provident, and mild. It would be like the authority of a parent, if like that authority, its object was to prepare men for manhood; but it seeks, on the contrary, to keep them in perpetual childhood. . . . [W]hat remains but to spare them all the care of thinking and all the trouble of living?. . . (the state) covers the surface of society with a network of small, complicated rules, minute and uniform . . . such a power does not destroy, but it prevents existence. . . . [I]t compresses, enervates, extinguishes, and stupefies a people, till each nation is reduced to nothing better than a flock of timid and industrious animals, of which the government is the shepherd. . . .[11]

Let me apply a principle of Aristotelian political science to the universal and homogenous state. As I said earlier, Aristotle argues that man is by nature a political animal, and that a man without a city must be either a beast or god. In the theory behind the universal and homogenous state, politics disappears and the state becomes divine, but in practice the state becomes bestial. The horrors of the twentieth century inflicted by national and international socialism reflect these utopian expectations and the attempt to perfect the human condition.

Some argue, like Kojève and Hegel, that the world state is inevitable and desirable. Others wonder if the world state is really possible and worry that it is utopian. My conclusion is that the world state is undesirable because it would be inevitably tyrannical. The theory behind it is completely alien to the American political and constitutional tradition. Citizenship gives way to fearful and timid subjects; limited government to the unlimited state; consent falls by the wayside. The universal and homogenous state, seeing itself as the source of right, becomes increasingly therapeutic, and proceeds by satisfying and stupefying man, using technology as its tool, and abolishing liberty in the name of egalitarianism.

It should not come as a surprise that I believe that our current policy debates and policy decisions ought to take their bearing from the principles of the American Founding and not the utopian, statist, tyrannical theory of the universal and homogenous state. Insofar as globalization means the spread of property rights, open markets, and free trade, we should follow George Washington's advice in his Farewell Address, to expand our trade with other nations but to avoid any political entanglements. Insofar as globalization means the expansion of international organizations under bureaucratic elites such as the World Court, the International Criminal Court, or the World Trade Organization, thus undermining America's national sovereignty, it must be rejected.

We must remember that for the left, globalization means something very different from what it means to free marketers. We ought not to give up our national sovereignty. The danger is not the nation–state, but rather the state unlimited by constitutional principles, the state informed by utopian expectations. What this means is that in spite of the utopian dreams of the philosophers of the universal and homogenous state, the world is what it always has been—a place of opportunity and danger, a place of war and peace. It is a place with good guys, bad guys, and fence sitters. "Constitutional Government does not induce visionary expectations from government (thus Constitutional prudence does not envision either wars to end all wars or vesting power in an elite bureaucracy implementing the will of the master race, master class, or even the progressive social justice of Independent Regulatory Agencies), nor is Constitutional Government contemptuous of politics, but it teaches the responsibilities of citizenship."[12]

What Constitutional Government requires of us is to be vigilant and prudent citizens. What it requires of us is that we demand of ourselves and our government that liberty and constitutional order be preserved and restored, especially in the United States. How are we to do that?

Notes

[1]This interpretation of the Declaration derives primarily from the writings of Harry Jaffa. See especially, "The Universal Meaning of the Declaration of Independence" in *Crisis of the House Divided: An Interpretation of the Issues in the Lincoln–Douglas Debates*, 3rd edition (Chicago: University of Chicago Press, 1982); "The Nature and Origin of the American Party System" in *Equality and Liberty: Theory and Practice in American Politics* (New York: Oxford University Press, 1965); "What is Equality? The Declaration of Independence Revisited" in *The Conditions of Freedom* (Baltimore and London: The Johns Hopkins University Press, 1975); "Equality as a Conservative Principle" in *How to Think About the American Revolution: A Bicentennial Cerebration* (Durham, NC: Carolina Academic Press, 1978); "Another Look at the Declaration: in *American Conservatism and the American Founding* (Durham, NC: Carolina Academic Press, 1984); and "What Were the 'Original Intentions' of the Framers of the Constitution of the United States?" and "'Who Killed Cock Robin?' A Retrospective on the Bork Nomination" in *Original Intent and the Framers of the Constitution* (Washington, D.C.: Regnery Gateway, 1994).

[2]*The Federalist Papers,* Clinton Rossiter and Charles Kesler, eds. (New York: New American Library, 1999), p. 290.

[3]*The Portable Thomas Jefferson,* Merrill D. Peterson, ed. (New York: Penguin Books, 1975), p. 534.

[4]Quoted in *American Political Rhetoric,* 4th edition, Peter Lawler and Robert Schaefer, eds. (Lanham, MD: Rowman & Litlefield Publishers, 2001).

[5]Papers of Alexander Hamilton.

[6]Harry Jaffa, *Original Intent and the Framers of the Constiution,* p. 273.

[7]Alexandre Kojève, "Tyranny and Wisdom," in *Leo Strauss On Tyranny,* revised and expanded edition, Victor Gourevitch and Michael S. Roth, eds. (New York: The Free Press, 1991).

[8]See Bryan-Paul Frost, "Is a Global Liberal Democratic Order Inevitable?" this volume.

[9]Kojève, op. cit., p. 161.

[10]Quoted in John Marini, "Bureaucracy and America: Leo Strauss on Constitutionalism, the State and Tyranny," in *Leo Strauss, the Straussians, and the American Regime*, Kenneth Deutsch and John Murley, eds. (Lanham, MD: Rowman & Littlefield, 1999).

[11]Alexis de Tocqueville, *Democracy in America*, Volume 2 (New York: Vintage Books, Random House, 1990), pp. 318–19.

[12]Marini, op. cit.